Jim Crow Terminals

Jim Crow Terminals

THE DESEGREGATION OF AMERICAN AIRPORTS

Anke Ortlepp

The University of Georgia Press

ATHENS

© 2017 by the University of Georgia Press
Athens, Georgia 30602
www.ugapress.org
All rights reserved
Set in 10.25/13.5 Minion Pro by Graphic Composition, Inc., Bogart, Georgia

Most University of Georgia Press titles are
available from popular e-book vendors.

Printed digitally

Library of Congress Cataloging-in-Publication Data
Names: Ortlepp, Anke, author.
Title: Jim Crow terminals : the desegregation of American airports / Anke Ortlepp.
Description: Athens : The University of Georgia Press, [2017] | Includes bibliographical
    references and index.
Identifiers: LCCN 2017003726| ISBN 9780820350936 (hardback : alk. paper) | ISBN 9780820351216
    (pbk. : alk. paper) | ISBN 9780820350943 (ebook)
Subjects: LCSH: Airports—United States—History—20th century. | Air travel—United
    States—History—20th century. | Segregation in transportation—Southern States. |
    Discrimination in public accommodations—Southern States. | Airports—Law and
    legislation—United States. | African Americans—Segregation.
Classification: LCC HE9797.5.U5 O77 2017 | DDC 387.7/3608996073075090045—DC23
    LC record available at https://lccn.loc.gov/2017003726

CONTENTS

ACKNOWLEDGMENTS

I owe many thanks and much gratitude to the numerous institutions, colleagues, and friends who have supported me during my research and writing of this book. They have helped me transform an abstract idea into material pages between two covers. I am deeply grateful for the support and encouragement I have received over the years, without which I would not have been able to bring this project to fruition.

I would like to thank the University of Kassel, Ludwigs-Maximilians-University in Munich, the German Historical Institute in Washington, D.C., and the Smithsonian National Air and Space Museum. These institutions provided the institutional and financial support that enabled me to write this book. I was very fortunate to be awarded the National Air and Space Museum's Verville Fellowship for 2011–2012. The museum provided an inspiring and relaxed environment within which to think, talk, and make words. In particular, my thanks go out to Dom Pisano, who encouraged me to apply for the fellowship, supported my work throughout the process, and shared his knowledge of aviation history. I would like to give a shout-out to Collette Williams, who helped me settle in and became my friend. My thanks go to Chandra Bhimull and Jim Thomas, my fellow fellows, who were a wonderful support group. I enjoyed attending the Writers' Group, which helped me stay focused. Thanks to Margaret Weitekamp, Paul Ceruzzi, Roger Launius, and Martin Collins for their critical feedback and to Richard Paul for sharing some of the experiences of writing a book.

I would also like to thank the librarians and archivists who helped me access the materials on which my story is based. I am particularly indebted to the staff at the Moorland-Spingarn Research Center at Howard University; at the Law Library, the Science and Business Reading Room, and the Manuscript Division at the Library of Congress; at the National Archives in College Park, Maryland, Atlanta, Georgia, and Fort Worth, Texas; and at the libraries of the Smithsonian National Air and Space Museum, the National Museum of American History, the National Museum of Natural History, and the National Museum of American Art. My thanks also go to Katharina Kloock, who as librarian of the German Historical Institute helped me balance my travel budget by assisting me with interlibrary loans. I would also like to thank Karin

Hellmann, Sebastian Knecht, and Christoph Grill at dpa Picture-Alliance for assisting me with my image and permission requests in such speedy fashion. Moreover, I am grateful to Cathy Miller at the National Archives at Atlanta and Bill Fox at the Greenville News for providing image scans and granting permissions.

I would not have been able to write this book without the advice and feedback of my colleagues and friends. Phil Tiemeyer, Michelle Engert, Dom Pisano, and Jim Thomas read drafts. Phil, who shares my enthusiasm for aviation history, also shared materials, good times, and the occasional beer. Michelle shared her legal expertise and good energy. I am also grateful to Steve Hoelscher and Bryant Simon for providing critical commentary and suggesting revisions. Moreover, I profited from the critical feedback from colleagues at conferences and workshops. Whereas any errors I may have produced are exclusively my own fault, my book has become better thanks to the feedback I received.

Furthermore, I would like to thank the University of Georgia Press for bringing my manuscript to publication. I am grateful to Mick Gusinde-Duffy and Beth Snead for their support, for their patience, and for making the review process a productive experience. I am also grateful to Bryant Simon and Jane Dailey for including my book in their book series. And my thanks go to John Joerschke and Thomas Roche, my project editors, who were a pleasure to work with.

I would also like to thank members of my staff at Kassel University and former colleagues at the German Historical Institute. Bryan Hart at the GHI assisted me with the initial research for this project. Jane Parsons-Sauer and Anna Müller helped me put the finishing touches on the manuscript. Jane Parsons-Sauer proofread it, and Anna Müller assisted me in getting permissions for the images that illustrate this book.

I could not have done this without my friends. Uta Balbier, Phil Tiemeyer and Shaun Crouse, Michelle Engert and Michael Brenner, Anna Engelke and Jörg Thadeusz, Marion Schmickler and Frank Whitelock, Collette Williams, Kerstin Schmidt, Katharina Kloock, Richard Wetzell, and Larry Joseph. Thanks for being there!

And last but not least I want to thank my family, who have always encouraged me and enthusiastically participated in my adventures.

Kassel, November 2016
Anke Ortlepp

ABBREVIATIONS

ATS	Air Terminal Services
CAA	Civil Aeronautics Administration
CAB	Civil Aeronautics Board
CCF	Civic Case Files
CORE	Congress of Racial Equality
DOC	Department of Commerce
DOJ	Department of Justice
DOT	Department of Transportation
FAA	Federal Aviation Agency
FAAP	Federal-aid Airport Program
FOR	Fellowship of Reconciliation
ICC	Interstate Commerce Commission
IMA	Interdenominational Ministerial Alliance
LDF	Legal Defense Fund, NAACP
LOC	Library of Congress
NAACP	National Association for the Advancement of Colored People
NARA	National Archives and Records Administration
NARACP	National Archives and Records Administration College Park
NASM	National Air and Space Museum
SCLC	Southern Christian Leadership Conference
SNCC	Student Nonviolent Coordinating Committee
WPA	Works Progress Administration

Jim Crow Terminals

CHAPTER 1

Introduction

In a sworn affidavit to the Department of Justice in 1961, civil rights leader Ralph Abernathy testified on his repeated inability to use the facilities at Dannelly Field Airport terminal in Montgomery, Alabama, during the 1950s. Abernathy related a confrontation with the airport manager over access to the "whites only" drinking fountain. Abernathy had been drinking from the fountain one day in March 1960 when the manager yelled, "Boy, get away from that fountain, what are you doing drinking that water?" Undeterred, Abernathy went on drinking until the manager "came over to me, put his hand on my shoulder, and said, 'can't you read?'" An exchange of words followed this physical confrontation, according to Abernathy: "I said, 'sure.' Then he said, 'can't you see this is white water?' I said, 'yes.' He asked, 'then why are you drinking it?' And I said, 'because I am thirsty and that's the kind of water I drink.'" The enraged manager went to a nearby phone to report Abernathy's subversion of spatial norms and violation of accepted behavior to the police. Before the police arrived, Abernathy and his wife, Juanita, had already caught their flight to Syracuse, New York. However, stepping up to the fountain and drinking its water had unequivocally expressed Abernathy's rejection of the airport's racial segregation policy. It further demonstrated that he considered it his right as a citizen and a consumer to use the airport on an integrated basis.[1]

Conditions at Dannelly Field were not exceptional. Racial segregation was a reality at most airports across the American South in the postwar period. As the number of African American air travelers began to rise noticeably after World War II, many airports across the region converted to separate facilities for blacks and whites, thus incorporating terminal buildings into the southern landscapes of segregation. Although travel by airplane was considered the most modern form of transportation, for southern segregationists it also represented the latest manifestation of an increasingly nationalized and standardized interstate travel culture whose integrative forces they struggled to resist. Much like railroads and buses, airplanes carried people, ideas, and consumer goods to and from the South, yet they did so at an unprecedented speed. At a time when the region was continuing to experience massive structural changes due to urbanization, agriculture's loss of significance, and population shifts, segregationists reacted with an affirmation of white supremacy, an ideology that formed the basis of their social, political, and economic life. Rather than allowing for the proliferation of experiences and identities that travel encouraged and enabled, segregationists applied the familiar tactic of inscribing racial difference onto the landscape of emerging southern geographies of aviation in an effort to communicate and insist on local definitions of whiteness and blackness. They did so with an urgency that set air transportation apart from railway and bus transportation. This urgency was partly a reflection of the quickly shifting legal landscape of the postwar decades; but it was also a reaction to increasing numbers of African American airline customers and their growing agency as citizen-consumers.

As Ralph Abernathy's testimony demonstrates, the racialization of airport spaces did not go uncontested. Black air travelers resisted discrimination in ground facilities, which stood in stark contrast to the equal service they received from the airlines themselves as federally regulated businesses. There is little more than anecdotal evidence to suggest that cabin seats were assigned according to passengers' racial backgrounds.[2] "Even to the orthodox," C. Vann Woodward observed, "there was doubtless something slightly incongruous about requiring a Jim Crow compartment on a transcontinental plane, or one that did not touch the ground between New York and Miami."[3] Free to choose their seats in the airplane cabin, African Americans resented and often avoided duplicate terminal facilities and exclusionary spatial practices. These features seemed at their most questionable when they appeared in the newly constructed modernist airport terminals that opened their doors in cities across the South in the 1950s. Here modernity clashed with the retrograde social philosophy that inspired the terminals' layout and design. Seasoned by decades of protest against discrimination in transportation and public accommodations, African American travelers protested against airport segregation. They engaged in direct action at local airports, transforming terminal buildings into protest territory. They also sought relief in the courtroom and solicited support from the federal government in their fight for airport desegregation. Following a court order, the airport in Shreveport, Louisiana, eventually became the last airport to integrate. The last signs leading air travelers to separate spaces marked "colored" and "white" came down in July 1963.[4]

The history of Jim Crow airports and their desegregation has escaped scholarly attention. Historical accounts of racial discrimination in transportation and the fight for integration have focused instead on railways, buses, and streetcars; terminal facilities, such as train stations and bus depots; and other public accommodations. Scholars have looked at consumer boycotts like the Montgomery Bus Boycott, protest campaigns like the Freedom Rides, and litigation to trace the long process that led to the abolition of racial segregation in interstate and intrastate travel.[5] It is important that we add airplanes and airports to this narrative about the right to travel, because the nascent jet age was rapidly reorganizing Americans' travel patterns in the late 1950s and 1960s. In the postwar period, growing numbers of Americans came to rely on air transportation. Passenger numbers soared from 17.3 million in 1950 to 62 million in 1960. Air travel quickly developed into the preferred way of long-distance travel. The year 1960 was the first year when more Americans began to choose airplanes over railways and buses for personal and business travel exceeding 500 miles.[6] America's increasing reliance on air travel as a mode of mobility expressed shifts in consumer culture, left an imprint on material culture and the built environment, and contributed to the formation of individual and collective identities.[7] For many Americans in the 1950s and 1960s, air travel became a symbol for participation in a modernist utopia of stylish, carefree cosmopolitanism. In a booming national marketplace of goods and services, it was advertised as a form of transportation that allowed consumers to connect face to face more quickly and conveniently than ever before, which enabled them to explore the world. Much more than trains and buses had done, or so the airlines promised, air travel had the potential of connecting the international and national to the regional and local.

During the 1950s and 1960s, however, air travel's culture of mobility was mostly a white upper-middle-class phenomenon. High ticket prices placed a trip by airplane out of the reach of most consumers of other backgrounds. This reflected the uneven (racial, ethnic, class, and gender) dynamics of the expanding postwar consumer society, as highlighted in studies by Lizabeth Cohen and others.[8] For African Americans to claim a stake in the consumption of air travel meant having to overcome class and racial barriers. Analyzing these barriers is the concern of this book. When and to what extent, it asks, were African Americans able to participate fully in air travel's modernist utopia? Why were the ground spaces of air transportation not fully accessible to them at the beginning of the jet age, even as they enjoyed free access to aircraft cabins? Which larger shifts in the postwar social, economic, and political order, as they find spatial expression in the built environment, are reflected in the struggle over nondiscriminatory ground access to the air travel experience? In addressing these questions, this investigation of segregated air terminals and the struggle for their integration argues that we have to read the fight for airport desegregation and the demand for equal access to air transportation as central issues in contentious debates over active participation of black consumers in the postwar consumer culture; over notions of African American citizenship; and over the construction of modernist (racial) subjectivities.

This critical intervention follows a number of interlocking trajectories. One such trajectory traces the evolving landscapes of transportation in the South. It investigates how aviation's ground infrastructure developed in relation to spatial patterns and spatial practices established in other means of transportation and their terminal facilities. The work of Blair Kelley has shown that segregation in rail traffic began in the North in the 1840s and 1850s as an effort to control new customers—emancipated former slaves. African American riders of trains and streetcars were relegated to the outdoor platforms of coaches even when the cars were empty. While public transport in the North was integrated by the end of the Civil War, Jim Crow transportation was revived in the South in the struggle over the renegotiation of racial identities in the postbellum period. Around the turn of the century, Kelley shows, most cities across the South racially separated their streetcar riders, a practice that met with anger and resentment from local black communities. Kelley also offers a useful framework for the interpretation of streetcar boycotts. Rather than dismiss them "as futile middle-class efforts at inclusion" in a period of accommodation, she conceives of the boycotts as a cross-class struggle not only against Jim Crow streetcars but also as part of the "larger attack on black citizenship" that white supremacists waged at the time.[9]

Kelley's work echoes observations that scholars Grace Hale and Katherine Barnes have made with regard to transportation on the railroads. The case of Homer Plessy, in particular, showed how racial segregation was not only employed to question the purchasing agency of African American railroad customers in the last quarter of the nineteenth century, as Hale has so aptly illustrated.[10] "White" and "colored" signs leading one group of customers to comfortable seats in first class and others to dirty wooden benches in third class were also designed to invalidate the citizen rights that black southerners were granted during Reconstruction. Plessy addressed this fact when he filed a lawsuit against the Louisiana railroad company that denied him the seat he had legally purchased. Rather than affirm Plessy's rights, the Supreme Court in *Plessy v. Ferguson* (1896) handed down a decision that acknowledged the right to ride but reinscribed racial difference into the Constitution. The Court did not take issue with the existence of separate accommodations on railways that state codes required as long as they were equal in quality. Thus, "separate but equal" became the law of the land.

A host of scholarship has shown how application of the new legal doctrine spread, and how quintessentially unequal most transportation facilities, public conveyances, and public accommodations became—communicating notions of whiteness and blackness prescribed by the ruling classes. When buses appeared as vehicles on transportation landscapes, they too were incorporated into the system of racially segregated travel—both intrastate and interstate. Abundant scholarship has also shown how individuals and communities, often in cooperation with civil rights organizations, resisted the humiliation of racial separation. They worked toward change by organizing boycotts, filing lawsuits, and pressuring federal regulatory agencies like the Interstate Commerce Commission (ICC) to stop discrimination. Protest action also began to include test drives on buses, such as the 1947 Journey of Reconciliation, which brought together an integrated group of riders in an effort to check the nature of on-board service and investigate the spaces and spatial practices of travel on the ground. Like the Freedom Rides, a more radical test drive that brought systematic discrimination against black travelers to national attention in 1961, these test drives focused on the issue of civil rights, as Derek Catsam has shown.[11]

The emergence of segregated airport terminal spaces and the struggle for their desegregation then was not an isolated development. It is part of a much longer history of racial discrimination in and beyond transportation. The forms of action activists and protesters subscribed to and called for were inspired by what was going on around them and what had happened before. Yet, this book also hopes to show that the story about airport desegregation stands out for its essentially postwar character; for the fact that segregated airports continued to open their doors at a time when other transportation facilities began to integrate; and for the urgency with which segregation was both implemented and contested. The story stands out for another reason: no other transportation sector implicated the federal government to the degree that commercial aviation did. A federally subsidized business sector almost from the start, aviation benefited strongly from support of the federal government for construction of its infrastructure. Federal dollars were dispensed through the Federal-aid Airport Program (FAAP) begun in 1946. Yet, the infrastructure this program helped build—the many new airports that popped up all across the South—fell under municipal, not federal, control. Nonetheless, the degree of federal involvement led civil rights activists to question the responsibility of the federal government in implementing segregation, as well as how it could be held accountable and forced to get involved in the struggle for airport integration.

Another trajectory follows the development of postwar cultures of consumption, in particular the shifting participation of black consumers in a national marketplace that offered growing numbers of goods and services. Air travel was one of the services that became more widely available to Americans of different backgrounds, African Americans included. As part of a growing middle class, black consumers like many others discovered flying as a convenient and fast (if often expensive) way of traveling in the 1950s and 1960s. Air travel also promised participation in a new lifestyle of mobility and affluence that airlines advertised in newspapers and magazines, most especially in the pages of *Ebony* magazine. This lifestyle transcended local and regional affiliations by literally lifting air travelers out of their everyday contexts and tying them into a national culture of air-mindedness that had begun to take shape in the interwar period but was reaching full bloom in the postwar years.

As such, air travel was not only a representation of modernity as it reached its peak moment. It also represented a national consumer culture whose lack of differentiation posed a threat to the South's relations of power and way of life. Grace Hale and Ted Ownby have shown how in the early twentieth century advertising, shopping, and railroad travel broke down what had been "personalized local relations of class and racial authority," as Hale puts it.[12] Pete Daniel has demonstrated how the consumption of popular culture such as music and fashion in the 1940s and 1950s complicated race relations deemed nonnegotiable by most whites. Victoria Wolcott has investigated how the use of recreational facilities like amusement parks, swimming pools, and skating rinks was not only "about integration and interracial friendship but about power and possession."[13] Black claims to these public leisure spaces destabilized racial hierarchies, which were often violently defined. Shared geographies of consumption like chain stores and department stores, where consumer goods were made available and that formed the core of many postwar southern towns, also blurred the color line. These previously unfamiliar purchasing environments helped break down what had been power relations based on agricultural economies and the dependencies of sharecropping. The unrestricted access to material goods enjoyed by both black and white customers in these commercial establishments threatened to foster social and economic equality among them. While African Americans enjoyed unmediated shopping of brand-name products in chain stores, buying the latest fashions via mail order, or taking the train to a family reunion, air travel offered an expanded avenue of exploring the quality and liberating potential of a standardized national service product.[14] Joining the new national trend of mobility, blacks in air travel found a way of questioning regionally distinct notions of racial difference as citizen-consumers. More than just movement through the sky as integrated territory, air travel functioned as a platform for the renegotiation of racial identities.[15]

Existing scholarship has also shown how white supremacists reacted to the renegotiations of whiteness and blackness in new forms of consumer behavior. Across the South, racial difference was codified into the law. Many cities and states regularly amended their segregation statutes to react to the shifting dynamics of the consumer society and marketplace. These segregation laws not only regulated human interaction but also shaped the built environment, as they required racial difference to be built into the landscapes of consumption in an effort to resist what Aniko Bodroghkozy has called the "urbanizing geography of anonymity" and its integrative forces.[16] This book will show why and how airports, as quintessentially urban spaces, were fit into southern landscapes of segregation. It will also look at how the spaces of aviation were eventually excavated from these segregated landscapes, with a focus on how the racialization of air travel's infrastructure on the ground and the struggle for its desegregation was a confrontation over the meanings of race and region. Fighting for unrestricted access to the air travel experience, African Americans called for the redefinition of their identities as American consumers. At the same time, they called for their recognition as modern subjects and American citizens.

A third trajectory follows the development of an urbanizing and modernizing New South, a process that entailed the racialization of public life. The story of how the South struggled to overcome economic backwardness from the last quarter of the nineteenth century and into the twentieth century has been the focus of an immense body of scholarship, which does not have to be recapitulated here. Scholars have pointed to the structural transformation of the agricultural economy, from sharecropping to agribusiness; the impact of an expanding consumer society; the growth of manufacturing; and financial support from the federal government as factors that helped reshape the Old South into the New, providing it with a reconfigured economic base. Slowly but steadily the South's economy lost much of its regional distinctiveness and became an integrated part of the national economy. David Goldfield and others have shown how simultaneously the region was transformed from a rural to an urban place, especially in the postwar decades. Cities like Atlanta, Birmingham, Montgomery, and New Orleans, which are among central locales in the struggle for airport desegregation, emerged as major urban centers during those postwar years. They did so as a result of the massive population shifts the region experienced when large numbers of poor rural southerners, both black and white, decided to turn their backs on the destitution and hopelessness of the countryside and move to the cities. By the end of World War II, urbanization had become one of the hallmarks of modernization in the South, and urban leaders across the region thought of their booming cities—and their airports—as symbols of progress.

Scholarship has also shown how, both before and after the war, economic modernization went hand in hand with racial discrimination and racial militancy. Modernization and the changes it brought to southern social and economic life threatened the sense of security white southerners had derived from making the color line the defining feature of the New South. Racially segregating the spaces of consumption was one way of maintaining the racial order in modern urban environments, as Grace Hale and Elizabeth Abel have demonstrated. Karen Kruse Thomas's study of the implementation of federal health care policy in the South focuses on Jim Crow hospitals as another way of inscribing racism into modernization. Accepting federal dollars as seed funds for construction of a health care system that had been largely nonexistent or in poor shape, white southern power-brokers rejected more immediate outside interference in southern racial matters and insisted on the duplication of medical facilities, much like airport managers would insist on separate airport facilities using federal funds. Although this development made good healthcare available to unprecedented numbers of African Americans of all class backgrounds, it was Jim Crow healthcare—upgraded or not.[17]

These patterns of racial discrimination continued to be accompanied by racial militancy, especially after World War II. Jason Ward has shown how white supremacists tried to use any means possible "to force African Americans back into their pre-war place."[18] These means included riots, bombings, and other acts of violence to push back with "massive resistance" any progress made by black consumers and the strengthening force of the civil rights movement. At the same time, a new generation of segregationists (e.g., Strom Thurmond) complemented militant white supremacy with a more refined rationale for racial separation, trying to save segregation while securing the South's share of postwar prosperity. These increasingly complicated negotiations between economic modernism, a retrograde social philosophy, and an exclusionary political system manifested in white supremacist contributions to debates about African American access to airports and the air travel experience. Radical white supremacists fought hard at home and in Congress to make sure that neither the new patterns of mobility nor the federal airport subsidies that enabled them would upset the racial order in the region. They had no respect for African Americans as consumers or citizens and were determined to maintain the status quo. More moderate white voices capable of recognizing the signs of the times in the post-*Brown* period, like Atlanta's mayor William Hartsfield, were willing to move in a more integrationist direction, but their politics tended to find fewer followers than the well-organized core of radical white supremacy. Looking at the responses of those opposed to integration, the following chapters acknowledge the work of Clive Webb, Jason Sokol, and others who have encouraged us to think of white supremacy not as a monolithic entity but instead as a fragmented force that produced more varied and nuanced pronouncements and actions than hitherto acknowledged. In its fragmentation and local variation, it was more comparable to the civil rights movement than previously assumed.[19]

A last trajectory follows the progression of the civil rights movement across southern landscapes. Mostly a familiar story, it provides context for the struggle for airport desegregation. While activists were challenging Jim Crow spatial practices in airport cafeterias, the denial of service at airport restaurants, the existence of separate waiting rooms, and "for colored" and "for white" signs on restroom doors and drinking fountains, protesters elsewhere were fighting for the integration of buses, schools, parks, beaches, golf courses, theaters, and lunch counters. They were also fighting for the right to vote—collectively demanding the desegregation of public life and political enfranchisement as groups and individuals working for change. Like the struggle against other forms of discrimination, the battle for airport integration was fought simultaneously in a number of places. One of the first battlefields was Washington, D.C., where in 1948 Helen Nash filed a lawsuit against the restaurant proprietor of National Airport after having been refused service in the airport's Terrace Dining Room. The conflict spread to Atlanta, Tallahassee, Greenville (South Carolina), Montgomery, New Orleans, and many other places before it drew to a close in Shreveport. There, in the summer of 1963, the last signs leading air travelers to segregated airport facilities came down. Some of the actors involved in the struggle—particularly representatives of national civil rights organizations and lawyers working for the National Association for the Advancement of Colored People's (NAACP) Legal Defense and Educational Fund (LDF) and the U.S. Department of Justice—waged several battles at once. They applied similar tactics and strategies to a broad range of discrimination causes.

As such, the struggle against airport segregation was part of the larger collective struggle for desegregation. Opposing this particular form of discrimination, local activists took inspiration from protest techniques developed by activists elsewhere or applied tactics recommended by civil rights organizations. The NAACP and the Congress of Racial Equality (CORE), two national civil rights organizations most heavily involved in the fight against Jim Crow terminals, stood for largely different approaches. The NAACP recognized litigation as the most effective route to integration. It supported individual (class action) lawsuits; it also lobbied for statutory and regulatory reform. CORE, in contrast, favored nonviolent direct action. Its field staff and local chapters organized on-site marches, sit-ins, and boycotts to protest against Jim Crow spatial practices at airports and elsewhere.

This book also investigates the involvement of the federal government and the federal judiciary in the fight for airport integration. As previous scholarship has shown, both came to play a role in the fight against racial discrimination—if only reluctantly so.[20] How the Truman, Eisenhower, and Kennedy administrations addressed the concerns of air travelers; how the Federal Aviation Agency, the Department of Justice, and Congress reacted to the pressure of civil rights organizations; and how federal justices handled cases brought to them are concerns addressed in the following chapters. They explore the significance of federal and state forces as agents in the creation and dismantlement of racialized spaces of aviation.

This study also addresses the role of other actors such as airport planners, architects, airport managers, air travelers, and civil rights activists in shaping aviation's built environment and the practices informing its use. It conceives of airport terminals as sites of conflict—as territories of confrontation over the renegotiation of racial identities in postwar America. As such, it situates itself in the scholarly debate over the multifaceted entanglements of "race" and "space." Drawing on the understanding that both concepts are historical constructs whose meanings and shapes fluctuate due to conflicting social forces that monopolize their definitions and enforce them as normative, cultural landscape historian Dianne Harris has suggested that we pay more attention to the built environment as a reflection of ideas about race and as an agent in their construction. To understand the shifting notions of race and the forms of racism they entailed, Harris encourages us to study how Americans, both black and white, created, inhabited, and used spaces in the "performance of everyday life."[21] She also wants us to pay attention, however, to how built form has shaped the behavior of historical actors. Existing spatial parameters not only directed their daily movements but also helped define their place in society—whether defined by exclusion and marginalization or inclusion and privilege.

From this perspective, landscapes and architecture are never neutral, although they may appear as natural. Instead, "built form and ideologies of race (as with class and gender) become complicit in the manufacturing of societal norms."[22] In order to deconstruct this complicity, Harris and other cultural landscape historians have employed the analytical categories of space and place to excavate social, political, and economic power relations based on race embedded in the landscape.[23] As a result of their efforts, racially based practices of discrimination and privilege in a number of spatial contexts have received scrutiny (e.g., slave landscapes, suburbs, parks, streets and freeways, urban ethnic enclaves, inner city neighborhoods and the effects of urban renewal and gentrification on these neighborhoods).[24] This study shifts attention to the landscapes of air travel. It looks at airports as racially coded geographies of mobility and consumption and scrutinizes the ways in which their spatial ordering and material fabric affected both black and white Americans. It conceives of aviation as a spatial apparatus that not only reflected racism but also created a modernized version of racial discrimination as a southern way of life. This way of life came under attack in the postwar decades when the civil rights movement questioned ideologies of race and also claimed and repurposed the (segregated) spaces that gave built expression to these ideologies. Airports became sites of conflict in this struggle against the discrimination of African Americans as citizens and consumers. As such, the following pages show that we have to see the fight for the integration of Jim Crow terminals as part of the larger effort toward the renegotiation of racial identities based on equality. In efforts to shift boundaries and remove "whites only" signs in terminal facilities, civil rights activists aimed at altering the physical features of airport terminals. At the same time, they sought to change the conceptual framings of the relationship between black and white Americans.

This book builds on a wide variety of materials. Oral histories, memoirs and autobiographies, newspaper reports, papers of individuals and organizations (mostly civil rights organizations), and government records form part of the body of primary sources. This body also includes laws, statutes, regulations, and court records. These records provide some of the most detailed insights into the struggle over spatial configurations of American airports. Court records, in particular, provide the views of black litigants whose rights as air travelers and airport patrons had been violated—often with details difficult to find elsewhere. They also offer for analysis the legal arguments presented both by the proponents of the status quo and those who fought for change. The latter recognized litigation, statutory reform, and regulatory reform as the most effective tools to address discriminatory practices in air travel's ground facilities. Similar to railroad desegregation but in contrast to the strategies employed in the fight for the integration of interstate bus transportation and other facilities, nonviolent direct action was important, though not to the extent that it brought national attention to the issue or triggered intervention by the federal government. That is why litigation and statutory and regulatory reform receive due attention in the following chapters.

Rather than provide a legal history of airport integration, however, this study aims at interlacing the history of space and place, and the formative roles they have played in racial formation, with the history of laws and litigation. Taking inspiration from the work of David Delaney, it combines investigations of the built environment with explorations of postwar legal landscapes. Delaney conceives of legal landscapes as geographies of power defined "in the terms received from and recognizable through legal discourse" or legal action. He recognizes law as a specialized rhetoric of political discourse that shapes social reality and its spatial conditions. The law, then, becomes an important agent in formulating what he calls the "geopolitics of race." Ideological rather than neutral laws provide the legal framework for the construction of ideas about race and their expression in the spatial ordering of the physical world. From this perspective, the examination of legal arguments in courts and legislative debates in Congress sheds light onto "actual attempts to project contested visions of social reality onto the world in order to shape the world."[25] After all, in litigation lawyers try to redefine and recategorize events, relations, persons, things, and their meanings and identities. These redefinitions are the most contentious when the transformation of inherited hierarchies of power and privilege is at stake. The legal battles between black air travelers and airport proprietors, legislative standoffs in Congress, and new federal regulations challenged these hierarchies of power and privilege based on racial difference.

Legal challenges to the status quo had a particular significance when they were brought forward by African American lawyers. Kenneth Mack has shown how in the twentieth century the legal profession provided narrow avenues of opportunity for blacks (albeit mostly men) when other professional opportunities remained closed. Many became civil rights lawyers. As "representative men" and "representative women," these lawyers encapsulated their cultural groups' highest ambitions and aspirations. At the same time, they were expected to serve as legal trailblazers and craft "legal precedents that would restore the lost promise of the civil rights laws and constitutional amendments of the Reconstruction era."[26] Some of these civil rights lawyers, Mack argues, became respected members of the legal community, in both the North and the South. They transcended race as representatives of a profession—Mack calls it "the brotherhood of the bar"—while they litigated on behalf of not only their clients but also their entire racial group. In that context, courtrooms became transformative spaces in themselves. In this story civil rights lawyers appear as African American agents of change along with black travelers, grassroots organizers, and local protesters.

CHAPTER 2

The Emergence of the Jim Crow Airport

The segregation of airport terminal buildings emerged as a pattern in the late 1940s. As the number of airports in the South grew, and as airports expanded their facilities to accommodate the increase in passengers, this relatively new building type was incorporated into the existing spatial order of white supremacy. Because the administration of airports was a responsibility of local municipal authorities rather than the federal government, each southern city was able to define its own policies regulating access to and use of terminal facilities. Local practices therefore varied widely. While some cities began to practice discrimination when their airports started serving the public, others did not. And while some introduced segregation at a later date as a reaction to the growing diversity of patrons, others never did. Moreover, the availability of services—such as restaurants, restrooms, waiting rooms, water fountains, and taxis—provided to African American passengers on a nondiscriminatory basis varied from city to city.

These variations notwithstanding, by the mid-1950s racial segregation in airport terminal facilities was the rule rather than the exception across the South. Discrimination against black travelers had become a deeply entrenched feature of regional transportation services. After Reconstruction, southern states and cities implemented new laws that required black and white southerners to use separate spaces set aside for them on trains and streetcars and in stations and depots. In 1881, Tennessee was the first state to codify railroad segregation.[1] Then, in 1887, Florida was next with a law that required railways to provide equal but separate accommodation for white and black passengers.[2] Other states like Mississippi and Texas soon followed suit.[3] If for a moment in the late nineteenth century it seemed as if opportunities increased for African Americans, the spaces necessary to realize those opportunities were fragmented by implementation of the color line. For many black travelers, unequal access to the means and facilities of travel was not only a frequent inconvenience; it also confronted them with humiliating experiences, a reminder of their precarious status as second-class citizens.

Among those who commented on the presence of the Jim Crow car and waiting room well into the twentieth century, the thoughts of novelist Charles W. Chestnutt and sociologist W. E. B. Du Bois still resonate. In his 1901 novel *The Marrow of Tradition*, Chestnutt recounts the journey of a young black physician from New York to North Carolina and the indignities the character suffers along the way. It was not so much the material inferiority of the car that affected him but the injustice of being spatially separated, "set apart from the rest of mankind upon the public highways, like an unclean thing."[4] Du Bois echoed these sentiments in his writings when he bemoaned the existence of the Jim Crow car, whose "discomfort lies chiefly in the hearts" (and not the bodies) of those who rode it, as the embodiment of a racist social order in the American South.[5] According to Grace Hale, Du Bois crafted the image of the middle-class African American in a Jim Crow car into "a complex definition of the very meaning of race in America."[6] For black travelers in the South, the segregated railroad car with its lack of comfort and security signified racial difference as it moved across the landscape.

When buses began to appear in southern transportation networks in the 1920s, the Jim Crow car found an equivalent in segregated cabins. Cities and states were quick to create a web of laws that mandated segregation no matter whether buses traveled on municipal, intrastate, or interstate routes—a web that due to its many local variations presented travelers with the pitfalls of unfamiliarity. These laws also applied to waiting rooms at stations and depots. Although usually the seating order on buses was not fixed by spatial partitions, but malleable according to the numbers of black and white passengers traveling on each bus, the rows in the back of a bus signaled the inferior status of occupants. The back rows of seats did not convey inferiority because their physical features were different—bus companies usually offered the same types of seats to all riders—but because a larger distance separated them from the front door. This arrangement invested bus drivers with the authority to enforce the color line on any bus and to do so by force if necessary. There is much documentation of black riders involved in physical altercations, their evictions from buses, and their arrests by local law enforcement. Weariness over these conditions and the accompanying collective fatigue prompted Rosa Parks to refuse to give up her seat for a white rider on a municipal bus in Montgomery, Alabama, one evening in December 1955.[7]

At a time when National Airport in Washington, D.C., became the first airport to attract national attention as a segregated terminal facility, legal ground on transportation issues was beginning to shift. In a landmark decision in *Morgan v. Virginia* (1946), the Supreme Court declared that segregation on interstate buses was unconstitutional.[8] But many communities were slow to adopt the new ground rules for surface travel, allowing Jim Crow to ride on, "despite court rulings telling him to get off."[9] The ruling did not apply to commercial aviation. The industry's laws, established by the Civil Aeronautics Act of 1938, prohibited discrimination of airline passengers on the basis of their racial backgrounds by air carriers.[10] And apparently—there is little evidence to suggest otherwise—airlines abided by these rules.[11] Jim Crow rode railroads and buses, but he did not travel by air. Federal laws and regulations were mostly silent, however, with regard to passenger rights on the ground. Airports, with the exception of National Airport, fell under municipal rather than federal control, an American peculiarity rooted in the history of airport development in the United States, which in many cities was driven by private initiative (boosterism) or by public-private partnerships.[12] Still, questions about what kind of spaces airports should be and what their appearance in southern cultural landscapes was meant to signify had both local and national dimensions, especially after the mid-1950s. Whereas the white establishment weighted their compatibility with the status quo, many black travelers and civil rights advocates wondered about the meaning of airports as national symbols of progress, modernity, and equality.

These issues were brought to national attention when National Airport opened to the public in 1941 as a segregated facility. Built to serve as the gateway to the nation's capital, it was the only airport in the country that fell under federal ownership and authority.[13] An elegant art deco structure, the terminal and surrounding airport infrastructure sat on federal land located in Arlington, Virginia. The main building was a perfectly symmetrical, four-story, boomerang-shaped form, its upper two stories receding from the two main levels. Facing the circular access road, the building's front was defined by eight pillars, which referenced the Big House at Abingdon Plantation on whose former grounds the airport was situated. Two canopied walkways extending from either side of the building sheltered arriving and departing passengers. In its design features, the terminal appeared to be a link between a bucolic past and the modern present—a link, however, that might have been designed but was not utilized as a release from the region's history of racism. Its interior featured a grand hall with large panorama windows facing the apron and runway. The airlines' ticket counters and waiting areas were located in this large, open space. Set off toward the building's wings were the gates, the president's lounge, the airport restaurant ("The Terrace Dining Room"), the coffee shop, and baggage and maintenance facilities.[14]

Whereas initially all areas of the terminal were accessible to all passengers, the restaurant's proprietor, Air Terminal Services Inc., began to discriminate against black travelers shortly after the building's opening, denying them any kind of service. In justification of the new practice, the company argued that Virginia's state ordinances rather than federal law regulated the use of terminal space. Section 1796a of the Virginia Code provided that the races had to be separated in all public halls and public places.[15] Maintaining an open access policy for the rest of the building, the federal government acknowledged the legality of its tenant's new course whenever questions about the policy arose. In the fall of 1945, Harold Young, a solicitor for the Department of Commerce—the CAA's home at the time—wrote in response to an inquiry by the National Commission on Interracial Cooperation: "The Supreme Court of the United States has held that where property was secured by condemnation, as the airport property was, the Government is without authority to compel an operating company to ignore or violate State laws." He went on to point out that the Commerce Department did not condone Jim Crow practices, but that his department lacked "the authority to compel the company operating the restaurants to ignore or violate the laws of the State of Virginia," which would have resulted in fines and, if the violations continued, shutdown of the proprietor's business.[16] The Commerce Department also lacked the will to intervene in any other way that would have brought relief to black travelers, reflecting the federal government's slow pace, if not reluctance, to deal with segregation on the federal level and within its own institutions.[17]

It was not until 1947 that African American patrons were able to obtain a meal at the aiport. The Air Terminal Services opened a separate cafeteria for them in the basement of the terminal building. Until then, they had to go without food or make do with provisional arrangements of the sort Mamie Davis encountered in the summer of 1946. Davis was a secretary of administrative affairs for the Young Women's Christian Association (YWCA) and as such traveled frequently. When the return flight of her business trip from New York to Washington was delayed, she received a coffee shop voucher from her carrier, American Airlines. She took the voucher to the coffee shop and presented it to one of the hostesses on duty, who refused to serve her. Unable to eat, Davis returned to the American Airlines ticket counter to file a complaint, which produced two results: she was offered a lunch box and a place to have her meal in the office space behind the ticket counter.[18] Whereas airport authorities were unable or simply refused to deal with the physical necessities of black air travelers, such as having a meal, American Airlines offered temporary relief from the experience of spatial exclusion. It did so in a way that was makeshift at best and not designed to accommodate larger volumes of passengers. But hiding Mamie Davis in an office space behind the counter also marginalized her existence as an air traveler. The opening of a coffee shop reserved for the exclusive use of African Americans institutionalized this strategy of marginalization at National Airport. As a result, the airport's dining facilities continued to generate complaints from African American passengers.

The Virginia Code also applied to Norfolk's Municipal Airport. In fact, in 1950 Virginia became the only state among the southern states to update its statutes in reaction to the appearance of airports in the built environment. Section 56–196 of the Code (1950) required "the establishment of separate waiting rooms at stations or depots [of aircraft carriers] for the white and colored races by the operators of such stations or depots."[19] However, this mandate for segregation in "waiting rooms and other public facilities" rested on a "may" requirement, which granted airport authorities and proprietors some leeway concerning its implementation. Given this flexible legal framework, the new airport terminal that opened its doors in May 1951 was an integrated facility;[20] plans to provide two sets of restrooms were scrapped after the NAACP's Norfolk chapter threatened to initiate legal action against the airport, in cooperation with the Women's Council on Interracial Cooperation, for violations of interstate travel provisions, which in their eyes made state segregation laws void.[21] Days after receiving the protest note, Norfolk's city manager confirmed that "the toilets have been rearranged so that there will now be (none) with a racial designation."[22] This reaction was noteworthy in a city where race relations were tense.[23]

This integrationist approach was challenged two years later when Costas Maroulis, the proprietor of the airport restaurant, the Azalea Room—which was named after the azalea gardens that surrounded the airport—and the coffee shop, asked the airport's Board of Commissioners for permission to spatially reorganize the restaurant in order to make room for a colored section. Maroulis, an immigrant from Greece, failed to provide an underlying rationale for his request. One possible explanation for his desire to redesign his dining room could have been complaints from white patrons, who resented encounters with black customers in his restaurant. The changing racial status of ethnic Greeks in American society likely provides an alternative explanation. Although Greek Americans entered the white mainstream during and after World War II, Greek American whiteness continued to be renegotiated throughout the twentieth century, as Yiorgos Anagnostou has argued. Whiteness was a relatively stable category in the postwar period, but it could come under pressure in times of crises, such as the Cold War, when communist Greeks were ostracized from white middle-class ethnic respectability.

Most Greek Americans, Anagnostou argues, understood the mechanics of U.S. American social hierarchies based on race.[24] This understanding led to various forms of interethnic contact. Whereas Greek Americans reached out to African Americans in places such as Detroit and Tarpon Springs, Florida, to mitigate the effects of racial discrimination, elsewhere "Greek Americans quickly learned Jim Crow."[25] Costas Maroulis may have well been an example of a man who had learned quickly.

The board signaled a willingness to accommodate Maroulis's request after its general counsel Marshall T. Bohannon supplied a legal justification for the reversion to Jim Crow. "Segregation should be and can be legally effective in the restaurant at Norfolk Municipal Airport," he advised.[26] It all depended on whether one considered an airport restaurant as a public facility or a public place—a significant difference—for a different section of the state code applied to public places, which made segregation mandatory.[27] Compromising its earlier approach, the board agreed to this verbal ploy and the grave material consequences. Following its decision, curtains were put up in the Azalea Room, a form of architectural partitioning long popular as a simple spatial strategy of white supremacy. These curtains marked most of the restaurant as off-limits to African American patrons, wrapping them into a small space reserved for their use. Black and white air travelers who may have sat in adjacent seats on the same airplane became invisible to one another on the ground. Ironically, the new policy was not applied to the coffee shop, which remained integrated, a fact that underlined the arbitrary nature of maintaining the color line.[28]

The irony of this arrangement did not escape the black community. The pastor of Norfolk's Bank Street Baptist Church, John B. Henderson, pondered the rationale behind the new policy in an editorial in the city's black newspaper *Journal and Guide*:

> Are our good white southern friends afraid to eat in the same dining room with us for fear some of our black will rub off on them? . . . Well if that is it, why are they using the fastest form of transportation known to man, a form of transportation that within less than an hour will carry them out of their beloved southland to other sections where they will have to eat in the same room with Negroes; or else eat out of the garbage can as that is the only place where they won't be disturbed by the presence of Negroes? It doesn't make sense.[29]

In the eyes of an increasingly mobile black middle class, spatial partitioning at an airport facility made no sense at all. For many black consumer citizens, airports signified the change that was slowly beginning to reshape southern cultural landscapes. At the same time, airports and the transportation services they offered provided an exit strategy from the confines of an oppressive southern social order. From a white supremacist perspective, however, the same airports signified a change that had to be contained. Mobility posed the most serious threat to a society whose internal cohesion was forced by local dependencies.

It was mostly because segregation laws had imposed restrictions on the mobility of African Americans that blacks found it difficult, if not impossible, to escape local communities and their racialized social and economic dependencies, even if only temporarily. These included vagrancy laws and segregation requirements in intra- and interstate transportation facilities and services. Vagrancy laws were initially introduced by southern authorities "to control the black population and prevent the collapse of the sharecropping system following the abolition of slavery."[30] Anyone without work had to hire themselves out to an employer. After the turn of the century these laws also became a tool to control the workforce in urban environments. Segregation requirements in intra- and interstate transportation made travel cumbersome and unpleasant for black travelers. And although travel by any means of transportation continued to be beyond the means of most blacks in the 1950s, more middle-class blacks who could afford to go away had to plan around segregated services and facilities. These were the groups that brought the most pressure on existing local dependencies. Equal access to air travel as the newest form of mobility would further increase the pressure brought to bear on the southern way of life in the postwar period, as air travelers would literally be able to lift themselves out of that way of life. Haphazard measures to shape and reshape airport terminal space indicate the desire of proponents of the status quo to keep things the way they were and to control the changes of modernization.[31]

In the early 1950s, patterns of spatial segregation and discriminatory practices also existed at other airports. A number of incidents that disclosed these practices were reported by Gloster Current, the director of branches for the NAACP. In his position, Current traveled to cities all across the country to visit the organization's local chapters, and as such he was among the growing number of African American business travelers. At the Oklahoma City airport, he encountered "whites only" service at the Sky Chefs restaurant in the fall of 1952.[32] He was also denied service at the dining room run by Dobbs Houses, Inc., at the airport in Birmingham, Alabama, two years later. The systematic nature of discrimination at Birmingham was confirmed by reports that the restaurant repeatedly refused to serve African American military personnel.[33] Incidents like these were not isolated, but part of a larger trend, as the black press pointed out to its readers. The *Cleveland Call and*

Post portrayed segregation at airports as a growing problem. "In some border airports," an article pointed out in January 1954, "there are signs welcoming Latin-American visitors in Spanish. Signs requiring racial segregation of colored United States citizens are displayed with equal prominence." Not only was this humiliating to black passengers: "The effect of this on visitors from Latin-American countries is extremely damaging."[34] The *Pittsburgh Courier* also lamented a general lack of integrated airport facilities. While there was a "veritable crazy quilt of contradictory policies" as to waiting rooms, restrooms, and transportation services, "there is almost no exception to the rule that Negroes cannot eat in lunchrooms and dining rooms."[35] This, the article stressed, led to all kinds of absurd scenarios, such as one at the airport in Fort Worth, Texas, where black passengers could use the waiting room but had to eat in the employees' cafeteria, "the overwhelming majority of whose patrons are white!"[36]

To understand more specifically how pervasive airport segregation had become by the early to mid-1950s, a number of surveys were conducted. The first was initiated by the NAACP's Executive Secretary Walter White in the spring of 1953.[37] Having long been involved in the struggle to integrate travel, in that year his organization began to look at airports more systematically as spaces that were being reorganized to include Jim Crow features. Noting the disconcerting trend "that segregated restrooms and other facilities for Negro passengers at airports are spreading," White called on fifty local branches to investigate the spatial conditions at their local airports. Segregation struck him as particularly "unnecessary and absurd" in light of the fact that even in the Deep South, passengers were treated equally in the aircraft cabin.[38] Based on the findings of the survey, the NAACP planned to initiate protest action against airport authorities in an effort to hinder the incorporation of the spaces of air travel into the landscapes of racial difference. While the small number of survey returns confirmed the expanding nature of spatial reapportionment at airports along racial lines, they also showed the myriad of ways in which the color line was drawn. Patterns of spatial organizations varied widely from airport to airport with the exception of airport restaurants and coffee shops, where segregated facilities or a lack of services for African Americans were the rule.

The findings submitted by members of the Memphis NAACP branch merit particular attention, not only because they provide information about the ground conditions at the airport terminal building;[39] they also illustrate the rules of social interaction between African American visitors to the airport and white airport staff. Although the branch's investigative committee did not come as travelers but as researchers, their treatment by the airport manager reflected southern racial etiquette. This behavior illustrates the condescension and disrespect African Americans of all social backgrounds were exposed to in their daily interactions with whites. The investigative committee included four members, respectable representatives of Memphis's black middle class: Utillus R. Phillips, the branch's president; Hollis Price, the president of Le-Moyne College, a historically black school;[40] J. W. Bowden, who ran the local office of the Universal Life Insurance Company; and J. F. Estes, an attorney. The terminal they came to investigate was a structure built in the late 1930s.[41] Like Washington's National Airport, Memphis Municipal Airport was designed in the art deco style typical of the time. But the terminal was a much smaller building—a three-story edifice with two wings and a concourse extending out in a ninety-degree angle, giving the airport the shape of a giant "T."[42] Its size reflected the city's status as a small regional transportation hub. Upon inspection of its passenger facilities, the committee encountered restrooms set aside for the use of "colored men" and "colored women." It also discovered that the dining room was spatially divided into areas reserved for white and African American patrons. Only the snack bar was integrated. The segregation of services included limousine transportation that was available for white passengers only; black air travelers were relegated to the use of black-owned taxi cabs. These patterns reflected the larger trend.

In their report, Estes and Phillips moreover described the committee's reception by the airport manager who had agreed to discuss conditions at the airport with them, as one "of an old line southern custom." He welcomed its members with the line, "Come in Boys, take a seat," a standard greeting for African American males irrespective of their age. Stetson Kennedy has interpreted this and other forms of interracial etiquette as compulsory rituals denoting first- and second-class citizenship.[43] During the conversation, the manager moreover frequently used the phrase "'I like a good 'Nigger' and 'Nigra'" (italics in the original). According to the report, he also pointed out that as long as he was in charge, African Americans were going to be treated like whites.[44] Given the conditions the report describes, this was obviously not the case. Blacks were neither treated respectfully nor allowed equal access to the entire range of airport spaces and services. The airport manager's remarks illustrate the conviction that, from a white supremacist perspective, things were perfectly fine the way they were. Segregation reflected the natural order of the southern world, whose notions of whiteness and blackness depended on the existence of the color line.[45] That this line was also drawn at Memphis Municipal Airport must have seemed inevitable to the manager. From his perspective, African Americans had obviously come a long way as consumers of the most modern means of transportation. The fact that his airport reflected the customary ways of organizing space in public facilities therefore needed no critical reconsideration. Members of the NAACP committee disagreed, even though their organization did not proceed (right away) to initiate legal or direct action. But the committee's findings were revisited when the CAA investigated the use of federal funds in the construction of the airport's new terminal building in the mid-1950s.

Even foreign nationals were not spared the humiliation of receiving second-class treatment at southern airports, as the case of the Indian ambassador Gaganvihari Lallubhai Mehta taught a shocked nation in August 1955. Stopping over in Houston on his way to Mexico City, Mehta was shown to a separate section of the airport restaurant instead of being seated in the main dining room where he had requested service.[46] As the *New York Times* reported the next day, to the restaurant supervisor, "the Indians had looked like Negroes and 'the law is the law.'"[47] Although Mehta apparently mistook the action as a courtesy and only in hindsight realized that he had been the victim of racial discrimination, the incident received unprecedented media attention and put Jim Crow airport terminals into the national spotlight. In a playful twist of the story that underlined the "foolish fallibility" of segregation, ABC radio broadcaster Edward Morgan reflected on what would have happened if "the lady in charge of the restaurant had mistaken a Negro for the Indian ambassador, and thus had not required him to seclude himself in a segregated private dining room." An African American would have actually come to sit in the white section of the airport dining room. Instead, Morgan went on, the incident illustrated the sad fact that black air travelers could not get a meal at the airport without discrimination.[48] He and other commentators agreed that this was an embarrassment for the city of Houston, which celebrated the fortieth anniversary of its "world port" airport the night the incident happened.[49]

The disrespectful treatment of Ambassador Mehta was also a major embarrassment for the Eisenhower administration. It highlighted the consequences of an official policy that shied away from the formulation of a strong domestic civil rights agenda. The abolition of racial discrimination was not given a high priority by the administration. Instead, it endorsed the same double standard to which previous administrations had subscribed. Promulgating a tough Cold War rhetoric internationally, which stressed democratic values and condemned the Soviet Union for its human rights violations, the Eisenhower administration turned a blind eye to the situation of millions of black Americans at home who were denied their citizenship rights on a daily basis.[50] Civil rights organizations had protested against this double standard during World War II when they initiated the "Double V" campaign, an effort that supported the American fight against fascism in Europe while demanding policies designed to end racial discrimination on the home front.[51] In 1955, civil rights advocates and critical media voices also pointed to the international perspective and squarely framed the Houston events in a Cold War context.[52] Incidents like the one involving the Indian ambassador created "ugly publicity for the United States abroad," Edward Morgan commented.[53] They did so not only because a foreign government official was involved but also because segregation per se was an injustice that had to be abolished. Whether they shared this assessment or not, Roy Hofheinz, the mayor of Houston, and John Foster Dulles, the U.S. secretary of state, issued apologies to Ambassador Mehta and the Indian government.[54]

In the spring of 1955, only a few months before the Houston incident, Charles C. Diggs Jr., the newly elected Democratic representative from Detroit, Michigan, conducted a second survey.[55] Committed to ending racial discrimination and critical of the Eisenhower administration's record on civil rights, Diggs became involved in a number of civil rights causes during his freshman year, and the fight against airport segregation was among his chief concerns.[56] To him, it seemed like an anachronism that customary patterns of discrimination against African Americans, which relegated them to separate and often inferior parts of the built environment, were applied to this new building type that symbolized modernity and progress like few others. In air travel's initial years, Diggs wrote in a letter of complaint to a number of airline CEOS, he had been gratified to see that passengers were treated equally and the aviation industry was "not falling into the old pattern of segregation and discrimination established by railroads and buslines." As the postwar years progressed, however, so did the spread of "undemocratic practices," which irritated him. The more common air travel became, he insuated, and the more people traveled—African Americans among them—the further Jim Crow's hand reached into reshaping terminal space. In his observations, Diggs undoubtedly recognized the connection between the expansion of the consumers' market, the growing mobility of Americans, and the extension of the color line by southern whites into spaces where it had not demarcated difference before. The urgency with which the forces of white supremacy extended this line to reaffirm the status quo needed to be countered with similar urgency by the proponents of equality.[57]

Diggs approached the airline presidents a few weeks before sending out the airport survey forms. In his letter, he expressed his frustration regarding segregated facilities across the South. Describing a general pattern that denied black air travelers equal access to restrooms, dining facilities, and ground transportation services, he also commented on his visit to the airport in Chattanooga, Tennessee. Diggs was irritated by a spatial arrangement that allowed African Americans to eat in the airport restaurant without restriction but required them to use separate restrooms. He wondered why "we can consume food and beverage in the same place, but we must eliminate the same in separate facilities."[58] Other establishments were much more careful in making sure that black and white bodies did not consume food and water together or use the same restroom facilities. Elizabeth Abel has argued that this was done to prevent a mixing of bodies and body fluids. She frames it as an effort to underline the nonnegotiability of constructions of race even on the most basic level of human wants.[59] Diggs urgently requested the airlines to use their influence to bring an end to these discriminatory practices.[60]

In their replies, the airline presidents and industry representatives expressed varying degrees of concern. A common theme in their reaction was the rejection of responsibility for the ways in which spaces were administered and practices enforced locally. General Counsel S. G. Tipton stated the point clearly on behalf of Harold Pearson, the president of the Air Transport Association of America: "We have no control over these facilities, and airline policy cannot be enforced upon them." Tipton explained that airlines held tenant status at airports across the country. Since they did not own airport buildings but rented terminal space, they were themselves dependent on "local customs and local laws."[61] Concerning the attitude toward practices of spatial exclusion based on race, the statements varied widely. While some airline executives stressed their company's record of fairness, others made no secret of the fact that they actually subscribed to white supremacy and condoned segregation. Eastern Airlines' president Thomas A. Armstrong assured Diggs that "Eastern does not and will not engage in practices of segregation and discrimination with respect to any public services or facilities." The scope of that statement was somewhat narrowed by the caveat that followed. The airline would and could apply this policy only to the spaces it controlled. The letter went on to state, however, that Eastern would "take such steps as we properly may to assure that all of our customers receive fair, adequate and nondiscriminatory treatment."[62] What these steps would entail remained vague. C. R. Smith of American Airlines also stressed his airline's ongoing efforts to "do our best to discourage discrimination." He acknowledged that local laws and regulations often provided difficulty, producing patterns of racial discrimination. As the executive officer of an airline that operated out of Dallas and provided service to quite a number of cities across the South, he accepted this fact. His remark that "we do our best to live well under them [local laws]" described a coping mechanism designed to ensure his company's local well-being, not the well-being of its black passengers. In no way does his letter suggest his intention to take a more active stand against Jim Crow practices.[63]

The reaction of Collett E. Woolman, president of Delta Airlines, was different, somewhat surprisingly so. With its headquarters located in Atlanta, Delta was the most southern airline as far as both its route system and its theme of southern hospitality for inflight service was concerned. As the biggest regional carrier, Delta served many of the cities where segregated terminal spaces emerged in the late 1940s and early 1950s. Woolman indicated in his letter that he was perfectly aware of this development. Stating that his airline took pride in its policy of treating all passengers equally, he also admitted: "Recognizing that areas of difficulty do exist, we have earnestly endeavored to approach our mutual problems on a realistic basis." When it was within the power of his company to make its own rules based on equality, it did. But as a tenant, it often had no influence on how local regulations were applied: "We do not encourage the practices of which you complain . . . where local laws require separate facilities . . . we do make every effort to insure the provision of equal and acceptable facilities by the governmental owners of the airport properties."[64] These efforts included the reimbursement of extra expenses to those passengers who had trouble getting limousine services and brought it to Delta's attention. However, realism according to Woolman dictated the airline's willingness to accept separate-but-equal facilities when it could have pushed harder for integration—an economically risky strategy he must have avoided in order to keep his company's market share. Any canceled service contract with a southern airport unwilling to accommodate Delta would have steered business toward one of its competitors.

Among these competitors was possibly National Airlines, whose president George T. Baker was the most confrontational in his response to Diggs. His airline was also based in a southern city, although National downplayed the concept of region in its corporate identity. It ran its business out of Miami, Florida, a city known for a racial caste system that extended beyond the African American community to include Afro-Caribbeans and Latinos. Although Miami was not in the Deep South and its racial traditions were complex, it was governed by a white establishment eager to defend the color line.[65] Baker presented himself as a representative of that establishment. His letter made clear that he was in no way concerned about Jim Crow laws or spatial discrimination based on race. If the majority of voters in a city supported the way in which their elected officials conducted public affairs—one is to assume that segregating public spaces was one such affair—was that not true democracy, he asked Diggs. Oblivious to the fact that in most cities few African Americans were allowed to vote, he went on to state that he saw no substance in Diggs's complaint about segregated facilities: "Negroes who live in the South want it that way." Baker, instead, reprimanded Diggs for pushing the issue of integration too hard, which was not "beneficial." He construed the congressman's fight as personally motivated and out of touch with the realities of people in the South, underlining the fact that Diggs represented constituents in Michigan, not Florida. Baker encouraged Diggs to back off: "If the zealots and radicals of both races would discontinue their mountain-climbing on mole hills, rapid progress could be made." He issued assurances that they both shared a desire for change. But before they were going to change people, they had to change themselves. "Being absolutely honest in determining what is right, instead of who is right," Baker wrote, "has solved many knotty problems for me, as it will for you." He therefore asked Diggs: "Please try it."[66]

Diggs did not try it. Instead, he turned to the airports directly. His office sent out questionnaires to over one hundred airport managers in thirteen states. Outside of the Deep South, the list of states included Arkansas, Kentucky, Maryland, Oklahoma, Virginia, Ohio, Missouri, and Tennessee. The survey was designed to track changes in the legal landscape and their ramifications in the built environment. It consisted of three parts. Part one inquired about the prevailing policies at the time of the airport's opening. Was there any discrimination "based on race, creed or color" as far as the use of taxi services, restaurant facilities, waiting rooms, restrooms, and water fountains was concerned? Part two asked about changes to the original policies and the reasons for such changes, and part three inquired about present policies regarding access to the spaces and services named above.[67] The survey results trickled in over the course of the next few weeks. While they cannot be considered comprehensive because only about 45 percent of the addressees replied, and the number of returns varied by state, they provide a unique perspective on local spatial practices and the rationale behind them.[68]

The survey showed, first of all, that the racial segregation of airport space was a transregional phenomenon. It was practiced mostly in the South but not exclusively. Airports in the North and the West also discriminated against black air travelers. One example was the airport in Cincinnati, Ohio, where black and white passengers had to use different eating facilities and restrooms in the year the airport opened in 1947. Quickly thereafter, however, the policy was dropped in reaction to pressure from local civil rights organizations.[69] At some airports where racial discrimination had never shaped spaces, local administrators sported a segregationist attitude notwithstanding. In a postscript to his survey reply, the manager of the airport in Cumberland, Maryland, remarked freely: "Personal—am in favor of segregation."[70] The survey also showed that airport segregation was not a uniform phenomenon. Spatial patterns and practices varied from place to place even within states, reflecting the local character of the legal landscape. States, cities, and sometimes airport managers made the rules. Local customs defined by airport patrons and administrators added another layer to notions of acceptable use of space by blacks and whites.

Over half of the airport managers who responded claimed that the use of their facilities was not shaped by Jim Crow practices. I say "claimed" because in some cases the information provided in the survey forms does not match other sources. Some managers admitted that integrated spaces existed only because the number of African American passengers was too small for anyone to mind.[71] Others stressed compliance with federal laws. J. Mark Wilcox, the general counsel for the Dade County Port Authority, the agency in charge of Miami's airport, assured Diggs that "at the present time, we believe that the operation of the Airport is fully within the applicable laws of the United States of America and that there is no discrimination exercised." He admitted, however, that ground transportation was an exception, as it sat on a different legal basis—state laws—but that concessionaires were bound to provide fair services by a contractual statement that guaranteed adequate transportation to all arriving passengers irrespective of their racial background at all times.[72]

Ground transportation was a problem at a number of other airports—mostly in Florida, Mississippi, Louisiana, and Alabama—that claimed to be fully integrated otherwise. Here state codes and city ordinances prohibited integrated transportation services as they did in other parts of the South. But enforcement patterns seemed to vary widely. Administrators blamed their lack of authority for the situation but also stressed that rarely, in their perspective, had the lack of appropriate limousine and taxi service caused passengers any problems.[73] Testimony from travelers who had experienced discrimination suggests otherwise. One example is Ralph Abernathy's description of conditions regarding ground transportation at the airport in Atlanta. Rather than wait for a black-owned taxi to pick him up from the airport after an evening arrival and with a connecting flight the next morning, he often preferred to spend the night in the airport waiting room. Abernathy resented the fact that, at least during the 1950s, limousine services for African Americans were not a regular airport service feature but were available only on demand.[74]

Other airport directors freely admitted that racial discrimination was a reality that black passengers had to cope with. The manager of the Sarasota-Bradenton airport did not even bother to go through the lines of the questionnaire. He simply scribbled "yes we do" on the form.[75] Others provided more information and also explained changes in policy. At the airport in Mobile, Alabama, segregation had been a policy since the opening of its passenger terminal in 1947. The airport was in compliance with the Alabama State Code, as the airport manager pointed out.[76] The airport at Jacksonville, Florida, had offered integrated facilities to air travelers initially, but in the late 1940s "as colored passengers increased separate facilities were provided to comply with State Law."[77] In Richmond, Virginia, the terminal restaurant at Byrd Field became segregated a few years after the airport began to operate in 1932, also in an effort to comply with local laws.

Elsewhere airport managers referred to customary patterns of behavior to explain spatial practices. At Fort Lauderdale, segregation did not exist de jure but de facto since "the small number of negro patrons using the airport appear to generally follow local custom," airport manager Lee Wagener explained. Tying his remarks into a long tradition of vindicatory segregationist rhetoric, he went on to point out that African Americans seemed to prefer facilities and services reserved for their use.[78] How little the existence of segregated or integrated spaces had to do with what black travelers preferred is illustrated by the remarks of Hot Springs, Arkansas, airport director Ralph Disheroon. He assured Diggs that his airport was integrated when he pointed out that "the class of colored people we have use our airport has never caused anyone to offer an objection. This is the reason for my handling this as I do." Disheroon framed the use of airport facilities as a class-specific activity, not a practice that was informed by people's racial background. For the moment, he seemed to be at ease with this new class of consumers who frequented his airport. His statement left no doubt, however, that access to integrated facilities was not the individual right of each citizen of the United States but a privilege that could be granted in a patronizing gesture or be taken away ad-lib by representatives of the white ruling class.[79]

As the last statements illustrate, the Diggs survey moreover showed that patterns of spatial exclusion in many places emerged in reaction to the rising numbers of African Americans like Diggs himself, who discovered the airplane as a convenient and modern means of transportation in the postwar period. While their numbers remained relatively small compared to the hundreds of thousands of predominantly white air travelers who flocked to the skies following World War II, and can only be estimated due to the lack of exact figures, air mobility increased in the black community as well. This mobility was greater in the North where an affluent black middle class able to purchase tickets was larger, had more opportunity to travel for leisure and business, and was less rigidly bound by laws that restricted movement. But southern blacks also came to rely more on air transportation for travel within and out of the South. Mostly representatives of the professions, business travelers, well-to-do leisure travelers like Birmingham business tycoon A. G. Gaston, and nationally and internationally known celebrities like Ella Fitzgerald, Harry Belafonte, and Sidney Poitier traveled by air in the immediate postwar years.[80] Their numbers came to include travelers of more moderate means and backgrounds.[81]

This clientele became the addressee of advertising campaigns sponsored by the airlines. Beginning in the late 1950s, TWA and American Airlines, two of the major carriers with headquarters outside the South, began to reach out to black customers. They did so in very target-group-specific ways, which increasingly came to characterize advertising more generally. Their ads appeared mostly in *Ebony* magazine, the black-owned monthly with a predominantly African American readership. Unlike ads published elsewhere in the press, which framed air travel as lily-white, these advertisements featured African American air travelers in interracial environments where they mingled with other airline patrons and interacted with airline service personnel. The black travelers in the ads are young, good-looking male and female professionals who travel by air for business and leisure. "Her job is precise, so is her airline," pronounced a TWA ad published in 1964. It included two images showing a black woman checking test-tubes in a lab in one and standing at the check-in counter in the TWA Terminal at John F. Kennedy International Airport in New York in the other. Another ad showed a business traveler making a phone call and arriving at the airport. The copy explained that traveling by air was the only way this successful salesman could handle a "crowded schedule," which included trips to two or three different cities per week. A third example showed a black business executive sitting at his desk in a skyscraper office and then comfortably settled into his seat in an integrated cabin aboard a TWA flight, accepting a beverage from a friendly white flight attendant. "Meet a man on the way up . . . and one way he got there: TWA," the caption reads, suggesting a narrative of upward mobility—both socially and three-dimensionally—that featured African Americans as its protagonists. To fly was to be modern, urban, and on the move.[82]

Another such protagonist appeared in an American Airlines ad in 1963. It showed Dorothy Height, the president of the National Council of Negro Women, entering an aircraft cabin where she was being greeted by an American Airlines flight attendant: "Good to have you with us again, Miss Height." The caption alluded to Height's frequent flyer status as a regular commuter between New York, her home, and Washington, D.C., the seat of her organization's headquarters. It also hinted at the importance of air transportation for the representatives of black civic, political, and social organizations. "Flying's the only way that I can meet a busy schedule that takes me all around the country," Height was quoted as saying in the ad's copy. As a civil rights and women's rights activist of national prominence, her visibility, nationwide reach, and local impact depended on access to a fast and convenient means of transportation—or so her comment suggested.[83]

As such, she exemplified a group that swelled the ranks of black air travelers after the mid-1950s when civil rights activists became frequent airline passengers. In the papers, memoirs, and autobiographies of many of those engaged in the struggle for black equality, travel by air begins to appear as an activity during that period. Some representatives of the civil rights movement soon relied heavily on air transportation to enhance their mobility, within the South and beyond it. Ralph Abernathy, for instance, whose altercation with Montgomery Airport's manager was related earlier, makes more than two dozen references to flying in his autobiography. He does so mostly in passing ("I was too late to catch a flight back," "I flew back early the next morning"), for his use of airplanes had become so commonplace—or appeared as such in hindsight—it deserved little commentary. Abernathy frames himself as a modern individual who used whatever new transportation technology was at his disposal. There are only a few instances when he contextualizes his own behavior as somewhat extraordinary at the beginning of his career as a young minister in Montgomery and Atlanta. Describing West Hunter Street Baptist Church, where he was appointed pastor in 1961, he writes: "For a sophisticated city church, the congregation was surprisingly naïve. I was the first pastor they ever heard of who went from place to place in an airplane."[84]

Martin Luther King Jr. also referred to flying rather matter-of-factly. As the chairman of the Southern Christian Leadership Conference (SCLC) and an increasingly visible leader following the Montgomery Bus Boycott, his writings reflect a busy national travel schedule whose connecting dots were the nation's airports.[85] But King was not only a frequent flyer. Like many others before him and many of his contemporaries, he drew inspiration from the "winged gospel."[86] His imagination fed on the possibilities and the promises an airborne civilization held. In a number of sermons he reflected on the peculiarities of travel by air, its significance, and its potential meaning in a political and social context. In a sermon outline drafted in April 1959, King writes about a five-and-a-half-hour flight from New York to London during which he and his fellow passengers were informed by their pilot that their return flight would be four hours longer. Breezy tailwinds were carrying them to London; strong headwinds would slow them down on the way back. Pondering the direction and force of transatlantic winds, King drew larger lessons from the adversities a jet plane had to face on the journey to its destination:

> But I started thinking about the fact that if, even if that plane is four hours late, it battles through that wind somehow, and it gets to New York. . . . And this,

I think, we find in this a parallel to life: that often we have strong tailwinds, and we move through life with ease, and things work in our favor, and everything is bright, and everything is happy. The sunshine of life is glowing radiantly in our eyes. These are bright and marvelous and happy days. But there will come moments when life will present headwinds before you. It seems that as you move something is blocking you. Circumstance after circumstance, disaster after disaster, stand in your path and beat up against you. And who is the man of creativity? He is the man who is determined to move on in spite of the headwinds.[87]

From this perspective, the jet plane's struggle against the elements became a metaphor for the civil rights movement's struggle against white supremacy. While few others in the movement as explicitly framed air mobility in the jet age as a signifier for a new age in social relations, traveling by airplane appears as an accepted convenience of postwar life in the autobiographies, writings, and biographies of other civil rights leaders and grassroots activists.[88] Traveling by air also greatly facilitated the work of the lawyers working for the Legal Defense Fund whose heavy caseloads often required them to commute between different courts and the fund's office in New York.[89] Airplanes moreover helped spread news. Reporters, photographers, and film crews who had previously relied on cables and wires could now easily travel between their newsroom and the theaters of action. The presence in the media, and in particular on television, greatly facilitated the civil rights cause.[90] By the early 1960s, civil rights activists and lawyers had come to rely on air transportation to participate in activities and events on short notice, to commute between different theaters of activity, and to combine their civic activism with their personal lives.

Efforts to document the shape of aviation's built environment like those of Charles Diggs were appreciated by the civil rights community. The results of his survey provided an impression of the pervasiveness of airport segregation in the mid-1950s. They also gave him and others an understanding of where the struggle for integration needed to take place. Diggs would focus his attention on Congress and use the means at his disposal as a U.S. representative to strive toward desegregation. His congressional work also gave inspiration to those who had been engaged in this struggle with limited success. O. L. Sherrill, the executive secretary of the General Baptist State Convention of North Carolina, wrote to Diggs in the fall of 1955. Regretting that the "feeble voices" of his organization's previous efforts had been ignored, he thanked Diggs for his activism: "We are proud to have someone in an official capacity who knows our problems, our sufferings, and the humiliation which segregation causes one to experience. We have nothing but admiration for your technique and approach to the problem."[91] Diggs's efforts also resonated with federal administrators. His probes and frequent communications with the CAA leadership eventually led the agency to look into discriminatory practices at airports across the South.

The NAACP also kept track of the ways in which the landscapes of air travel changed. In 1957, the organization sent out a follow-up to its earlier survey designed in particular to document changes that occurred in response to a ruling by the Interstate Commerce Commission (ICC). Following years of pressure from civil rights organizations, the ICC had finally banned segregation on interstate public transportation and mandated the integration of ground facilities (with the exception of restaurants) in 1955.[92] Although the ruling did not refer to air transportation or airports specifically and its applicability had yet to be tested, Roy Wilkins, the NAACP's new executive secretary, used the opportunity to explore airport terminal spaces in the second half of the 1950s.[93] The findings, which due to the fragmented nature of the survey returns have to be read in conjunction with the NAACP's case files documenting airport discrimination, show that patterns of spatial segregation based on race continued to be widespread. Although some airports had desegregated—the airports in Knoxville and Nashville, Tennessee, abandoned segregated floor plans in 1954, for example—most terminal facilities de facto continued to be firmly locked into the southern landscapes of segregation until the 1960s.[94]

Airport restaurants and cafeterias turned out to be the most rigorously segregated spaces as reports by NAACP officers and complaints from individuals show. Maintaining the color line continued to mean that whites and blacks had to eat and drink separately from one another. Whether fixed or temporary partitions separated them, or duplicate facilities existed, varied from place to place. Yet, many airports practiced some form of racial discrimination at their eating facilities. In early 1959, Chester Lewis, the state legal counsel for the NAACP, was denied service at the McPherson, Kansas, airport restaurant while traveling with a colleague. In a protest note to the mayor of McPherson, he described the experience as humiliating and emotionally distressing. Linking space, race, and demeanor, Lewis stressed that he and his colleague had been well dressed and well behaved, which served for him to illustrate the purely racist motivation of their discrimination (in response to his complaint the airport was integrated).[95] Gloster Current had a similar experience at Charleston Municipal Airport in late September the following year. Upon entering the airport's dining room, he was told by a waitress that the restaurant did not serve Negroes and was kicked out by the airport manager.[96] Lillian Voorhees, a drama professor at Fisk University, also encountered racial discrimination at the airport in Baton Rouge in early May 1963.

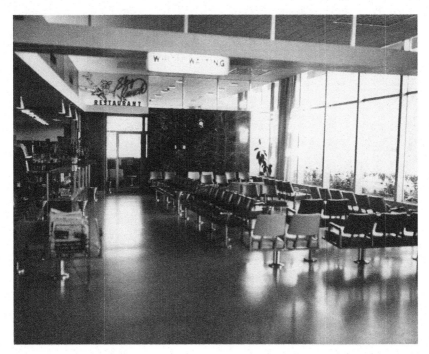

FIGURE 1. Waiting area reserved for white airport patrons at Dannelly Field Airport in Montgomery, Alabama (case files, *United States v. Montgomery*, NARA Atlanta).

When Voorhees, who was white, and her travel companions, a black student and her parents, entered the airport restaurant, they were asked to leave by the waiter. To make up for the lack of service in the proper dining area, the waiter suggested that the interracial group have their meal in the kitchen, an offer that they rejected.[97]

The Sky Ranch restaurant at Dannelly Field Airport in Montgomery, Alabama, was also a "whites only" eating establishment. It sat in the wing of a newly constructed terminal building that had opened its doors in 1958. Like the terminal structures in Charleston and Baton Rouge, it represented a second wave of airport construction initiated and funded through the Federal-aid Airport Program, which began dispensing funds in 1946. Like them, it was a modern structure that included the most up-to-date safety features and consumer amenities. More than these two buildings, however, the terminal in Montgomery serves to show that modernism and racial discrimination did not exist in binary opposition because it is the only structure whose visual documentation has survived. In a more immediate way than other sources, photographs of the terminal interior illustrate that racial segregation was an integral part of modernism and modernization. It was literally built into the

FIGURE 2. Airport entrance area with sign to waiting room for black airport patrons at Dannelly Field Airport in Montgomery, Alabama (case files, *United States v. Montgomery*, NARA Atlanta).

terminal, whose floor plan and design features affected the actions and movements of white and black patrons in the space.

Entering through the main door, travelers found themselves in the entrance area, which gave them access to the ticket lobby and the main waiting area. An illuminated sign reading "White Waiting" clearly demarcated this area as off-limits to African American travelers (see fig. 1). Like other signs it gave race a graphic body that shaped the meaning of its abstract terms.[98] Rows of mid-century modern chairs, plants, newspapers stands, and a gift counter created a pleasant and open space that also afforded access to the Sky Ranch restaurant. A much smaller sign reading "Entrance Colored Waiting" directed black clients to the waiting area reserved for black airport patrons, which was around the corner from the main area and not immediately visible from the terminal's main door (see fig. 2). This waiting room was a drab and contained space behind glass windows, accessible only through a door. To remind black travelers of their precarious status, airport management had posted a note: "We reserve the right to refuse service to anyone." Just outside this area, the restrooms reserved for the use of blacks were located. An illuminated sign reading "Colored" in big letters emphasized the purpose of their existence. A smaller second line reading "Men & Women Rest Rooms" indicated that the airport management was generous enough to provide separate toilets for men and women. The restrooms for white travelers were located in the ticketing lobby, the most centrally located area. Signs reading "White Men Rest Room" and "White Women Rest Room" indicated their limited availability to a select clientele. Two water fountains stood in the same area. In their complete identicalness, they functioned as the most obvious and absurd symbol of the "separate but equal" doctrine to which Montgomery's airport management subscribed. Like the waiting rooms and rest rooms, their duplicate existence signified the racial hierarchy that lay at the core of the airport's spatial organization. The Jim Crow terminal consisted of an arrangement of clearly demarcated spaces designed to marginalize and even make invisible the existence of African American air travelers. They also show how a facility built to function as the gateway to the most modern means of transportation at the same time gave expression to the retrograde social philosophy that dictated rules for its use. Thus, the "Airgate to Dixie," as the airport liked to call itself, also served as the gateway to the status quo.[99]

In the early 1960s, not only were airports mostly segregated territories whose individual shape varied according to the surrounding legal landscapes. Southern landscapes of transportation more generally formed a "jungle of law and custom," as the New York Times put it. De jure regulations and de facto practices varied so widely throughout the region "that uncertainty often leads him [the Negro] to surrender to tradition even where racial barriers are nonexistent."[100] White Southerners often exploited this insecurity to argue that African Americans preferred segregated facilities. For many black travelers, it was particularly confusing that Jim Crow laws not only varied from city to city but from one means of transportation to another along with the ground facilities connected to them. To ease their concerns about travel being more risk than pleasure, Victor H. Green, a civic leader from Harlem, had begun to publish the Negro Travelers' Green Book in 1936. The Green Book reviewed accommodations, restaurants, and other travel facilities. It also discussed transportation services focusing on air travel in its 1953 edition. But more than a consumer guide was necessary to challenge racial segregation and integrate the nation's airports not one by one but once and for all. As part of a multifaceted strategy aimed at the desegregation of the landscapes of aviation, civil rights groups and grassroots activists applied strategies of nonviolent direct action.

CHAPTER 3

On Location

Direct Action against Airport Segregation

Civil rights advocates understood that the fight against airport segregation would have to be waged on a case-by-case basis, airport by airport, just like the fight against other forms of racial segregation. This case-by-case approach had two dimensions: nonviolent direct action, a new protest strategy that emerged from the civil rights movement in the second half of the 1950s; and a focus on litigation, which was favored by the NAACP and eventually supported by the Department of Justice. Forms of nonviolent direct action were built on traditional protest forms such as marches and boycotts. Whereas leaders like Bayard Rustin, the co-organizer of the 1941 March on Washington, and Martin Luther King Jr., who came to national prominence during the Montgomery Bus Boycott, laid the philosophical groundwork for this new phase of resistance to the status quo, the Congress of Racial Equality (CORE) and the Student Nonviolent Coordinating Committee (SNCC) experimented with new protest forms such as sit-ins and Freedom Rides.[1]

Most campaigns between the mid-1950s and mid-1960s focused on the South and were designed to tackle two forms of racial discrimination: political disenfranchisement and spatial segregation. Integrating southern landscapes, including buildings, businesses, and services, became a goal of local civil rights groups all over the region. Transportation and its infrastructure had for some time been an area that local organizers and their national allies focused on because—as Gunnar Myrdal observed—unequal access to transportation services was the most bitterly resented form of segregation.[2] After the integration of railroads, attention shifted to challenging segregation in local, intrastate, and interstate bus transportation, which campaigns like the Montgomery Bus Boycott and the Freedom Rides accomplished.[3] The Bus Boycott, which started in December 1955 and ended a year later, successfully integrated municipal transportation services in Montgomery, Alabama.[4] The Freedom Rides, a series of protest rides by interracial groups of riders on interstate buses going into deep southern territory in 1961, brought about the integration of interstate bus services like Greyhound as well as the desegregation of local ground facilities such as bus depots. What tragically made the Freedom Riders very effective were the intensely violent incidents they triggered in communities on their itinerary, such as Anniston, Birmingham, and Montgomery. Scores of riders, along with federal monitors sent to Alabama to monitor the protests, were physically abused to such a degree and with apparent approval of the local police that the Kennedy administration stepped in to protect the riders.[5] It also pressured the ICC to enforce a court ruling that had mandated integration on interstate buses six years earlier.[6]

As the number of African American air passengers began to increase, many discovered that ground access to air travel was defined as much by Jim Crow laws as bus and train travel. In an effort to protest against exclusionary politics built into the architecture of aviation, activists targeted airport terminal facilities for direct action. Local organizations had protested against airport segregation by appearing before city councils and airport authorities (e.g., in Nashville and Memphis). But they had not staged protest action at the locations and in the actual spaces where black air travelers experienced discrimination. The airport terminal was new protest territory.

One of the first airports to become a target for direct action was Atlanta Municipal Airport. The airport had practiced segregation since the opening of its first passenger facilities in the late 1920s. However, due to the negligible number of black passengers, no separate spaces were built in terminal buildings, whose size and form constantly changed in the 1930s and 1940s as planners were expanding spatial capacity in reaction to growing numbers of white patrons. After the end of World War II, one of the hangars previously used by the military was converted into the airport's main passenger terminal. This was somewhat of a surprise move by the municipal leadership under Mayor William B. Hartsfield, a civic booster otherwise never shy about putting Atlanta on the map. But the conversion of the hangar saved both money and time.[7] It created capacity quickly at little cost and gave airport administrators an opportunity to think about facilities appropriate for the anticipated jet age. It was the terminal's interior rather than its shell that offered airport patrons a design spectacle. The building featured the country's longest airport ticket counter. Above the counter, large murals of the city and surroundings embedded the building in local history. Renderings of downtown Atlanta, Stone Mountain, the Georgia mountains, plantation homes, and the Okefenokee

Swamp adorned the walls. Scattered throughout the large rectangular space of the terminal were waiting areas, a gift shop, telephone booths, and other services, most of them available on a segregated basis only.

At the western end of the building the Dobbs House restaurant was located, run by the Dobbs Houses food company. Dobbs Houses, Inc., was a national business based in Memphis, Tennessee. The company started as a restaurant franchise in the 1920s and later expanded into airline catering. Airport restaurants formed one of the company's divisions.[8] Integrated into the terminal's theme park environment, featuring tangible local history, the Dobbs House restaurant gave built expression to the Lost Cause. Every feature was designed to recreate the Old South. As a welcoming gesture, the Dobbs House restaurant placed a bale of cotton by the door. Next to it, jingling a dinner bell, sat Alfonso Smith, an elderly African American man who impersonated Uncle Remus—the docile storyteller in the collection of animal tales and oral folklore published by Joel Chandler Harris in 1881.[9] *Jet* magazine in 1955 gave voice to the outrage of black travelers, many of whom considered the daily performance of this stereotype "disgusting."[10]

Originally a plain door, the restaurant's entrance by the mid-1950s was framed by a pillared canopy, a design feature referencing plantation architecture *en miniature*. Inside the restaurant, more reminders of Georgia's plantation past were supposed to provide ambience. Just like the ticket lobby, the walls featured large murals depicting scenes of plantation life. The murals transported restaurant patrons back to the antebellum period, portraying an idyllic southern country life, a happy past where whites and blacks got along—as masters and slaves. African Americans inhabited the space as figures looking down from the murals on the walls, frozen in time. As contemporaries, though, they were unwelcome. The Atlanta Dobbs House management practiced racial segregation, barring black patrons from having their meals at the "whites only" eatery. Just like other airports across the region, Atlanta Municipal Airport reflected the status quo in the ways in which its passenger facilities were spatially organized. Here, as elsewhere, the color line kept black travelers from enjoying equal access to air travel.

Atlanta Municipal Airport was poised to become the busiest airport in the country in the mid-1950s and the major hub for travel into and out of the South. Thus, Atlanta's airport became an increasingly important aerial gateway for African American air travelers.[11] Members of the city's black business elite and large middle class flew in unprecedented numbers, often purchasing tickets through Henderson Travel, Atlanta's first black-owned travel agency established in 1955.[12] The airport also served members of the emerging civil rights movement and the occasional northern black doing business in the

South. For many black visitors, even those who were nationally recognized celebrities, the restaurant turned out to be a source of frustration and humiliation.

One such example is the experience of actor Sidney Poitier. After wrapping up the filming of the movie *Blackboard Jungle*, Poitier was sent to Atlanta by his studio to promote the movie in the black community. In his autobiography *The Measure of a Man*, he relates that, after his newspaper and radio interviews, he went back to the airport where he hoped to eat dinner at the Dobbs House restaurant before his departure. Upon entering the eating establishment, he noticed that all waiters, including the head waiter, were black. Yet when the latter came to meet him at the door, obviously recognizing the actor, he confessed his inability to treat him like other (white) patrons: "Mr. Poitier, I'm sorry. I could give you a table, but we're going to have to put a screen around you." "What do you mean?" Poitier replied, barely able to contain his astonishment. "Well," the waiter explained, "it's the practice here; it's the law." What aggravated Poitier, who declined the service offer, was the fact that one African American man had to explain the rules of racially motivated spatial exclusion to another. Relegated to a low-paying service job in a white-run business, the head waiter had to function as the spokesperson for the white establishment. "It must have hurt," Poitier concluded, who walked away allegedly feeling sorry not for himself but for his compatriot. He admitted that he felt outrage and anger too. "Yes, but I took it in stride—because this moment of absurdity was, in fact, so totally unremarkable. To African Americans in 1955 this kind of insult was old hat." In conclusion, Poitier writes how he was able to digest the incident and go on with his life because he felt that he had to. But accommodation to racial segregation, he points out, was impossible.[13]

Martin Luther King Jr. had similar experiences on several occasions. As a frequent traveler who in the mid-1950s was emerging as one of the leading figures of the civil rights movement, he often used the Atlanta airport. Writing to Atlanta attorney Sylvester Robinson in early October 1956, King recounted an episode that had taken place a few days earlier. On his way from Montgomery to a speaking engagement at the Hampton Institute in Virginia, he had to change planes in Atlanta. Faced with a delay, King, who specifically mentioned that he had been the only black passenger on the flight, proceeded to the Dobbs House restaurant hoping to use the lunch voucher his airline had provided. There, however, a scenario quite similar to what Poitier had experienced unfolded. King was offered "a seat behind a dingy compartment which totally set me off from other passengers." Neither his refusal to eat under segregated conditions nor his conversation with the restaurant manager about his status as an interstate passenger made a difference. The manager insisted that the city ordinance and the state law that implemented the color line in Atlanta's restaurants should not be violated. King left the dining space going without food for the better portion of the day. What he labeled a tragic inconvenience also struck him as an excellent case for a lawsuit. To that end he talked to the head waiter, the other waiters, and the hostess, the only white service person on duty, in an effort to recruit possible witnesses.[14] In 1959, he again was refused service at the Dobbs House restaurant, on one occasion in the company of his brother A. D. King and father Martin Luther King Sr., and again he did not seek redress.[15] By then, however, a civil action against the airport was underway. H. D. Coke, not an Atlanta resident but an interstate traveler from Birmingham, Alabama, who had tried in vain to eat at the restaurant, filed an antidiscrimination suit against the airport in 1958.[16]

By then, black Atlantans had fought for decades against racial segregation in their city. Grappling with Atlanta's reputation as the New South's urban powerhouse "too busy to hate," their struggle involved various organizations.[17] It also produced powerful campaigns and significant outcomes, for the city's can-do stylization as the regional center of racial harmony and integration was largely a myth. The city's white elite might have practiced forms of racism that differed slightly in comparison to those in Montgomery or Birmingham; but essentially, African Americans in Atlanta existed as much on the margins of society, spatially and institutionally, as they did elsewhere. The size and heterogeneity of the black community, however, made possible a considerable measure of autonomy and self-sufficiency especially with regard to education, which helped establish Atlanta as a regional center of black culture and higher learning. The efforts of an older generation of civil rights leaders that came of age before World War II focused on achieving equality through the law. It included most notably A. T. Walden, the president of the Atlanta branch of the NAACP, who espoused an approach that Tomiko Brown-Nagin has called "pragmatic civil rights." It amended legal activism with pragmatic forms of engagement that were designed to preserve economic self-sufficiency and personal autonomy while expanding political influence. Rather than fight against racial discrimination in the courts exclusively, these leaders sought reform of the status quo, often negotiating black civil rights through the confines of Jim Crow. Within the limits of this approach, civil rights leaders brought about change with regard to voting rights, housing, public recreation, and transportation. The slow pace of integration in the post-*Brown* years, however, positioned this older, accommodationist leadership against a new generation of leaders—many of them students—who saw grassroots organization and direct action as means toward quicker, comprehensive change that did not stop short of full equality.[18] Weary of the NAACP and its activities, these younger voices found a home in the local CORE chapter and would soon help to establish a local SNCC chapter. CORE activists were among those who brought direct action to the restaurant at Atlanta Municipal Airport.

The Atlanta airport protest was a CORE initiative. It is best described as an eat-in to promote interracial eating (the terminology would be invented a few years later). Shared meals were one of the city's most strictly enforced social taboos. The eat-in was carried out by an interracial group of five activists who intended to have lunch at the Dobbs House restaurant on August 8, 1959. Members of the group included James R. Robinson, CORE's executive secretary; the Reverend Wyatt T. Walker, the Virginia state director of CORE; James T. McCain, CORE's Georgia field secretary; and two others who were not CORE officers, Guy Hershberger, an American Mennonite theologian and professor at Goshen College,[19] and Elmer Neufield, the executive secretary of the Mennonite Central Committee Peace Section. All five were on their way home after attending the Leaders Institute against Segregation, a training conference cosponsored by CORE; the SCLC; and the Fellowship of Reconciliation, an interfaith peace organization dedicated to peaceful conflict resolution.[20] The Mennonites, a religious group dedicated to pacifism and community building, formed a strong presence in the latter organization, and their presence in the group of protesters is therefore not surprising. The church was supportive of the African American civil rights struggle, and members participated in a number of other protests.[21]

When the group sat down at a table in the restaurant's main dining room, James Robinson related in an interview, the assistant manager informed them that only its white members would be served. The African Americans would have to find seats at another table—the same screened-off table Sidney Poitier had been shown years earlier. "We told him that the five of us were together and had no intention of being separated to comply with jimcrow [sic] laws."[22] In reaction, Robinson, Walker, and McCain were allowed to stay in the "whites only" section of the dining room but were not served. They ate anyhow, sharing the meals their white colleagues were able to order. The group's action triggered only a mildly hostile reaction from airport management and restaurant staff. One of the waitresses on duty expressed what can be read as a mix of astonishment and admiration: "You know, Negroes before have refused to sit behind the screen, but no one ever got so far as you people."[23] Most other restaurant patrons took little notice according to a newspaper report, not seeming to mind integrated food service. Although the protest had no immediate effect on the integration of the notorious airport restaurant or the city's public accommodations in general, its participants nevertheless encouraged others to imitate it. "We all agreed," James Robinson said, "that it was the best coffee we had ever had—the extra tang of drinking your coffee interracially across the Georgia color bar is highly recommended!"[24]

Four months later, in January 1960, CORE targeted the airport in Greenville, South Carolina, in cooperation with the Interdenominational Ministerial Alliance (IMA), a faith-based ecumenical association invested in the struggle for civil rights with branches across the country. At the time of the protest, South Carolina had emerged as one of the battlegrounds for the civil rights movement. In fact, Peter Lau argues that South Carolina had "represented an important strategic and symbolic site in the bourgeoning southern movement" since the end of World War II.[25] Black Carolinians were highly organized and had scored victories primarily in the realm of labor relations. Not content with improvements in the workplace, they also fought for voting rights and against pervasive segregation. This fight, which met with strong resistance across the state, had also mobilized blacks in Greenville, where civil rights organizations, most importantly the NAACP and CORE, had built a strong presence.[26] Incensed over recurring incidents of racial discrimination at the local airport terminal, civil rights activists began to focus their attention on that particular space and explored strategies that would bring about its desegregation. One effort focused on the courts and supported Richard Henry's lawsuit against the airport, which was filed in 1958 but still pending. Henry, a civil servant employee of the U.S. Air Force, was denied access to the terminal's waiting area on several occasions.[27] In another effort designed to underscore the urgency of their issue, the local CORE and IMA chapters turned to direct action as a protest strategy. On January 1, 1960, they pulled together several hundred protesters to hold a "prayer pilgrimage" at Greenville Airport to demonstrate against racial segregation at the terminal building.

Greenville Municipal Airport was a small regional airport. It opened in 1928 and began scheduled flights in the late 1930s, when Eastern Airlines arrived, followed by Delta Airlines a few years later. By the mid-1950s, the airport offered about two dozen weekday departures. With the exception of a connection to Richmond, however, no flight out of Greenville exceeded 200 miles. That the airport attracted an interstate visitor like Henry was largely the result of the Air Force base that was established in the city in 1942.[28] The airport's predominantly local significance as an aerial gateway was reflected in its built form. The new terminal that opened its doors in 1954 was a small building, a two-story tiered structure topped by an air traffic control tower. It was a typical example of small town airport architecture, funded in part by the FAAP. The terminal featured a modestly designed modernistic exterior, unassuming in its functionalism. The same functional simplicity characterized the building's interior, a big open space where the waiting area and the ticket counters were located. Checkered vinyl flooring and wood paneling on the walls gave the area a sober ambience. Interior designers had added a decorative touch by hanging large photographs on the walls. These photographs embedded the building in local history in ways similar to the murals at Atlanta Municipal Airport. Rather than depicting natural landmarks, the art at Greenville Airport rendered impressions of the industry that defined the city: the cotton mills. The photographs showed panoramic views of gigantic loom workshops. The rows of looms looked like abstract art, producing shapes that tied in with the checkered patterns of the floor. The photographs gave visual expression to Greenville's identity as a proud New South city, an identity that was also reflected in the city's marketing slogan as the "Textile Capital of the World."[29]

Much like the textile mills, the rather sterile environment of the terminal was mostly a white space, reserved for the use of white airport patrons.[30] The airport restaurant, the Redwood Dining Room, was a whites-only facility as well. Although Greenville Municipal Airport provided separate facilities for African American passengers, the "colored lounge" formed a tiny percentage of the terminal's square footage. The "lounge" was a room off the main entrance of the terminal, a duplicate space containing chairs, telephones, and restroom facilities. The room's features spelled out a simple message: it requested the occasional black air travelers to arrive at the airport just in time for departure rather than spend much time in the terminal. The fact that black passengers were sometimes allowed to linger in the waiting room reserved for whites only underlines the arbitrary nature of the politics of racial segregation, but it did not make Greenville Airport an integrated facility. Instead, it was a racially exclusive space where black travelers were marginalized spatially and their existence systematically denied.

To protest against this form of discrimination, the prayer pilgrimage was held. The organizers deliberately chose January 1, 1960, as the date for the event, for it marked the ninety-seventh anniversary of Abraham Lincoln's Emancipation Proclamation, which had freed southern slaves in 1863. The prayer pilgrimage not only was designed to express the black community's growing impatience with the city's Jim Crow regime but also, more specifically, was meant to voice outrage over the airport's humiliating treatment of retired baseball star Jackie Robinson the previous fall.[31] Robinson, who was hugely popular not only in the African American community but in the general population, had come to town in late October 1959 on the invitation of the NAACP to attend its South Carolina State Conference and speak to the delegates. When Robinson returned to the airport to catch a flight back to

New York, accompanied by NAACP director of branches Gloster Current and a number of other conference participants, he was asked to leave the main waiting area by the airport manager, O. L. Andrews.[32] Andrews approached Robinson while he was signing autographs and talking to fans, according to a report later filed by Current. Anything but starstruck, the manager threatened to arrest Robinson, Current, and their company if they refused to leave the area. He ignored the group's insistence that as interstate passengers they were entitled to use all terminal facilities on an integrated basis. Rather, Andrews insisted that local laws barred them from spaces designated as "whites only." Confronted with his imminent arrest, Current, as detailed in his report, declared his willingness to go to jail. No arrests were made, however, and the situation did not escalate before it became time for Robinson and company to board their flights.[33] What made the difference in this case was not so much the intensity of the confrontation with the airport manager. Rather, it was the prominence of one of the victims of racial discrimination that set events in Greenville apart. Local organizers recognized the importance of Robinson's celebrity status and seized the opportunity, hoping to use his high-profile status as a tool to generate publicity for their protest.

The "prayer pilgrimage" followed a choreography that was becoming a signature characteristic of civil rights protests. It began with a mass rally at Springfield Baptist Church, for in Greenville as in many other communities the black churches stood at the center of activities. Among the almost two dozen speakers who represented major civil rights, labor, and business organizations was Ruby Hurley, the southeastern regional director for the NAACP, who reminded listeners that South Carolina was among the least integrated states in the South. He called for immediate change and encouraged all in attendance to send a message to those in power by casting their vote against incumbent South Carolina Governor Ernest F. Hollings in the next election—a difficult task given widespread disenfranchisement and low voter participation.[34] Following the rally, about three hundred protesters drove to the airport in cars, left their vehicles about half a mile away from the airport, and marched to the terminal in what CORE's James McCain described as bad weather conditions in the *CORE-lator*.[35] They battled low temperatures and sleet along the way, singing "America the Beautiful," one of the most beloved American hymns, an ode not only to the country's natural beauties but also to its democratic tradition. To express their patriotism and claim their stake in the American project, demonstrators sang about brotherhood, liberty, and freedom in law. Heroes in the past, the song suggests, in their "liberating strife" had put their country's needs above all else and loved "mercy more than

FIGURE 3. Delegation of ministers at Greenville Municipal Airport during the prayer pilgrimage on January 1, 1960 (*The Greenville News*).

life."[36] Brotherhood and mercy were needed now to rectify the mistakes of the past and liberate African Americans.

Getting to the terminal, which was heavily guarded by local police and filled to capacity by an expectant crowd of mostly whites, which included members of the Ku Klux Klan, a delegation of fifteen ministers and a few marchers entered the building. Inside, the ministers congregated in the entrance areas, coming to stand in front of one of the big loom workshop panoramas, where they prayed and read a resolution (see fig. 3).[37] The resolution strongly played on familiar themes of patriotism and citizenship, framing access to integrated facilities as an unalienable right and not a privilege. C. D. McCullough, a minister from Orangeburg, South Carolina, declared: "We are only demanding that which is the due of every citizen of the U.S. We should be base citizens, indeed, unworthy to be called Americans, if we acquiesced in the degradations which southern tradition would impose on us."[38] He went on to point out that blacks refused to be satisfied with what he called the crumbs of citizenship while others enjoyed "the whole loaf by right of a white-skinned birth."[39] J. S. Hall, the pastor at Springfield Baptist Church and the chairman of CORE's Greenville chapter, added that his group had come to demonstrate "that we still have some of freedom's fire in our blood. The Negro is restless and will not be satisfied until every public sign that says 'colored' and 'white' is burned and the smoke is in the clouds."[40] On that note the group left, and the protesters returned to town.

Abiding by the principles of nonviolent direct action CORE subscribed to, the prayer pilgrimage was conducted in a manner that was peaceful, orderly, and dignified. It brought local leaders and their mass base together for concerted action to issue an unambiguous message: racial segregation was unjust and unacceptable. Nothing but its abolition would do. The time for action had come. To stress the urgency of this message, civil rights activists upset Greenville's spatial order, if only for a day. With their motorcade and their march they sketched a path from the town's black community to the airport. Thereby they established a direct link between the two, claiming air travel was something black consumers desired as much as white consumers. The hundreds of marchers who participated in the pilgrimage seemed like a prediction of the swelling ranks of black travelers. But the protesters also claimed the terminal as they had claimed other spaces: as a symbol of white supremacy and the denial of black equality. For a few hours then, the terminal became protest territory, a battleground in the fight over postwar racial identities—both black and white—and African American citizenship. Both sides knew what was at stake. How much Greenville's whites feared change became apparent in the massive turnout of onlookers who came to the airport to "welcome" the prayer pilgrims.[41] Like elsewhere, members of the Klan and local law enforcement verbally and nonverbally tried to articulate the nonnegotiability of white supremacy.[42] The airport management turned the airport into a fortified bastion, lowering both the U.S. and South Carolina flags as protesters approached the terminal and locking all but one entrance door. By letting only fifteen activists into the building, the representatives of the status quo resisted the short-term integration of the terminal as much as the black protesters forced it upon them—albeit without resorting to violence.[43] For the moment, the airport terminal would remain segregated. While activists continued the struggle to integrate other parts of Greenville's (public) service infrastructure like the public library, the Kress department store's lunch counter, and the skating rink, the contrast between the airport's modernistic architecture, which the *Cleveland Call and Post* commented on in its reporting, and the anachronistic spatial practices that defined its use, would continue to exist.[44]

In the summer of 1961, Jackson, Mississippi, and Tallahassee, Florida, emerged as locales for direct action protests. The airports in both cities became test sites for CORE Freedom Ride activists. One group of Freedom Riders hit Jackson airport with a "Freedom Fly-In" to test airport facilities on June 7, 1961. A few days later another group arrived at Tallahassee airport by bus with a similar mission. In May and June 1961, these Freedom Riders traveled through the Deep South mostly on interstate buses to test service conditions in terminal facilities. The Freedom Rides were organized by CORE, although SNCC-affiliated activists from Nashville joined the cause after the first group of riders experienced massive outbreaks of violence during their journey; and the NAACP and the SCLC came to support them, too. CORE considered the Freedom Rides a dramatic way of applying its nonviolent protest strategy that "came about as a logical extension of the student sit-in movement," as Derek Catsam has argued.[45] The organization also hoped to generate national attention for a largely local civil rights movement by tying the places of the movement together as stops on a protest journey.

The Freedom Rides were designed to bring a new challenge to Jim Crow transportation. Since the landmark decision in *Morgan v. Virginia* (1946) that integrated interstate buses, further progress in the fight against segregation had been made. *Henderson v. United States* (1950) reaffirmed the illegality of Jim Crow laws in interstate transportation. In 1955, the ICC weighed in on the issue, banning segregation in trains, buses, and station waiting rooms. Conditions on the ground in bus depots and airport terminals still left much to be desired, however, due to a lack of compliance.[46] The civil rights community hoped this would change after the Supreme Court declared the unconstitutionality of segregation in restaurant facilities and terminal services in *Boynton v. Virginia* (1960).[47] Modeled on the 1947 Journey of Reconciliation, a joint effort between CORE and the Fellowship of Reconciliation to test adherence to *Morgan v. Virginia*, the Freedom Rides were designed to test compliance with *Boynton v. Virginia*. CORE sent integrated groups of riders into southern territory to investigate facilities and bring national attention to the racialization of the built travel environment. Mostly interested in exploring the service options and spatial order of bus terminals, a few Freedom Riders set out to investigate the conditions at local airports.

The first group of riders was supposed to travel from Washington, D.C., to New Orleans. They left Washington on May 4, 1961. Whereas their journey through Virginia was largely uneventful, the riders began to experience hostile reactions in the Carolinas. Hostility turned into extreme violence once they entered Alabama territory. Buses were bombed and riders severely beaten in Anniston and Birmingham, forcing them to complete their journey by plane. These events did not deter other activists from following their example. Instead, more groups set out to travel to cities and towns across the South, forcing the Kennedy administration into action in an effort to protect their rights as well as their lives.[48] Jackson, Mississippi, was high on the list of places to be targeted by the Freedom Riders. It had a reputation as the "hard core capital of segregation," as the *Boston Globe* put it, reporting on the Freedom Rides.[49] The newspaper echoed assessments made by a number of critical observers, among them C. Vann Woodward, who considered Mississippi "that irreducible citadel of Southernism."[50] The state was a hotbed of white supremacy. In reaction to *Brown v. Board*, the forces of massive resistance had created a political and social climate of impermeability, in which change seemed impossible. Across the board, representatives of the white establishment, among them Governor Ross Barnett, articulated only one message: integration would never become a reality in this bastion of the status quo.[51]

Like Greenville, Jackson Municipal Airport (Hawkins Field) was a small regional airport, although it served as the aerial gateway to Mississippi's state capital. Its passenger terminal was built in 1936 with the support of the Works Progress Administration (WPA).[52] The original building was a small, two-story neofederalist structure with two wings. The front and back entrances were protected by pillared porticos, classical in front, art deco–inspired in the rear. These design features served as reminders of the southern plantation past, just as they did at airports in Atlanta and Washington, D.C. After the war, the building's wings were extended to increase its square footage. Unlike other airports, however, Jackson was slow to invest further in the expansion of its terminal facilities during the 1950s, which reflected the city's financial situation. Passengers and airlines had to make do with a structure that survives as one of the few remaining examples of 1930s airport architecture. The terminal probably felt as outdated architecturally to the Freedom Riders in 1961 as Mississippi's racist laws and practices.[53] Rather than arouse a sense of nostalgia, the building evoked anger and frustration in black travelers because its facilities were segregated. Nonmalleable Jim Crow features were added during a renovation of the terminal in the mid-1950s. Inquiring about a possible misuse of federal funds, Representative Charles Diggs received assurances from the CAA, which cosponsored the renovation, that "the construction and alteration to the waiting room, dining-kitchen and sanitary facilities are not included in the approved project, and that the Federal Government will not participate in the cost of such facilities."[54] The city of Jackson added the facilities anyhow, paying for the construction with local funds. At this point, the CAA did not get in the way of the reconfiguration of the terminal—which it would in 1963. Nor did it act to prevent the discrimination against black passengers that would follow. Instead, the Jackson airport management was enabled to redesign passenger service facilities as a strategy to invalidate the existence of black air travelers. The duplication of service facilities here, as elsewhere, led to the spatial marginalization of African American travelers in the airport terminal.[55]

To investigate and test these facilities was the mission of the three Freedom Riders who flew into Jackson Municipal Airport on June 7, 1961, the first day of the Fly-In. Gwendolyn Jenkins, Robert Jenkins, and Ralph Washington arrived on a Delta Airlines flight from St. Louis two weeks after the first waves of riders had hit the city and protesters were beginning to fill the city's jail.[56] After disembarking, the Freedom Flyers proceeded to the terminal, where they fanned out in different directions in an effort to integrate simultaneously the building's segregated service spaces. Robert Jenkins, a student at St. Louis University, went to the airport restaurant and was arrested when he refused to leave without having been served. Ralph Washington, a pathology attendant at St. Louis County Hospital, successfully integrated the restrooms reserved for the use of white men; and Gwendolyn Jenkins, a receptionist at a St. Louis law firm, was prevented from entering the restrooms marked "women white" by a team of police officers who then arrested her and Washington.[57] As the only gender-integrated team to carry out nonviolent direct action at an airport terminal that included a black woman, Jenkins, Jenkins, and Washington carefully staged their airport protest performances. To sustain the increasing media attention the Freedom Riders received after the events in Alabama, the local CORE branch regularly sent out press releases to announce the arrival of new groups of riders in Jackson. It also informed the press of the impending trip of the St. Louis Freedom Flyers, who were met not only by a police contingent but also by a number of media representatives disposed to record their activities.[58] All three presented themselves camera-ready, decked out in carefully chosen outfits and displaying a demeanor that was as composed as it was dignified. The photograph showing the group before their departure in St. Louis is a familiar version of protest imagery that framed (and tamed) the African American civil rights subject on location (see fig. 4).[59] It is part of a larger visual archive showing civil rights activists peacefully integrating eating establishments and waiting rooms.

Another image shows Gwendolyn Jenkins standing in front of Jackson Municipal Airport's racially exclusive women's restroom, which is guarded by two police officers. It invokes the nexus between mobility, race, and gender. Jenkins's activities communicated that African American women wanted to and did travel by air like an increasing number of their contemporaries. She looked just like the young woman shown in those TWA advertisements in *Ebony* magazine, gainfully employed and eager to consume. But her presence in the unwelcoming territory of the airport terminal signaled a second nexus: the intersectionality of space, race, and gender that motivated her actions.

FIGURE 4. Freedom Flyers Gwendolyn Jenkins, Ralph Washington (standing in front), and Robert Jenkins go aboard a Delta Airlines plane in St. Louis on June 7, 1961, for their trip to Jackson, Mississippi (picture alliance/ Associated Press).

Hoping to integrate the women's restroom, Jenkins not only protested against racial discrimination in the landscapes of (air) travel. Insisting on access to that particular sanitary space marked "women white," she also claimed a status of womanhood long denied African American women: the status of a lady. I agree with Elizabeth Abel, who has argued that Jenkins did not strive to undermine the category of "the lady" by showing that its margins compromised the center. Rather, Jenkins appropriated the signifiers of that center by delivering a careful performance of attitude, grooming, and manners.[60] The image shows her carefully poised in a black-and-white striped skirt-suit and white gloves, holding a tote bag and a suitcase. Her dress, accessories, hair, and countenance make her a perfect example of a black lady who has every right to be considered equal. Her facial expression is the only indication of the doubts she might have about the police officers' willingness to share her vision. They stand in front of the restroom door, guarding the access to the toilets, thus serving as representatives of the status quo who are unwilling accommodate her. The sign "women white" hovers between the police officers and Jenkins, like a floating signifier of the racial and gender biases that produced the airport space.

The first Fly-In was unsuccessful, but it was repeated the next day. On June 8, Mark Lane and Percy Sutton flew into Hawkins Field from Montgomery, Alabama. Lane, who was white, was a New York State legislator. Sutton, who was African American, served as president of the NAACP's New York branch and as legal counsel for CORE's office in Harlem. Both were or would become notable civil rights attorneys.[61] Their fact-finding mission included Sutton's attempt to use the restroom reserved for white men, which got both arrested on charges of breaching the peace.[62] A third group of protesters went to the airport six weeks later to focus on the airport restaurant as the space to be integrated. Rather than orchestrate another Fly-In, the group of Freedom Riders around Rabbi Alan Levine seems to have formed somewhat spontaneously and with the encouragement of local CORE members after an afternoon lecture by Martin Luther King Jr. at Tougaloo College on July 21, 1961. Assembling a racially integrated, interfaith group of eight, Levine took them to the airport, where the group arrived around 7:00 p.m. hoping to have dinner.[63] However, J. L. Ray, the same police captain who detained Gwendolyn Jenkins, arrested the group after he warned them of going into the restaurant, which they attempted to do anyhow. Ultimately, none of the three groups of Freedom Flyers was able to make a difference. Whereas their appearance at the airport marked a new level of engagement that increasingly brought civil rights activists from across the country into southern communities, the action failed to have an immediate impact on the spatial configuration of the airport terminal, which continued to exist as a segregated facility for the next two years. For now, Jackson's forces of massive resistance prevailed, which included city commissioners and the airport authorities appointed by them.[64]

A week after the Freedom Fly-Ins, a group of Freedom Riders staged a sit-in at the airport of one of the many other Freedom Ride destinations: Tallahassee, Florida. The Interfaith Freedom Riders, an interracial group of ministers and rabbis recruited by CORE, reached Tallahassee on June 15, 1961.[65] They had set out from Washington, D.C., a few days earlier to test facilities along the way, and in particular to investigate conditions at Tallahassee's bus depots and airport. Their journey turned out to be largely uneventful. In Tallahassee, they encountered segregated facilities in the Trailways and Greyhound bus terminals but were able to eat and use the restrooms, although the restaurant proprietors overcharged them for their meals, and the police first had to disperse a hostile crowd at the Greyhound depot.[66] Planning to fly back home after their integration of the bus stations, the group went to the airport, where they hoped to have a meal at the Savarin airport restaurant before their departure.[67] Their service inquiry was denied because the airport manager had received instructions from city officials to close the restaurant

FIGURE 5. Reverend Arthur L. Hardge and another Freedom Rider look over the "closed" sign on the door of the Savarin restaurant at Tallahassee Municipal Airport, June 15, 1961 (picture alliance/Associated Press).

rather than to serve the Interfaith Freedom Riders as his downtown colleagues had done. Although Union News Co., the restaurant's proprietor, had declared its willingness to provide service in negotiations with CORE beforehand, the protesters were personally rejected by the manager. They also encountered a big sign in the door that said "Closed" while they saw other patrons finishing their meals behind the glass windows of the restaurant (see fig. 5).[68] Obviously, the restaurant's closure was a pretense to avoid conflict and to hide the practices of racial discrimination and spatial marginalization to which the airport subscribed. It was then that ten of the original eighteen riders decided not to leave on their scheduled flights but to stay until the restaurant was made available to them. With their sit-in, they hoped to draw attention to the crack in what Glenda Rabby has called "the thin veneer of compliance with the desegregation ruling" in the city of Tallahassee.[69]

CORE's interest in civil rights matters in Florida derived from the state's own history of segregation. Often relegated to the sidelines of histories of southern Jim Crow, Florida deserves to take center stage if only to show that its history of racial discrimination was not exceptional—at least in the central part of the state that was "more southern" than the rest of it. Most cities and towns enforced racial ordinances, which relegated African Americans to the margins of urban society.[70] And as Ralph Abernathy has pointed out: "It was St. Augustine and Tallahassee rather than Miami and St. Petersburg that produced the racial headlines during the 1950s and 1960s."[71] Florida's state capital neatly fit into deep southern geographies of racial separation. Although Tallahassee's black residents had successfully organized a bus boycott in 1956, challenging segregation in public transportation, and had continued to fight for integration in a number of other areas employing different protest techniques, most of the city's public institutions and private businesses continued to practice Jim Crow until the mid-1960s.[72]

The airport, as the Interfaith Freedom Riders found out, was no exception. The surveys conducted by the NAACP and Representative Charles Diggs in the mid-1950s exposed Tallahassee as being among a number of Florida airports where duplicate facilities existed and some form of racial segregation was practiced.[73] Since then, the airport had built new facilities including a new terminal building, which opened in April 1961, two months before the Freedom Riders came to Tallahassee. This new building replicated the old terminal's patterns of spatial organization designed to discriminate against African American passengers.[74] John Collier, one of the riders and a black minister from Newark, New Jersey, described the new terminal's segregated facilities during a court hearing later that year:

> As you went in the main entrance to the right where [sic] the ticket counters . . . to the left was a sign indicating that the colored waiting room was just ahead. There were four doors which were doors to restrooms, marked colored man [sic], colored women, white ladies, white men. There was an area in which there was a counter around which were six or seven stools which indicated colored dining area.[75]

These retrograde features contradicted the building's otherwise pleasant ambience. Much like Montgomery's air terminal, the terminal building at Tallahassee Municipal Airport was a modestly designed modernistic structure. Its interior consisted of a sequence of spaces—check-in lobby, rental car lobby, waiting area, and restaurant—mostly separated by glass walls. These created a sense of transparency and openness, which was contradicted by the more hidden spaces reserved for use by African Americans. Its built form and interior design tied the building into a midcentury modernist aesthetic typical of airport architecture at the time. Murals created by painter Artemis Jegart tied the building into local landscapes with colorful representations of local landmarks. To make the airport construction possible, city leaders had drawn on FAAP subsidies like their colleagues in cities such as Jackson and Montgomery. However, in an effort to subvert the FAA's desegregation regulations with regard to airport terminal buildings, they raised private funds for construction of the terminal's segregated service features, which included the spaces described by John Collier.[76] This clever use of private funding rendered enforcement of nondiscrimination policies complicated for the federal government. Commenting on the situation at Tallahassee airport in an interview, Burke Marshall—head of the Civil Rights Division of the Justice Department—explained that the federal government lacked the tools for immediate intervention because "the Federal Aviation Agency was not a regulatory agency in the sense that the ICC was."[77]

During the remaining hours of June 15, Collier and his fellow riders realized that the Savarin restaurant's manager Hubert Isdell would not meet his initial assurances to reopen the restaurant and serve them. Instead, he marked up the prices for sandwiches and cigarettes at the adjoining concession stand.[78] In protest, the group sent a telegram to the ICC asking that immediate steps be taken "to see that the rights of interstate passengers are protected at this terminal restaurant" without realizing that they were turning to the wrong federal agency, which lacked authority in aviation matters.[79] When the airport closed for the night, the riders decided to leave and return the next day. Concerned about their safety in view of a growing crowd of whites, they requested and received police protection. On June 16, events unfolded much like they had the day before. After a few hours, the clergymen found themselves surrounded by an increasingly impatient crowd of local whites. Instead of dispersing the crowd, city attorney James Messer asked the Freedom Riders to abandon their protest and leave the airport. Unwilling to comply and motivated by hopes the federal government would intervene, the protesters were arrested by the police on charges of unlawful assembly.[80]

Police Chief Frank Stoutamire later testified that only by arresting the clergymen did he think he could avoid the outbreak of a riot. He framed the Freedom Riders as perpetrators who had come to town as outsiders to cause trouble and upset Tallahassee's racial equilibrium. The white crowd's aggressive behavior and disorderly conduct, on the other hand, was nothing but an excusable expression of "local resentment" in his perspective.[81] Framing the sit-ins as a manifestation of outside aggression, Stoutamire articulated a white supremacist discourse that pitted local culture and the particular form of race relations it generated against the attitudes, opinions, and practices of all those who were not from Tallahassee. Stoutamire and his like-minded contemporaries ignored the changing nature of U.S. legal landscapes, which included the landscapes of transportation in the South. Instead they held on to a storyline that framed local whites as the victims of outside interference. This interference had to be contained by all means, which included the strategies of containment Stoutamire used at Tallahassee airport.[82]

Initially planning to stay in jail until their case would be tried, the Interfaith Freedom Riders—the "Tallahassee Ten," as the press came to call them—posted bond after a few days. "We're not trying to fill up the Tallahassee jail," a CORE representative explained, "but we do plan to get service at the restaurant."[83] CORE had to face the fact that direct action did not bring immediate change to the airport terminal or the city of Tallahassee. Rather than revise Jim Crow policies, city officials and Judge John Rudd used the trial in the municipal court as a spectacle to perform the non-negotiability of the color line. Strict racial segregation was enforced in the courtroom both in the audience and among the defendants. Taking seats together, the group was separated according to race.[84] Not surprisingly, the court found the defendants guilty.[85] Had they come to Tallahassee for a "noble Christian purpose," Rudd informed them during sentencing, he would have dismissed the charges. But they had forced their views on the community instead of cleaning up their "own back yard."[86] The Tallahassee Ten's appeal to the Second Circuit Court of Appeals failed to overturn the lower court's decision. Rather, U.S. Circuit Judge Ben C. Willis took issue with the persistence of the Riders, without which their sit-in would not have been effective: "When citizens press their demonstrations in behalf of a cause (however worthy they deem their objectives to be) beyond the bounds of fully and effectively delivering their message and reach the stage that they materially and harmfully interfere with the orderly business and lawful activities of others, who are acting in public or private capacities, then the conduct is disorderly and assembly for carrying it out is unlawful. Such was the case here."[87]

Although two further appeals to the Florida and U.S. Supreme Courts went nowhere, the Tallahassee Ten were ultimately vindicated. Their trial had never addressed the legality of segregation at the city's airport, focusing on their misdemeanor charge instead. The question whether a constitutional statutory basis for airport segregation existed was considered in *Brooks v. Tallahassee*. It was a lawsuit filed shortly before the Freedom Riders came to Tallahassee that rested on similar facts: in this case, the inaccessibility of the airport's Savarin restaurant for African American patrons. David Brooks and two other local ministers who had requested service at the dining room in vain successfully argued in their complaint against the airport that, by imposing discriminatory racial ordinances to regulate spatial practices in the terminal building, the airport management had violated their constitutional rights of equal protection under the Fourteenth Amendment.[88] Siding with the plaintiffs, the U.S. District Court for the Northern District of Florida ordered the airport's integration in October 1961. A month earlier, on September 22, 1961, after months of protests by the Freedom Riders, the ICC finally invalidated the laws that required segregated seating arrangements on interstate buses. It also ordered the removal of "whites only" signs from interstate bus terminals by November 1, 1961.[89] This ruling, it turned out, did not apply to airports. With the signs in Tallahassee gone, the fight for integrated terminals continued elsewhere. In Florida's state capital, the resistance against Jim Crow practices on site, in combination with a court challenge, brought about the dismantlement of the city's segregated landscape of aviation.

The last case study illustrates the ways in which civil rights activists in Durham, North Carolina, went beyond this chapter's repertoire of resistance against racial discrimination at airport terminals. In Atlanta, Greenville, Jackson, and Tallahassee, direct action initiatives that targeted air terminal buildings unsettled local communities. They brought the issue of racial segregation and the system of inequality it signified into the public spotlight, at times generating national attention. In these four cities, out-of-town activists were instrumental in shaping protest activities and helping to generate momentum. In Durham, in contrast, it was local groups like the Durham Committee on Negro Affairs and student chapters of the NAACP that rallied around the cause of airport desegregation in the fall of 1961. They managed to bring about integration of the facility the town shared with its neighboring city Raleigh, albeit in a manner different from previous examples. While the students could draw on the support—mostly moral support and legal advice—of their national organization, their leaders, grassroots supporters, and resources were local in origin.

Since opening in 1948 as a commercial airport, Raleigh-Durham Airport (RDU) provided separate spaces for the use of black and white air travelers.[90] As a Jim Crow facility, it fit neatly into North Carolina's landscapes of segregation.[91] Both Raleigh and Durham strictly enforced the color line in public transportation and public accommodations, although Durham held on to its reputation as "the capital of the black middle class," where African Americans made outstanding contributions to the town's economic and community development.[92] The planning of the airport was a complicated affair originally. Rather than cooperating, the towns had competed against one another, each hoping to boost its profile by building an airfield. When construction of the airport finally got under way in 1941, the U.S. Army Air Corps took control over it and saw to its completion. In 1943, the airport became operational as an air base that was used mostly by the military but also allowed for limited use by commercial airlines.[93]

The original building was a simple, one-story balloon-frame structure, which looked more like roadside architecture than an airport terminal building. In its simplicity, it deviated from the art deco design standard found elsewhere, a style the Air Force seldom subscribed to for the construction of its mostly functionalist air-base buildings. A few years after the Raleigh-Durham Aeronautical Authority regained ownership of the airport, plans for its expansion took shape. The new airport, whose construction was subsidized by the federal government (FAAP), opened in 1955.[94] Its infrastructure also included a new passenger terminal. Stylistically, this terminal was another representation of generic postwar airport architecture. In its unobtrusive modernism, it looked much like the terminal buildings in Greenville and Tallahassee. The terminal was a two-story rectangular building with canopied entrances in the front and the back. An air-traffic control tower sat on the roof.[95] In designing its layout, civilian planners applied duplication as one of the spatial strategies of white supremacy, much like their Army Air Corps colleagues had in the old terminal.[96] Hence, the building contained racially segregated facilities including restrooms. These restrooms featured signs that the NAACP's executive secretary, Walter White, had first observed in the old terminal.[97] The signs read "Ladies," "Gentlemen," "Women," and "Men." Although the qualifier "colored" was missing from the signs, airport patrons, both black and white, no doubt knew which restrooms to use. The terms "Ladies" and "Gentlemen" were so exclusively used to refer to whites that they "could serve without further modification to signal racial difference."[98]

Groups like the Durham Committee on Negro Affairs and the Raleigh Citizens' Committee protested against these segregated facilities shortly after the terminal's opening. Fending off NAACP efforts to work on behalf of the black community, the Durham Committee formed in the late 1930s to pursue school integration and represent the interests of black teachers. Run by the representatives of Durham's black elite, it had pursued a number of causes since then, among them voter registration.[99] In a letter to Representative Charles Diggs, the Durham Committee's president J. S. Stewart brought the issue of racial discrimination at the newly opened terminal to the congressman's attention. He reported that representatives of his organization and the Raleigh

Citizens' Committee had appeared before the airport authority and voiced their concerns. They were given assurances that "the matter would be taken under advisement." Since then, however, nothing had happened. Instead, they received word from "confidential sources" that the airport's management had no intention of integrating the terminal. To Stewart, the existence of spatial patterns of racial discrimination seemed particularly outrageous in light of the fact that the airport authority continued to request federal funds for its infrastructure upgrade.[100] Having read about Diggs's fight for airport desegregation in the newspaper, Stewart hoped that by writing to the congressman he would be able to assist the groups in their cause. In reaction to Stewart's observations and information he had gathered himself, Diggs turned to the CAA to request an investigation into conditions at Raleigh-Durham and other Jim Crow airports across the South. The acting secretary of commerce, Louis S. Rothschild, then still in co-charge of aviation matters, promised Diggs to undertake an official airport study—a promise it would take the agency years to fulfill.[101] At RDU, no immediate action was taken, which would have led to the removal of the signs and thus changed conditions on the ground for African American air travelers. Although at some point the airport's management de facto stopped enforcing its racial policy, de jure and in appearance the restrooms remained segregated.[102]

A few years later, a group of student activists revisited the issue that had continued to upset Durham's African American community. The activists saw potential in exploiting a visit by President John F. Kennedy to the area to further their cause. On October 12, 1961, Kennedy was scheduled to visit the North Carolina International Trade Fair, hosted by Raleigh-Durham Airport. To get to the fairgrounds, the president would have to pass through the segregated terminal building. What better chance to draw national and even international attention to Jim Crow airports than the president's visit? Days before Kennedy was scheduled to arrive, representatives of two youth and student organizations affiliated with the NAACP—its North Carolina College chapter and Durham Youth Crusader chapter—sent a telegram to the White House drawing Kennedy's attention to conditions at the airport. They called on him to use his authority as the country's leader to protest against racial segregation by boycotting the fair. "We urge you as the leader of our Democracy," the telegram read, "to decline to open an International Trade Fair within the walls of a state facility where African delegates as well as members of your staff would be subject to embarrassment and possible arrest."[103] Rather than frame the airport management's racist practices as a local issue, the telegram's authors John Edwards, Callis Brown, and Billy Thorpe put them into international perspective. Chairman of the Airport Board of Control James Patton's refusal to remove the racist signs from the airport's restroom doors was presented as an instance with potential to hurt the reputation of the Kennedy administration in a Cold War context. The leader of the free world, the underlying argument went, was unable to guarantee the civil rights he was enforcing abroad to his own citizens at home. Arguing along these lines, the student activists tied the telegram into a decades-old discursive protest tradition.[104] The president's failure to deliver not only caused local air travelers and black visitors from across the United States to suffer indignities at Raleigh-Durham Airport. Foreign dignitaries on their way to visit the International Trade Fair would potentially be humiliated as well.

On a more practical level, the students announced a direct action initiative. They would picket the airport during Kennedy's visit should the airport fail to remove the racist restroom signs before then. Probably aware of the Kennedy administration's interventionism on behalf of the Freedom Riders in Alabama only a few months earlier, the young NAACP members hoped that the president and his attorney general would feel morally obligated to do something about the situation at their airport—although no violent confrontations had occurred. They may also have hoped that the Kennedy brothers would act pragmatically in an effort to protect the president's schedule, which included a visit to the University of North Carolina, Chapel Hill, where he was to receive an honorary degree. The students conjectured that the president would either cancel his visit to RDU or support their cause. They were correct in assuming that Kennedy would avoid the public embarrassment of being greeted by civil rights demonstrators upon his arrival at the airport.

While the student groups' preparations for the demonstration went ahead, administration officials began to negotiate behind the scenes with the airport's board of directors. The *New York Times* reported on the board's initial reluctance to respond to desegregation demands.[105] Claiming not to have enforced its racially discriminatory policies in years, the board felt disinclined to act and refused in particular to be pressured into action by a group of college students. This reluctance to cave to local and outside pressure notwithstanding, the board held an emergency meeting the day before Kennedy's visit. This illustrated if not a repentant attitude at least some discomfort at the prospect of being put in the national spotlight. To avoid the latter, the board decided to take down the Jim Crow signs in time for the presidential visit. This led the student activists to call off their demonstration. As a result of their peaceful confrontation with the airport board of directors and the Kennedy administration, the airport became integrated both visually and spatially. Its facilities became available to all air travelers without regard to their racial background. With the airport's integration, protesters had accomplished their goal. They did so peacefully and with the support of the federal government. In Durham as elsewhere across the Deep South, students and young African Americans emerged as the driving force behind local protests in the early 1960s, taking the lead from an older generation of community leaders, who were less radical and uncompromising. This was a role they would continue to play in the civil rights movement of the 1960s.[106]

Although the airport protests did not produce headlines quite as dramatic as those activists were producing in other contexts, they raised awareness about the racialization of the built environment and underlined the desire and right of African Americans as citizens and consumers to participate equally in the consumption of air travel. Even more than the bloody fight for integrated ground transportation, the struggle for unrestricted access to the spaces of air travel symbolized the desire to appropriate a mode of mobility that was increasingly considered as the essence of a modern American lifestyle. Airport desegregation continued to be a slow and piecemeal process, however, which is why civil rights activists continued to press on several fronts.

CHAPTER 4

In the Courts

Private Litigation as a Road to Desegregation

Civil rights activists resisted the incorporation of airports into the southern landscapes of racism by challenging Jim Crow on site at airport terminals. They also tackled the issue in another location: in the federal courts. They did so in an effort designed to change cultural landscapes on the ground. Their goal was to reshape the built environment in ways that erased the color line as a spatial signifier of difference and inferiority, which found expression in racist signs and racially exclusive spaces. But they also did so in an effort to change the legal landscapes of segregation. Recognizing the ideological rather than neutral nature of laws, legal discourse, and legal action, they hoped to challenge the legal framework that was the source of ideas about race and their expression in the spatial ordering of the physical world. Regarding the law and its interpreters as important agents in shaping racial and spatial norms, civil rights activists used legal challenges to airport segregation as crucial tools in the geopolitics of race.[1]

The NAACP had long championed litigation as an effective road to integration. Its legal branch, the Legal Defense Fund (LDF), helped plaintiffs bring suit when its lawyers saw any potential in the case. Cases won established precedents for future lawsuits. But litigation was a slow and tedious process, and the focus shifted from case to case. Working their way through the appellate courts, some cases took years to be decided. Rather than ending segregation per se, a court could narrowly integrate a specific place or an area of public life without an immediate broader application to other similar circumstances unless new lawsuits were brought. *Brown v. Board of Education* best illustrates this point. In its seminal 1954 decision, the U.S. Supreme Court declared segregated schools were unconstitutional, thereby invalidating the "separate but equal" doctrine set forth in *Plessy v. Ferguson* in 1896.[2] It mandated the integration of public education not only in Kansas but also across the country. The Court failed, however, to set a timetable for desegregation, only requiring that the ruling be implemented "with all deliberate speed." This broadly phrased provision slowed the process down considerably as many states and municipalities stalled on implementation and held on firmly to separate facilities in other areas of public life.[3]

In order to expedite the process of airport integration, civil rights activists and organizations continued to litigate whenever and wherever possible. This resulted in a number of individual suits for monetary damages against airport administrators and proprietors filed during the 1950s. The NAACP's LDF supported almost all of the legal actions brought against airports by private individuals between the late 1940s and early 1960s. For most individuals, the expense of litigation and appeals were out of reach without institutional assistance. The cases included *Nash v. Air Terminal Services* (1949), *Coke v. Atlanta* (1960), *Henry v. Greenville Airport Commission* (1960), *Turner v. Memphis* (1962), *Adams v. City of New Orleans* (1962), and *Shuttlesworth v. Dobbs Houses, Inc.* (1962).

National Airport became the first target of a desegregation campaign in the late 1940s. To many observers, it was a particular embarrassment that foreign dignitaries had to pass through racially segregated spaces at a federal facility that served as the gateway to the nation's capital. The fact that at the time segregation was practiced in the District of Columbia and in parts of the federal government did not weaken the criticism.[4] It rather exposed the federal government's role in the implementation and perpetuation of segregation. The NAACP called on the Truman administration to take action repeatedly, pointing out its responsibility to secure the rights of its citizens on an equal basis at the nation's flagship airport.[5] As a part of its focus on litigation, the NAACP also supported Helen Nash's lawsuit against the airport in 1948.[6] Civil rights advocates in particular focused on discriminatory practices in the airport's restaurant and cafeteria. Since the opening of the airport in 1941, the proprietor Air Terminal Services had refused to serve African American and black air travelers. The complaints by Mamie Davis, who had been unable to eat in the airport in the summer of 1946 and had brought her unpleasant experience to the attention of American Airlines president P. S. Damon and others, had not produced results. The federal government had yet to become involved, even though the year before it had admitted being in "disagreement with the wisdom and the propriety of this practice [i.e., separate lunchrooms]."[7]

The government's idleness was due in large part to what the Department of Justice believed to be limited federal authority over a property that was located in the state of Virginia. Federal authority over federal property located in the states was not per se restricted. It was limited when the land had origi-nally been seized by the federal government through eminent domain, as was the case with Gravelly Point, the area on which National Airport was built. It was moreover circumscribed by the Assimilative Crimes Act, which made "state law applicable to conduct occurring on lands reserved or acquired by the Federal government . . . when the act or omission is not made punishable by an enactment of Congress."[8] Thus, all Virginia criminal laws were adopted as federal criminal laws at the airport enclave.[9] Apparently, lawmakers had ne-glected to address this issue when they passed the District-Virginia boundary legislation in 1945 that settled the longstanding boundary conflict between the neighbors. The law established the airport as a "federal reservation" in Virginia but did not provide for statutory adjustments.[10] Under the Criminal Code of the United States, this made the area subject to all sections of the Virginia Code that required racial segregation. Thus, Jim Crow not only in-formed spatial practices at National Airport; airport administrators acknowl-edged that there was little they could do about it.

The NAACP's LDF lawyers saw a window of opportunity to revise this un-derstanding following the decision in *Morgan v. Virginia*, which the Supreme Court handed down in 1946. Ruling that segregation on interstate transpor-tation—in this case, on buses—presented an undue burden on interstate commerce, the Court invalidated the practice, legally reshaping an important part of the transportation landscape. Writing to the Secretary of Commerce Averell Harriman, the Defense Fund's Assistant Special Counsel Franklin Williams pointed out that the decision could very well be applied to National Airport as it too placed an undue burden on travelers: "The restaurant facili-ties at the Washington National Airport are clearly for the accommodation of passengers traveling in interstate commerce." Ergo, he concluded, the racially specific patterns that informed their use was illegal and unconstitutional.[11] The Commerce Department initially disagreed. Its solicitor, Adrian Fisher, wrote: "I do not believe that the application of the Virginia statute to an airport restaurant has an effect upon interstate commerce similar to the effect of the statute involved in that case."[12] The dissimilarity he referred to was that buses like the one Irene Morgan had taken to travel from Virginia to Maryland liter-ally transported people across state borders. Any state law designed to define the quality of that transportation service—like statutes mandating segregated seating—directly affected interstate commerce in peoples and goods.

Restaurants were an altogether different matter, mostly due to their local and immobile character. Their services were offered in connection to trans-portation services, but the nature of that connection remained to be explored by legal experts. Moreover, *Morgan v. Virginia* did not specifically apply to public accommodations. The Commerce Department was thus disinclined at the time to recognize it as a legal precedent that required a change in the segregated conditions at National Airport's eating establishments. Acknowledging the urgency of the matter, however, Fisher promised to bring it to the attention of President Truman's Committee on Civil Rights.[13]

The Commerce Department eventually used a different legal route to change the status quo at the airport. Secretary Harriman first turned to Congress to propose legislation in the fall of 1947, which would have invalidated the Virginia segregation laws that applied to the aviation facility as a consequence of the Assimilative Crimes Act.[14] Pointing out in a letter to Speaker of the House Joseph Martin that "the Department of Commerce is placed in the position of requiring the segregation of white and colored persons," he underlined: "This, I believe, is contrary to the policy of the Federal Government." He also insinuated that he considered racially discriminatory practices at the airport's dining facilities a national embarrassment.[15] Congress, however, stalled on the initiative, mostly because its southern members resisted any federal assault on segregation. Instead, the administrator of CAA, Delos Rentzel, took action (he then still worked under the roof of the Department of Commerce).[16] Navigating around the complex legal issues concerning state and federal authority, on December 27, 1948, the Truman appointee ordered the integration of the airport by way of amending the federal regulations pertaining to operation of the airport.[17]

Unsure of the breadth of his statutory power, Rentzel had initially not considered a segregation ban an option but recognized it as a course of action after a legal review by the Department of Justice. The amendment to the General Regulations of Washington National Airport added a new section that specifically applied to racial discrimination and segregation. The new section, which became effective immediately, provided: "In the operation of all facilities of the Washington National Airport, services shall be rendered without discrimination or segregation as to race, color, or creed."[18] The NAACP's Walter White applauded the action and highlighted its symbolic significance. Washington, D.C., he wrote, was "a world symbol of democracy."[19] Eleanor Roosevelt, writing in her regular newspaper column, agreed: "It is indeed a relief to find the Civil Aeronautics Administration has had the courage to ban racial segregation at the Washington National Airport. This a substantial step forward in the fight that must be waged to bring our National Capital into line with what must be Government policy."[20] Action taken here, both suggested, would send a message to the rest of the world, and it would, more importantly, send a message to the rest of the country. Rentzel's actions were a reminder that federal laws and regulations were not static and eternally valid.

They could be changed—bypassing the political process if necessary when one branch of government refused to engage. At this point in time, the open question was: Would there be more change strong enough to shift and reshape the legal landscapes of segregation?

More immediately, the amendment failed to bring an end to discrimination. Air Terminal Services, the restaurant's proprietor, decided to question the legality of Rentzel's segregation ban and to challenge the CAA's regulatory authority in federal court. At the same time, it announced that it would continue to deny service to African American passengers and airport patrons. As the company's vice president and general counsel, Frederick Ball, explained to the *Washington Post* a day after the ban, "Our position has been that only a court of competent jurisdiction can pass on the validity of the Virginia segregation statute. It's very doubtful that the Administrator of CAA can waive a Federal or State statute. Until this is clear in our minds, we'll maintain our position."[21] A service test of the Terrace Dining Room that same day confirmed Air Terminal Services' commitment to this position. When Margaret Davis Bowen, Velma Davis Perkins, and Patricia Huggins went to the dining room to have dinner, accompanied by a reporter, photographer, and counsel, they were stopped by a waitress and asked to leave by the restaurant's manager. The women were in town for a national meeting of the Alpha Kappa Alpha sorority, the oldest sorority established by black college women.[22] To protest against such refusal of service as the sorority sisters experienced, Edgar G. Brown, director of the National Negro Council, and his son Frederick staged an all-day sit-down at the airport cafeteria's food bar the day after the service test.[23]

A court hearing was set for early January on the validity of the regulation. As the court date approached, observers vented their anger and frustration over the situation in the press. Civil rights groups began to organize protest activities should the segregation ban be struck down. But the U.S. District Court for the Eastern District of Virginia agreed with the CAA and upheld its regulation, which mandated integration. Dealing critically with a number of claims made by the government and the plaintiff, Air Terminal Services, U.S. District Judge Albert V. Bryan upheld the notion that the CAA order held precedent over state law.[24] The Assimilative Crimes Act, he elaborated, was intended to fill gaps in the Federal Criminal Code using state laws. It was not designed, however, to override other "federal policies as expressed by acts of Congress or by valid administrative orders." One of those federal policies was the effort to end racial discrimination. "The regulation of the Administrator," he concluded, "who was authorized by statute to promulgate rules for the airport, is but an additional declaration and effectuation of that policy."[25]

Somewhat surprisingly, Air Terminal Services accepted the ruling. Underlining in a statement that its actions had not been motivated by a desire to promote segregation, but by the necessity to protect itself from state prosecution had it abandoned the practice, the company did not file an appeal.[26] Thus, integration finally became a reality at National Airport on January 4, 1949.[27] Test eaters who returned to the airport's coffee shop the next day found it open to both white and black customers. Edgar Brown, who carried out the sit-down strike at the food bar only a few days earlier, criticized the preferential treatment white patrons received on the first day of integrated service. He and his companions had to wait for three hours before a waitress took their orders.[28] It seems that this more subtle form of discrimination subsided quickly as no further mention of it appears in the records.

It is worth noting that Judge Bryan's ruling did not apply to other airports. The CAA's regulatory order applied to Washington National Airport exclusively. That explains why Virginia's attorney general, J. Lindsay Almond, did not contest the court's decision.[29] He did not have to. The decision neither invalidated relevant sections of Virginia's criminal code nor did it challenge the state's segregation laws. Ignoring National Airport as a legal anomaly, the state's white supremacist forces continued to shape southern landscapes—both legal and physical—according to their worldview. Local airport administrators most certainly recognized the new federal regulation's lack of geopolitical consequences. Rather than pause, they eagerly applied Jim Crow laws to airport terminals, giving a familiar spatial structure to the newest building type in the cultural landscapes of transportation. Airport segregation schemes—as chapter 2 has demonstrated—were just about to get off the ground in the late 1940s.

Although Helen Nash, a retired school teacher from Washington, D.C., recognized the effectiveness of the federal segregation ban, she continued to press her individual suit against Air Terminal Services.[30] Her suit was one of three brought against the restaurant proprietor. All were filed by African American women who claimed that they had been discriminated against in their attempts to buy and consume food at National Airport. Whereas Sadie T. M. Alexander, a prominent lawyer and civil rights advocate from Philadelphia, and Lilly Cunningham from New York City chose to drop their cases after the integration of the airport, Nash carried on hoping to recover damages in the amount of $58,000.[31] Moreover, her suit (like the other two) presented an opportunity to explore some of the legal issues that the CAA's ruling and the legal dispute between the CAA and Air Terminal Services had not addressed.

Nash originally brought her suit in 1948 in reaction to an incident that occurred in February 1947.[32] While waiting for a delayed flight to New Orleans, she and her husband, a local physician, attempted to redeem Eastern Airlines food vouchers, but neither the Terrace Dining Room nor the coffee shop would serve them. Instead they were sent to the basement cafeteria reserved for African American travelers.[33] With their middle-class background, the Nashes were typical representatives of an increasingly mobile social group. Much like the other aforementioned individuals who attempted to eat at the airport's dining facilities, they typified a new facet of the postwar consumer spectrum: African Americans who had money and time to travel. Nash's example (as well as the examples of Alexander and Cunningham) demonstrated, moreover, that black women used air travel to cover long distances rather than travel by car or railway, which would have taken days. Given the time commitment, as well as the inconveniences and dangers of such a long journey, in particular to a Deep South destination like New Orleans, those who could afford it made the trip by airplane. Nash's case also demonstrates the overlapping identities of consumer and citizen. Her case connected the lack of courtesy she and her husband experienced as airline customers with the denial of their citizenship rights. Unlike white patrons, they were forced to consume their food in a marginal space set aside for them as members of their race.

Nash's suit claimed that her treatment, based solely on her race, violated her rights under the Fifth and Fourteenth Amendments to the U.S. Constitution and the Civil Rights Act of 1947. In separate complaints, it challenged the validity of the CAA's new regulations and Virginia's laws, which legalized segregation. The suit stipulated instead that, due to the nature of its business, Air Terminal Service had an obligation to serve every paying customer regardless of race even though it was a private company; and it averred a cause for action on the grounds that inequality of the eating facilities was unacceptable segregation—in essence demanding a "separate but equal" dining room where only a basement cafeteria existed. The case rested on the theory that discriminatory practices at National Airport constituted a form of federal regulation of interstate commerce that deprived African American interstate passengers of due process and equal protection under the laws, which the U.S. Constitution guaranteed. The Court dismissed most counts as not relevant to the case, while upholding the constitutionality of segregation. But it did consider the operational responsibilities of a private corporation that did business at an airport, essentially establishing airport concessions as "public actions" within the meaning of the Fifth Amendment.[34]

In this regard, the case became an important precedent for future decisions on state action. U.S. District Judge Bryan—the same judge who upheld the segregation ban—reasoned that unlike private businesses on private property, the eating facilities at National Airport were operated on public property in a building constructed with public funds and under a concession from the federal government. "In effect," Bryan stated, "the concessionaire here is conducting the facility in the place and stead of the Federal government . . . It is to provide food and refreshment to the public in travel and to complement the facilities offered by the United States Government in support of air transportation." Therefore, the restaurants were "too close, in origin and purpose, to the functions of the public government to allow them the right to refuse service without good cause."[35] Ironically, this interpretation did not invalidate Jim Crow practices per se, but it lent substance to Nash's claim that, according to the "separate but equal" doctrine, she had a right to be served in "eating accommodations substantially equal to those provided in the restaurants for whites."[36] Since segregation was in effect government action, and no acceptable provisions were made for her as a black patron, the judge agreed that she had been deprived of her rights without due process of law, contrary to the Fifth Amendment. Bryan found that Nash had stated a claim on which relief could be granted and allowed the case to proceed to a trial by jury for her damage claim.[37] In the end, however, she did not prevail. Helen Nash lost her trial because the jury failed to agree with her contention of fact that the dining facilities reserved for African Americans at National Airport were of inferior quality compared to the "whites only" restaurant and coffee shop. Following the defendants' line of argument, it considered them "substantially equal" and delivered a verdict in favor of the defendant.[38] Not surprisingly, it was an all-white jury that made this finding of fact about conditions at the airport.

As the issue of segregation at National Airport was being resolved, it became clear to observers that the case would not easily lend itself to bring about the abolition of discriminatory practices at other airports. There were challenges in dealing with segregation at a federally owned facility that differed from those faced by airports that were municipally owned. Following the integration of National Airport, civil rights activists continued to use litigation as a protest strategy. Though lacking substantial federal precedent, they understood that airport segregation would have to be fought on a case-by-case basis, airport by airport, just like the fight against other forms of racial discrimination. Although *Nash v. Air Terminal Services* had not settled satisfactorily Helen Nash's financial claims against the restaurant concessionaire, the court recognized segregation in airport terminal facilities—particularly in eating establishments—as a litigable issue. The location of airport restaurants

in a public transportation facility, the court had ruled, required their proprietors to abide by antidiscrimination policies as they provided services not as
a private enterprise but in lieu of a public airport operator.

Looking at this case, the NAACP's LDF also recognized *Brown v. Board of
Education* and *Browder v. Gayle* as cases that would help them argue in favor
of airport desegregation, even though neither case specifically applied to air
transportation—instead they dealt with school desegregation and the desegregation of municipal buses. In the 1950s, civil rights attorneys watched for
cases "which would establish the principle firmly that government-owned
airports could not legally segregate blacks."[39] Individual private lawsuits were
eventually filed in a number of places, some of them growing out of local
protests. While some cases went nowhere, a few cases stand out in significance.[40] They include *Coke v. Atlanta*, *Henry v. Greenville Airport Commission*,
Turner v. Memphis, *Adams v. City of New Orleans*, and *Shuttlesworth v. Dobbs
Houses, Inc.*

Coke v. Atlanta was filed in the United States District Court for the Northern District of Georgia in Atlanta in December 1958. It was a class action
lawsuit brought by H. D. Coke, an African American insurance executive
from Birmingham, Alabama, against the city of Atlanta, the Atlanta Airport
management, and the management of the airport's Dobbs House restaurant.
Coke sought injunctive relief against the racist practices he had been exposed
to during a layover at Atlanta Airport on August 4, 1958. On his way from
Birmingham to attend a business convention in Columbus, Ohio, Coke's itinerary took him to Atlanta where he had to change planes. While waiting for
his delayed connecting flight, he went to the the Dobbs House restaurant to
have a meal, for which he and other passengers had received vouchers from a
representative of their air carrier—Delta Airlines. He was joined by two black
colleagues he met at the airport on the way to the restaurant. Upon presenting
themselves to the waitress, she told them that she would not seat them at the
table of their choice. Instead, she attempted to direct them "to a single corner
table segregated behind a screen for the purpose of serving Negroes," according to Coke's affidavit—the same table Sidney Poitier and Martin Luther King
Jr. were shown a few years earlier.[41] The table sat "in the extreme far right end
of the restaurant," an area that was not well lit. Rejecting the table, Coke and
his company also rejected the idea of relocating to the cafeteria. Irritated by
the confrontation, Coke went back to the Delta Airlines counter, where the
company's representative encouraged him to return to the restaurant, assuring him that his service request would be met. This time around Coke was
met by the headwaiter, an African American, who rather than seat his party
in the main dining room confirmed the restaurant's practice of relegating

black patrons to a separate area demarcated by the screen. Like Poitier three years earlier, Coke received these spatial instructions from a fellow African American, which aggravated him even further. Appalled by the incident, Coke gave an affirmative answer to the waiter's question whether he would sue the restaurant and then left with his colleagues.[42] In their motion for preliminary injunction, Coke's lawyers moved the court to enjoin the defendants from giving preferential treatment to white passengers. Otherwise their client would continue to suffer "irreparable injury, loss, and damage," as he was a frequent traveler who regularly traveled through Atlanta Municipal Airport.[43]

Coke's case is significant given the frequent incidents of racial discrimination that fellow Atlantans—such as Martin Luther King Jr., his father Martin Luther King Sr. (who appeared as a witness in the case), Ralph Abernathy, and others—experienced with conditions at the airport restaurant. It took someone from outside of Atlanta to file a suit against the Dobbs Houses company and the parties responsible for the airport's administration. Coke's legal counsel was provided by the NAACP's LDF, which saw potential in the case. His legal team included the LDF executive director Thurgood Marshall and assistant counsel Jack Greenberg as well as Donald L. Hollowell and Peter Hall, who practiced law in Atlanta and Birmingham.

Like most of the other individuals who filed suits against airport authorities, Coke was represented by a legal team that included lawyers who worked at the LDF's headquarters in New York and local attorneys. These teams of civil rights lawyers brought their (brilliant) legal expertise, long experience, and deep local knowledge to bear on the cases. Involved in legal battles on several fronts and often with a heavy case load, the LDF lawyers and their local colleagues were not only familiar with the legal landscapes on hand but also knew or had dealt with the defendants' counsel and competent federal district judges before. Thurgood Marshall, who had received his training at Howard University Law School under the tutelage of Charles Hamilton Houston, was a veteran civil rights lawyer. He founded the Legal Defense Fund in 1940 and had served as its executive director since then. Among his most noteworthy accomplishments was a victory for the plaintiffs in *Brown v. Board of Education*, which he and his colleagues James Nabrit Jr. and George Hayes had argued before the Supreme Court. Jack Greenberg had received his education at Columbia University Law School and joined the LDF in 1949 as the only white lawyer. He served as Marshall's co-counsel in many cases and would succeed him as the fund's executive director in 1961. Donald Hollowell was a key figure in the Georgia struggle for civil rights. After graduating from Loyola University Chicago School of Law, he set up a practice in Atlanta in 1952. Among others, Hollowell successfully argued a case against the University of Georgia that led to its integration. He also served as legal counsel for Martin Luther King Jr. and civil rights activists in the Albany Movement. Peter Hall, who practiced law in Birmingham, worked on the NAACP legal team that defended Martin Luther King Jr. during the 1955 Montgomery Bus Boycott. He would later represent the civil rights protesters in Selma and become Birmingham's first black judge.[44]

Coke was an ideal plaintiff for the LDF in several respects. Like Helen Nash and her husband, Martin Luther King Jr., and some of the other African American travelers previously discussed, he was a representative of the growing southern black middle class. He was vice president of the Protective Industrial Insurance Company of Alabama, which was headquartered in Birmingham, as the insurance business was one of the few avenues open to African Americans who sought professional success and middle-class economic status. Coke lived in the College Hill section of Smithfield, a Birmingham neighborhood fought over intensely by black and white residents during the 1950s. Originally bound to certain areas by the city's residential segregation ordinance, middle-class African Americans began to push the boundaries of their settlement, triggering violent resistance. Coke was among those black residents who made inroads into a traditionally white middle-class neighborhood.[45] He was also an ideal plaintiff because he represented the growing group of African American frequent flyers. As an insurance executive and chairman of the insurance convention he had been en route to attend, Coke traveled frequently, "visiting many sections of the nation, planning for meetings, looking at convention sites." His usual mode of travel was by air.[46] As the busiest airport in the country and the major hub for travel into and out of the South, Atlanta Municipal Airport was the crucial aerial gateway for a business traveler such as Coke. And last but not least, Coke was willing to file a complaint. Allegedly, he had gone to the Dobbs House dining room not as an activist intent on investigating the spatial practices its management subscribed to, but as a regular customer who happened to be denied service on the basis of his race. Two days after the incident, Coke contacted his lawyer.

The plaintiffs rested their case on the Fourteenth Amendment, arguing that, in denying Coke access to the dining room, the state had infringed upon Coke's rights as a citizen of the United States without due process of law. The "denial of service" not only violated the Amendment's equal protection clause, it "constituted a burden on interstate commerce" in violation of the Constitution's commerce clause.[47] Coke's lawyers tried to show that the Dobbs House restaurant's policies, even if devised without consultation, were tantamount to government action, and the city could be held accountable for civil rights violations by its lessee. Besides contesting the factual evidence in the case, the defense's strategy, much like in *Nash v. Air Terminal Services*, was to question "whether the restaurant's Jim Crow policy was government action to which the constitutional ban on segregation would apply."[48] Interrogatories after the pretrial hearings presented the following questions: Did the lease between the city and the restaurant give the city the right to control or supervise the operation of the restaurant? Did the city in fact exercise the right? Did the city, owning and leasing the eating facilities to Dobbs Houses, Inc., act in a governmental capacity representing the state in action and liability? Or did it not act in a municipal or proprietary capacity?[49]

The defendants attempted to invalidate the plaintiff's claim that he was in fact a representative of a class of people denied service and as such entitled to injunctive relief.[50] In support of their own position, they argued that since neither the state of Georgia nor the city of Atlanta in 1958 had segregation laws applicable to public or private eating establishments, it was the restaurant proprietor's individual choice and right to define his customer base by race. If that excluded some potential customers from service, the city and the airport management had to accept this fact because the lease agreement between their party and Dobbs Houses was silent on racial discrimination.[51]

During the proceedings in mid-December 1959, a year after the suit was filed, Coke's leading attorneys Hollowell and Greenberg tried to emphasize the enormity of the injustice their client had suffered. They drew attention to the fact that Coke had not been alone but in the company of two colleagues he had met at the airport. Besides showing that more than one person's rights had been violated by the denial of food service during the incident in question, this aspect of the situation helped Hollowell and Greenberg in portraying Coke as a representative of the growing class of African American passengers that used Atlanta Airport on a regular basis for interstate travel. It was not just Coke who returned to the airport on multiple occasions. Other passengers like him—black, male business travelers—had done so as well, but without being able to enjoy the advantages of all of the airport's services.

To corroborate their claim further that Coke shared his circumstances with others, Coke's attorneys brought Freddye Henderson and Roselle Douglas to the witness stand. Henderson was the director of Henderson Travel Service in Atlanta, which had a predominantly African American customer base. Henderson presented her travel agency's volume of airline ticket sales for the period from January to November 1959, the months between the filing of Coke's complaint and the date of the hearing. She had sold tickets in the amount of $82,683 (real price conversion in 2015: $671,000), mostly for interstate travel originating in or destined for Atlanta Municipal Airport—even by today's standards not a negligible amount.[52]

Douglas, a Spellman College student and member of Spellman's social science club, was called as a witness to present the results of an airport passenger survey she and three others had been asked to conduct by Hollowell. The four women had counted the number of African American travelers passing through the Atlanta airport passenger terminal at different times on three recent November days. Although comparatively small if looked at in isolation, the numbers were designed to establish the steady flow of black passengers through the terminal. On November 20, 1959, nineteen passengers had frequented the space between 1:30 p.m. and 4:30 p.m. On the afternoon of November 23, 1959 (between 3:30 p.m. and 5:30 p.m.), the number of passengers was thirteen. On the third day, November 30, 1959, twenty-two passengers had passed through the terminal between 6:40 a.m. and 10:40 a.m.[53] The numbers served to show that blacks (like whites) traveled before, during, and after the Thanksgiving holidays and they did so at different times of the day. There was nothing exceptional about the data or anything that would suggest a particular pattern of use; rather, the numbers proved that black air travelers had become part of the norm. They formed a stable part of the growing body of American air travelers.

To round off their strategy, the plaintiff's attorneys framed Coke's experience not as incidental but as part of a larger pattern of discrimination at the Dobbs House restaurant. To prove that contention, they brought Martin Luther King Sr. as a witness. A moral authority in Atlanta and the father of Martin Luther King Jr., he gave testimony of his own unpleasant experiences at the dining room, which corroborated Coke's claim that the airport restaurant systematically discriminated against blacks.[54]

The defendants' strategy involved attacks on Coke's credibility and the credibility of the witnesses the plaintiffs called. Defense attorneys B. D. "Buck" Murphy and Newell Edenfield were representatives of the white legal establishment with a reputation as defenders of the status quo.[55] They tried to show that Coke misinterpreted spatial arrangements and their meaning. When asked by defense attorney Edenfield how the table to which he was led was different from all the others in the restaurant, Coke pointed out that none of the others were protected by a screen. "That is the only difference?" Edenfield asked. "There was another difference," Coke replied, "and the reason I objected: that table was reserved especially for negroes, so I was informed." Pursuing his aggressive line of questioning, Edenfield further wanted to know whether there were any signs saying that the table was reserved for black patrons. Coke replied: "The screen is the sign that said that." Had the screen had any printing on it, or "did you just know that is what it meant," Edenfield questioned. Coke confirmed that he not only had known what it meant but also was assured of the screen's meaning by the waitress.[56] As a frequent air traveler, his remarks suggested, he knew how to recognize and read the signifiers of segregation. He did not need to have them spelled out in actual words. Nor did he need any coaching on how to read other people's racial background. Asked by Edenfield, who identified himself as someone who had lived in the South all his life, whether he was sure simply by judging from people's complexions that none of the other patrons at the restaurant "at that time had any Negro blood," Coke gave his assurance: "I know a White man from a Negro when I see one, most times."[57]

Murphy's cross-examination focused on finding out whether Coke had come to the restaurant with the specific purpose of provoking a confrontation with the waitress and headwaiter. Part of his attack on Coke's credibility was the attempt to frame him as an activist whose lawyer had persuaded him to seek trouble. Murphy's efforts were moreover designed to trivialize state involvement in the definition of racially discriminatory policies at the airport restaurant. During his examination of the restaurant manager B. F. Buttrey, who had introduced Jim Crow dining, it seemed as if these policies were a personal matter. Murphy tried to downplay Buttrey's role as an agent who acted in lieu of the state.[58]

U.S. District Judge William Boyd Sloan ruled for the plaintiffs.[59] The opinion delivered on January 6, 1960, affirmed the plaintiff's status as a representative of his class. It ruled that although the lease between the city of Atlanta as the owner of the airport and Dobbs Houses, Inc., as the proprietor of the restaurant did "not reserve to the city the right to control the operation of the restaurant," the actions of the lessee were nonetheless "the conduct of the City of Atlanta and thus state action" because the city owned and operated the airport. Rather than provide eating services itself, the city had hired Dobbs Houses to do so in its stead. Following *Derrington v. Plummer*, the court ruled that any conduct by the restaurant proprietor was "as much state action as would be similar conduct of the City of Atlanta itself."[60]

Segregation at the Dobbs House restaurant was thus framed as discriminatory action by the government, "violative of plaintiff's rights as a Negro citizen under the equal protection provision of the Fourteenth Amendment."[61] The ruling, which entitled H. D. Coke to injunctive relief, led to integration of the Atlanta Airport restaurant shortly thereafter. A decree issued by the judge on January 20, 1960, permanently enjoined the city of Atlanta and Dobbs Houses, Inc., "from directly and indirectly making or enforcing any distinction based upon race or color against plaintiff, H. D. Coke, or any other persons, in the use of the restaurant facility of the Atlanta Municipal Airport including the Dobbs House Restaurant at said airport."[62] The decision and its consequences were hailed by the African American press as a major victory. Part of a series of desegregation cases (buses and trolleys, public schools) all decided in the plaintiffs' favor, the *Atlanta Daily World* saw it as another milestone that would help "to further corrode the hard core of segregation in Atlanta."[63] It was also a vindication for the CORE protesters who had tried to integrate the restaurant only a few months before.

Coke v. Atlanta also had broader implications. Whereas *Nash v. Air Terminal Services* recognized segregation in airport terminal facilities—particularly in eating establishments—as a claim for which plaintiffs could seek relief in the courts, Judge Sloan's ruling established that airport concessionaires, and in fact everyone working in the entire airport, were state actors. Airports and their facilities came to be defined not as private enterprises but as governmental entities. Moreover, as Robert Dixon has pointed out, airport restaurants were constructed as falling within the meaning of "city use."[64] These decisions, then, were beginning to reshape the legal landscapes of aviation. They redefined what constituted a municipal space; they also questioned normative notions of race as legitimate parameters in the design and use of that space. Admitting African Americans to the airport restaurant in Atlanta signified not only the recognition of their rights as citizens under the U.S. Constitution but also the recognition of H. D. Coke's rights as a consumer who was entitled to both the purchase of an airline ticket and the ability to purchase a meal at the airport restaurant if he so desired. It that sense, the decision marked a seismic shift in the geopolitics of air travel. At the same time, the order of the court brought about permanent changes to the Atlanta Airport; the restaurant's management chose not to appeal it because after desegregation of the dining room its business ran smoothly.[65]

Although it made the screen in the Dobbs House restaurant disappear, *Coke v. Atlanta* did not automatically erase the color line at airport restaurants across the nation. But it did establish an important precedent for other cases, some of which were pending at the time U.S. District Judge Sloan issued his decision. While the screen came down in the Dobbs House restaurant, other local practices of discrimination and questionable performances of race persisted. A report about the court-ordered integration of the airport restaurant by Atlanta's WSB television station not only showed the conflicting parties leaving the restaurant together—among them the plaintiff H. D. Coke, his attorney Donald Hollowell, and Atlanta Mayor William Hartsfield—but also, for a few seconds, the camera rested on the impersonator of Uncle Remus. He was still doing his job in front of the restaurant's canopied door and he would continue to do until the opening of the airport's new passenger terminal in 1961.[66]

State action was also found in *Henry v. Greenville Airport Commission*, a case that dealt with racial discrimination in an airport waiting room. It grew out of the resistance against airport segregation in Greenville, South Carolina. The suit Richard B. Henry brought against the Greenville Airport Commission and its members was part of a two-pronged strategy to fight the city's discrimination against black air travelers.[67] The "prayer pilgrimage" brought the issue into the streets, the public realm, purposely increasing racial tension for a short time to facilitate long-term change. Litigation was part of the larger national effort supported by the NAACP to end airport segregation through case-by-case judicial enforcement in an attempt to firmly establish the right to travel as a right included in American citizenship.

Henry, an African American civilian employee of the U.S. Air Force, was not from Greenville. He had come to the city on a business assignment from Detroit, Michigan, in November 1958. While he was waiting for his return flight in the Greenville airport's main waiting area, the airport manager O. L. Andrews ordered him to leave. "We don't allow colored people in here," Andrews told Henry, informing him of the existence of a waiting room for African American patrons.[68] The airport manager ignored Henry's insistence that as an interstate passenger he was entitled to use of the main waiting area, which lacked a "whites only" designation. Rather than use the "colored" waiting room, Henry left the terminal building and waited outside until his flight was ready for boarding.[69] When he brought his case to the attention of the LDF attorneys after his return to Michigan, they decided to take his case. A complaint was filed on January 24, 1959, seeking an injunction to restrain the defendants "from making any distinction based upon color in regard to services at the Greenville Municipal Airport," which was construed as a government-owned facility.[70] His case had potential, similar to H. D. Coke's case; it also complemented the NAACP's other local activities aimed at integrating the airport.

The case, which rested on the same legal basis as the Coke case (and was argued by Jack Greenberg, Thurgood Marshall, and Lewis C. Jenkins Jr. from Columbia[71]), is significant not only for the legal avenues it explored but even more for the rhetoric and behaviors displayed by the defendants and the court. Both leading defense attorney Thomas A. Wofford and U.S. District Court Judge George Bell Timmerman made no secret of their white supremacist leanings, at times transforming the courtroom into a stage for the performance of their racism.[72] Their attitudes permeated their handling of the case; their selective recognition and application of legal precedent; their conduct in the courtroom; and their treatment of the plaintiffs. The manners of both men were defined by a deeply ingrained disrespect for African Americans; they also expressed their rejection of any possible changes to the way of life that was threatened by such recent developments as the Supreme Court's school desegregation rulings. As such, Wofford and Timmerman represented the forces of massive resistance in the courtroom. The court hearings, in particular, were an opportunity for the defense lawyer and the judge to vent an anger that went beyond the specifics of Henry's case.

In his opening statement during the proceedings on July 20, 1959, NAACP attorney Jack Greenberg, who had also been on H. D. Coke's legal team, pleaded for the plaintiffs that he thought it was "now rather late in the day for anyone to argue that a governmental body may maintain racial segregation in any of its facilities."[73] Since the airport had undisputedly been incorporated by statute of the state of South Carolina and was as such a governmental institution, any discrimination against patrons based on racial prejudice in his and his colleagues' view was in violation of the Fourteenth Amendment's equal protection clause. Certain of the soundness of his legal argument, Greenberg was caught off-guard by the refusal of Judge Timmerman to admit further evidence (a number of affidavits) or hear the witnesses for the prosecution. Instead Timmerman attacked Greenberg's professionalism, accusing him of dilettantism: "Just upon what are you predicating your jurisdiction? . . . It looks like somebody had picked up a digest of cases or a digest of the constitution and just at random picked out a whole lot of provisions to plead."[74]

Denying the plaintiffs any further opportunity to present their case, he cleared the floor for defense attorney Wofford, who went on a rhetorical rampage in an attempt to tear the case apart, ridicule the plaintiff, and defend southern values. Although Wofford agreed with the plaintiffs that the airport was a state-owned and operated facility, he flatly denied that the airport's day-to-day business operations could be considered government action or that the airport owed their passengers any service beyond use of the landing field. Segregation, he further argued, was not a state mandate but a customary phenomenon. He concluded triumphantly: "The customs of the people of a state do not constitute state action within the prohibition of the 14th [sic] Amendment." If the plaintiff had suffered from the treatment he received at the airport, only he himself was to blame for it. He had been provided with a waiting room, a courtesy as hypocritically generous as Wofford's assertion that "we always have believed, Your Honor, in at least feeding them." If Henry as an African American from the North resented the company of other African Americans in the "colored" waiting room, he should not blame airport management for his experience. He should avoid traveling to the airport in the future. Wofford encouraged people from out of state more generally to mind their own business instead of getting involved in the affairs of Greenville, "a small, progressive Southern community that some people are bent, beyond all reason to destroy." Regardless of what the plaintiffs said, he reminded the court, Henry's case ultimately rested "on the sole proposition that the 'separate but equal' doctrine has disappeared forever under any and all circumstances." And that proposition was nothing but an attack on southern values and the southern way of life. Concluding his pleadings, Wofford reminded the court "that fortunately the separate but equal doctrine has not yet completely and entirely disappeared dispite [*sic*] the wishes and dreams of certain people in the United States."[75]

Judge Timmerman, in an opinion issued two weeks later, dismissed Henry's lawsuit for lack of jurisdiction. Although his verdict was becoming increasingly untenable, what speaks through the pages of his ruling much louder than this technical argument are his white supremacist racial biases. Timmerman wrote: "Even whites, as yet, still have the right to choose their own companions and associates, and to preserve the integrity of the race with which God Almighty has endowed them."[76] He pretended not to understand the meaning of the word "segregation" as used by the plaintiff in his affidavit. Henry asserted that he was required to be segregated. He used the term "segregated" as synonymous with "racially segregated." What, Timmerman wondered, did that "loose expression" mean? From whom had Henry been segregated? Friends, family, and people he did or did not know? If Henry's segregation had consisted of any spatial distance to people who did not care for his company, little could be done about it: "The right to equality before the law, to be free from discrimination, invests no one with authority to require others to accept him as a companion or social equal."[77] Here, Timmerman rephrased the arguments Supreme Court Justice Henry Billings Brown had brought forth to rationalize "separate but equal" in *Plessy v. Ferguson*.[78] He affirmed the acceptability of social ostracism as another way of framing racial discrimination at a time when the Supreme Court had reversed its course and declared "separate but equal" unconstitutional. Timmerman concluded that Henry, as a modern consumer (from the North), was not exempt from having to live with the consequences of a social dogma the judge deemed valid.

What accounted for such aggressive and biased behavior in the courtroom by representatives of the white legal establishment? On the part of Wofford, it was a strategy of defense that involved the attempted intimidation of the plaintiffs and the trivialization of their concerns. But one gets a sense of something beyond that, a simmering anger rooted in the understanding that the case was part of a moment of transition, in which deeply held convictions were being questioned and challenged by a seemingly hostile outside world. The southern way of going about daily business was in urgent need of defense. This attitude of defiance also became palpable in the performances of the court. Timmerman's words and actions were an affirmation of the status quo, an insistence that nothing would change and that the social order built around the color line would remain intact. For him and his like-minded contemporaries, any approximation between blacks and whites, not to mention social equality and political parity, were inconceivable. As Jason Ward, Clive Webb, and others have shown, in the postwar years the color line was most vehemently defended by the conservative white establishment, especially in states like South Carolina, Mississippi, and Georgia. This establishment joined forces with conservative white working-class southerners in an effort to resist change that was brought by processes of urbanization and modernization, the civil rights movement, and increased levels of federal involvement in the South. Other elements of southern society, like moderate whites (both middle-class and working-class), who also favored segregation but were generally more willing to accommodate black demands for equality, were sidelined by the efforts of die-hard segregationists to organize massive resistance.[79]

Whereas Wofford and Timmerman represented the legal and judicial arm of massive resistance, the plaintiff Richard Henry personified the change white supremacists resented so much. Like H. D. Coke, Henry was a representative of the new class of business travelers who depended on air travel to perform their jobs properly. He also was an interstate traveler, albeit from the North, who operated beyond the confines of local or regional systems of deference and dependency. Moreover, he belonged to a group of African Americans who in the postwar years had benefited from federal support: members of the military.[80] As a civilian employee of the U.S. Air Force, Henry was the embodiment of a model of African American masculinity whose emergence was made possible in part by the federal government after World War II. He was a civil servant, a status that for many blacks provided access to the middle class. He also worked as an information officer who was responsible for Air Force community relations in eighteen states. Based at the Tenth Air Force headquarters, Selfridge Air Force Base in Michigan, Henry traveled frequently; his job required coordinating and communicative skills.[81] In short, his professional profile was anathema to those who subscribed to ideologies of white superiority and black inferiority. Even more than Coke, Henry was proof that African Americans not only desired to become but already existed as consumers and citizens.

On April 20, the Fourth Circuit Court of Appeals reversed Timmerman's ruling, opining that Henry's "complaint was entitled to a more liberal construction than it received and that it was erroneously dismissed."[82] The judges accepted the plaintiff's allegation that he was the victim of discriminatory state action based on race and was therefore entitled to injunctive relief. They reminded the lower court: "It is now well established that property acquired, maintained and operated by a state or by its political subdivisions and agencies must be equally available to citizens without discrimination because of race."[83] They also remanded the case for further proceedings.

The second hearing was held on September 14, 1960. Richard Henry was finally able to take the witness stand. It turned out to be as much of a charade as the first one. Once again defense attorney Thomas Wofford and Judge George Timmerman dominated the proceedings, humiliating the plaintiffs and their witnesses. This time around, they attacked Henry's credibility by questioning the authenticity of his experience: Was his run-in with the airport manager not a deliberate attempt to provoke a confrontation sponsored by the NAACP? Timmerman accused the plaintiffs of fabricating facts and insinuated that they were part of a larger effort by "some groups of people" who were going "around instigating lawsuits here and yonder in which they have no primary interest."[84] In response to Jack Greenberg's rejection of any such motivation on the part of his client, the judge countered with a proverb: "It is the wicked who deny before they are accused." Timmerman framed the plaintiff as a perpetrator rather than a victim of racial discrimination.[85]

Timmerman also made a point of rejecting the idea that American citizenship encompassed the right to have free and uninhibited access to travel facilities, which the higher court had affirmed. He did so during the cross-examination of J. S. Hall. In his testimony Hall elucidated how he was discriminated against on a number of occasions. Every time he had gone to the airport in the past, including in October 1959 when he accompanied Jackie Robinson to the airport, he had insisted on using the main waiting area not only because it was comfortable and more open, and had views onto the airfield, but most importantly because he wanted to claim his constitutional privilege: "I am a citizen and I have the right, or I feel that I have the right, to use all of the facilities provided at the airport as long as I am not violating a law."[86] If that was so, the judge confronted him, why had he not made use of his right to use the other room? How did he know it was less comfortable if he had never used it? Had he actually never used it or "peeked" through the door to investigate its condition?

Few were surprised when, instead of granting the injunction, Timmerman once again dismissed the case. His order decreed that the plaintiff had failed to prove the damages he had suffered conclusively. The judge ruled: "Moreover, to issue the injunction would not maintain the status quo, but would change it."[87] Unwilling to change the status quo, he refused to provide injunctive relief. Relief was at long last provided by the Fourth Circuit Court of Appeals, which in a second per curiam decree once again reversed Timmerman's decision. The appellate court stated that it had no discretion to deny relief by preliminary injunction to a person who had clearly established "by undisputed evidence" that he was being denied a constitutional right.[88] In essence, the higher court was ordering the lower court to issue an order to end the segregation of the airport. In recognition of the binding effect the Fourth Circuit's mandate carried, on February 17, 1961, Timmerman finally issued his order to integrate the Greenville Municipal Airport.[89] A few months later, in October 1961, another court ordered the integration of the airport of Tallahassee (see chapter 3).

By the end of 1961, the decisions in *Henry v. Greenville Airport Commission*, *Coke v. Atlanta*, and *Brooks v. Tallahassee* had established important legal precedents. They significantly shifted the legal ground in the fight against segregated waiting and dining areas in airports. The decisions, some of which came against the resistance of U.S. district court judges, settled the question about the status of airports as government facilities. They defined the actions of both public and private actors as falling within the meaning of state action. Theoretically they left little wiggle room. But as Katherine Barnes has rightly pointed out, the rulings applied only to Atlanta, Greenville, and Tallahassee.[90] Airport administrators elsewhere were not bound by these decisions. To challenge practices of racial discrimination at airports in other cities, black air travelers had to bring suits. They did. Several more lawsuits were pending in late 1961. They included *Bailey v. Patterson*, *Turner v. Memphis*, *Adams v. City of New Orleans*, and *Shuttlesworth v. Dobbs Houses, Inc.*

Whereas *Bailey v. Patterson* brought a broad complaint against the city of Jackson, its transportation carriers, and its municipal airport, *Turner v. Memphis* narrowly focused on practices of spatial exclusion in the Dobbs House restaurant at Memphis Municipal Airport. Like *Bailey v. Patterson*, but unlike earlier cases, *Turner v. Memphis* involved state laws requiring segregation. Both cases serve to show how the shifts in legal discourse that began to emerge in the earlier cases continued to take shape. Over the course of their resolution, the Supreme Court had a chance to weigh in expressing its growing impatience with the lower courts' inclinations to find litigable constitutional issues with regard to racial discrimination at airport terminal facilities.[91] *Turner v. Memphis* can serve as an example to show the causes of the Court's exasperation. The case tipped the scale in favor of an understanding that segregation by state action was per se unconstitutional. This principle, Robert Dixon has pointed out, covered restaurant lessees in municipally owned airports simply because they were municipal lessees. No city control or direction needed to be shown.[92] The plaintiff, Jesse H. Turner, filed the case with the support of the NAACP's LDF in April 1960. He was represented in court by a legal team that included several young black lawyers and Constance Baker Motley, one of the LDF's most seasoned legal experts and its only female attorney.

The existence of duplicate facilities and racially exclusive spaces at Memphis Municipal Airport came to the attention of the NAACP in 1953, when members of the Memphis branch investigated conditions at their local airport. Utillus R. Phillips, the branch's president, and his team found segregated restrooms, separate taxi services for whites and blacks, and spatial partitioning in the Dobbs House restaurant. Only the snack bar was integrated.[93] Whereas the airports in Nashville and Knoxville gave up their segregated floor-plans in 1954, integrating their restaurants (run by Sky Chefs) and other facilities, Memphis Municipal Airport continued to discriminate against African American travelers.[94] The city's actions here reflected larger patterns of racial discrimination, which over the years had turned Memphis into one of Tennessee's most segregated cities. Constance Baker Motley remarked: "Its large black population could attest that racism was rampant."[95]

When Turner and two business associates went to the restaurant on April 28, 1959, to have a meal, they were led to the same small room adjacent to the main dining room Phillips had inspected five years earlier.[96] Unlike the screen in the Dobbs House restaurant in Atlanta, the blacks-only dining room in Memphis was not a malleable spatial arrangement. Although the screen also made African Americans invisible, a separate room set them apart even more firmly, eliminating even the sounds of a shared presence. Turner returned to the restaurant on a subsequent occasion. His experience on October 29, 1959, mirrored the earlier one. Asking to be served at the Dobbs House restaurant, a hostess once again led him to the dining room set apart for African Americans.[97] On both occasions, Turner talked to the restaurant manager inquiring into the causes for his treatment. Manager W. S. Haverfield each time cited Tennessee state laws as the legal reason for his staff's actions.[98]

Turner was another representative of the class of airport patrons on whose behalf he brought his complaint against airport authorities in Memphis. He was a middle-class African American who represented the city's large middle-class population. Turner attended LeMoyne College and then embarked upon a career that made him the executive vice president of the black Tri-State Bank of Memphis, a community-oriented financial institution whose business was infused with a social justice agenda. Turner was also a well-known civil rights activist. Under his leadership, the bank was involved in civil rights causes, for example providing loans to prospective black homeowners and bail money to civil rights demonstrators. As such, the bank was an important institution in the local civil rights movement.[99] Moreover, Turner served as the treasurer of the NAACP's Memphis branch and succeeded Phillips as its president. At the same time, he was a member of the Shelby County Democratic Executive Committee, the first African American to hold this post since Reconstruction. It was in this capacity that he had to travel by air, about four or five times a year according to his own testimony.[100] The suit he brought against the airport was not his first civil action. A few months before he sued the airport, Turner filed a complaint against the Memphis Public Library that led to the library's integration in 1961.[101]

Turner's case against the airport rested on the Fourteenth Amendment. His legal team argued that Dobbs Houses, Inc., as a lessee of a publicly owned facility was subject to the amendment and therefore had to refrain from discriminating against select customers on the basis of their race. Although *Coke v. Atlanta* had yet to be decided, Motley and her colleagues tried to establish that the question of what constituted state action in the Memphis context had been settled by citing, among other cases, *Derrington v. Plummer*.[102] Making her case in a hearing for motion of summary judgment, Motley told the District Court: "The Supreme Court . . . cited that case [*Derrington v. Plummer*] and other cases of similar nature for the proposition that wherever a state is involved through any arrangement, management, or participation by way of funds, the Fourteenth Amendment restrictions apply."[103] As evidence of the state's involvement, the plaintiffs brought the lease between the city of Memphis and Dobbs Houses, Inc., which specifically stated the restaurant lessee's obligation to provide services in lieu of the city. The evidence also included the Grant Agreement between the city of Memphis and the FAA, which demonstrated the degree to which the federal government was financially involved in the airport. In her efforts to elucidate how legal interpretations of state action had changed in recent years, Motley hoped to convince the court that the defense's attempts to invoke Tennessee Jim Crow laws to justify their actions had no merit. In her view, the unconstitutionality of state regulations requiring segregation of facilities on public property was obvious.

In contrast, the defendants intended to establish the constitutionality of the segregation laws in question. They included the written law, sections of the Tennessee Code § 53–2120 (safety of restaurants), § 62–710 (the right to refuse service to anyone), and Regulation No. R-18 (L) (racial segregation in restaurants). In order to do so, leading defense attorneys Frank Gianotti and John Heiskell from Memphis, who represented the city and the restaurant operator, initially focused on procedural matters in their defense strategy.[104] They requested the case be heard by a three-judge panel—as was necessary in cases involving state laws, which Motley argued was not the case in *Turner v. Memphis*. The defense hoped that in the next phase of proceedings, the federal court would practice abstention and let the state courts of Tennessee get the right to pass on the respective statutes. They argued that unless the state courts declared the segregation laws unconstitutional, Dobbs Houses, Inc., would not have to refrain from desegregating its restaurant or act in violation of Tennessee laws.

Motley was a brilliant lawyer, and as the LDF's principal trial attorney she brought years of experience to the case. Her capacity for legal reasoning, the clarity of her arguments, and the precision of her language are stunning, especially when she was speaking and arguing in court. Motley had participated in most of the major civil rights cases since the mid-1940s and a few months later would become the first African American to argue before the Supreme Court. Coming down to Memphis she knew that she would be dealing with a hostile court.[105] Among her Memphis colleagues, Marion Speed Boyd, a judge on the U.S. District Court for the Western District of Tennessee, enjoyed a reputation as a staunch white supremacist. Nominated to the bench by Franklin D. Roosevelt in 1940, Judge Boyd, like Judge Timmerman, represented the conservative white (Democratic) establishment disinclined to consider any changes to the status quo.[106] His ideological inclinations found expression not only in his decisions but also in his behavior in the courtroom. When Motley was in Boyd's courtroom for the first time in a Memphis school desegregation case, she recalled in her autobiography, she and her local colleagues A. W. (Archie Walter) Willis, Russell Sugarmon, Benjamin Hooks, and H. T. Lockett—the same attorneys who represented Turner—waited in vain for their case to be called at the early hour it was scheduled for on the court's calendar for the day.[107] Instead, they were passed over, and their motion was not heard until the end of the day and the end of the docket. "This was Judge Boyd's personal segregation policy: blacks were always last on his calendar." But Boyd not only practiced temporal segregation. He also displayed disrespectful behaviors, which were designed to shield him against the personal encounters he found difficult to endure. When H. T. Lockett rose to present his motion in the abovementioned case, according to Motley: "Judge Boyd closed his eyes, and they remained closed as Lockett spoke. When I got up to speak, the Judge at least opened his eyes, but he asked no questions. When we got out of court that day, the four lawyers with me burst out laughing and told me that was Boyd's way of dealing with black lawyers: he literally could not stand the sight of black people."[108]

During the hearings in the Turner case, Boyd treated Motley with more courtesy. He welcomed her to the courtroom and allotted her ample time to speak. But it was a superficial courteousness. Their exchanges were fraught with tension, which became tangible in the ways in which Boyd asked questions. He engaged with Motley but mostly ignored her legal reasoning and procedural concerns, not so much as a matter of substance but as a matter of principle. How could an experienced white male judge from the South possibly listen to an able black woman attorney from the North twenty years his junior in a civil rights case? The odds were clearly against Motley. Whereas black civil rights lawyers by then had become an accepted part of the "fraternity of lawyers/brotherhood of the bar," as Kenneth Mack has argued, an African American woman trial attorney like Motley remained an oddity in the eyes of the (white) legal establishment.[109] Unlike Timmerman, Boyd refrained from making racially insensitive remarks or verbally expressing his segregationist worldview. But he was clearly much more comfortable interacting with the defense lawyers, whose talents consisted mostly in ignoring the new laws of the land in their interventions in and beyond the courtroom. It came as no surprise that Judge Boyd granted the defendants' motion for the convention of a three-judge panel even though Gianotti and Heiskell had come across as ill-prepared, confused, and not particularly talented in oral argument.

The three-judge panel was composed of John D. Martin (chief judge of the Sixth Circuit Court of Appeals), William E. Miller (U.S. district judge for the District Court for the Middle District of Tennessee), and Marion Boyd. The panel also sided with the defendants.[110] After hearing the case on November 6, 1960, the court stayed all further proceedings invoking the doctrine of abstention in order to give Tennessee state courts the opportunity to deliver interpretations of those segregation statutes the defendants sought declaratory judgment for. Frustrated with this outcome, Turner's legal team filed notices of appeal to the Sixth Circuit Court of Appeals and the U.S. Supreme Court. The Supreme Court treated the appeal as a petition for a writ of certiorari to the court of appeals in a pending action, considerably speeding up proceedings and essentially sidelining the lower court. This was an unusual step, and for that matter it was quite noteworthy that the court heard the case in this procedural posture. The immediate public importance of the case justified this deviation from normal appellate practice requiring the Sixth Circuit Court of Appeals to consider the case first.[111]

The per curiam opinion handed down on March 26, 1962, left no doubt why the Supreme Court acted as expeditiously as it did. It was obviously weary of the lower courts' unwavering enthusiasm for finding litigable state action issues involving public facilities. The court flatly rejected the defendants' constitutional concerns. Whether or not Tennessee state laws fostered segregation in publicly operated facilities did not matter: "But our decisions have foreclosed any possible contention that such a statute or regulation may stand consistently with the Fourteenth Amendment."[112] In light of these prior decisions and "the undisputed facts of the case," no issue remained to be resolved by the state of Tennessee, a process that could have taken years. The court therefore remanded the case back to the U.S. District Court with directions to grant Jesse Turner injunctive relief against the forms of racial discrimination he had complained of. A comment in the *New York Times* put the court's action into perspective: "The manner of today's unanimous decision was as significant as the result. The Supreme Court indicated its shortening patience with racial segregation and its willingness to cut through procedural obstacles if necessary."[113] Two weeks later, on May 11, 1962, Judge Boyd issued a decree that "forever enjoined and restrained" the defendants "from segregating Negroes in the services and facilities of the Dobbs House restaurant or any other eating facilities located in the Memphis Municipal Airport."[114] Although the restaurant management continued to subscribe to practices of racial segregation while its case was pending—Carl T. Rowan, deputy assistant secretary of state, was the last black patron whose treatment at the restaurant made national news—it implemented integration without incident after having been court-ordered to do so.[115]

The last two lawsuits still pending when *Turner v. Memphis* was decided were actions brought in New Orleans and Birmingham. Mainly drawing on the *Turner* case and *Coke v. Atlanta*, both actions proceeded along similar lines, bringing victories for the plaintiffs. *Turner* signaled that the question whether segregation could be legally practiced at airport facilities was no longer open for litigation. *Adams v. City of New Orleans* and *Shuttlesworth v. Dobbs Houses, Inc.* serve to illustrate how, by the summer of 1963, the process of redefining the legal understanding of state action and public facilities had come to an end. These shifts in legal doctrine translated into the spatial reconfiguration of the cultural landscapes of air transportation. As black plaintiffs won in courtrooms all over the South, segregation signs came down; duplicate facilities and spatial partitions had to be abandoned. *Adams v. City of New Orleans* and *Shuttlesworth v. Dobbs Houses, Inc.* also show how hard local lawyers fought in the battle over integration of public facilities on behalf of the white establishment they represented. They did not give an inch, neither in New Orleans nor in Birmingham; the latter was referred to as the "Johannesburg of America" by *New York Times* correspondent Harrison Salisbury.[116] Both cases document the unwavering commitment of civil rights lawyers to using the law as a tool for change; the unshakable commitment of local attorneys to resisting change by interpretation of the law; and the evolving role of the federal judiciary as an agent of change.

New Orleans resident Thomas P. Harris and a second group of New Orleanians, consisting of William R. Adams, Henry E. Braden III, and Samuel

L. Gandy, filed complaints against the city of New Orleans, Interstate Hosts Inc., and the New Orleans Aviation Board in May 1960 with the support of the NAACP's LDF.[117] *Harris v. City of New Orleans* and *Adams v. City of New Orleans*, which were consolidated into one case in July 1961, asked for court intervention to end racial segregation at Moisant International Airport's upscale restaurant, the International Room; the Cocktail Lounge; and the tavern called "Le Bar." Each plaintiff had been prohibited from eating at the restaurant on at least one occasion. With integrated service available at the snack bar and the coffee shop, plaintiffs argued that these incoherent practices illustrated the "irrationality and arbitrariness of the type of segregation" the defendants had imposed. They also argued these practices violated the Fourteenth Amendment's equal protection clause. Rulings in other cases had by now firmly established that dining facilities formed an inherent part of services rendered by municipal airports, as argued by the plaintiffs' legal team, led by local attorney Alexander P. Tureaud and the LDF's Jack Greenberg.[118] The denial of service based on a patron's race as practiced by Interstate Hosts, Inc., the airport's restaurant concessionaire, was therefore unconstitutional.[119]

The defendants presented defenses to justify the existing spatial regime, which selectively excluded African American customers from certain airport dining facilities. Most of these defenses ignored legal precedent based on recent jurisdiction. The defendants argued that Interstate Hosts was a private enterprise able to select its own customers and therefore not bound by the Fourteenth Amendment. They claimed that the company did offer integrated services at two eateries, providing black customers with a choice, and that the whites-only facilities were luxurious, catering not to everyone but to a specialized clientele. Additionally, they argued that if the facilities were to become integrated, Interstate Hosts' business performance would suffer, jeopardizing the company's financial obligations toward its lessor, the city of New Orleans.[120]

The U.S. District Court for the Eastern District of Louisiana disagreed with this kind of reasoning. District Judge Herbert W. Christenberry, a Truman nominee who had already delivered important rulings in a number of civil rights cases, including one that desegregated the public schools in New Orleans, ruled for the plaintiffs, accepting their argument that the actions of Interstate Hosts were unconstitutional. In his opinion Judge Christenberry wrote: "The decisive question presented here is whether or not the action of the lessee, Interstate Hosts, may, in the constitutional view, be said to be the conduct of the City of New Orleans, constituting 'state action.' I find that it is." Judge Christenberry cited among other cases *Turner v. Memphis* and *Coke v. Atlanta*. "These authorities leave little doubt that plaintiffs in the case before this Court are entitled to injunctive relief as a matter of the law."[121] Judge Christenberry used measured language in his published opinion of August 2, 1962; but a year later, the U.S. Court of Appeals for the Fifth Circuit, to which the defendants had appealed, did not. The appellate court rejected their appeal using strong words, calling the defenses the appellants had brought forward "patently frivolous." It was clear that "the Supreme Court has 'settled beyond question that no State may require racial segregation of interstate or intrastate transportation facilities . . . The question is no longer open; it is foreclosed as a litigable issue.'"[122]

In *Shuttlesworth v. Dobbs Houses, Inc.*, a federal court granted an injunction against Birmingham Municipal Airport and its restaurant lessee two weeks before *Adams v. New Orleans* was decided. U.S. District Judge Harlan Grooms found the plaintiff proved that the airport discriminated against African American patrons in its dining facilities, including the dining room, lounge, and coffee shop, and ordered their integration.[123] His order affected Jim Crow spaces in the airport's old terminal as well as in its brand-new passenger facility, which had opened its doors on February 1, 1962. The action was the third private lawsuit the Dobbs Houses, Inc., restaurant chain was forced to defend. As in *Turner v. Memphis*, the case pitted the company (and Birmingham airport authorities) against civil rights activists: Fred L. Shuttlesworth, a minister and the president of the Alabama Christian Movement for Human Rights, who was heavily involved in local desegregation campaigns; his daughter Patricia Ann; and his attorney Len Holt. For years, the Alabama Christian Movement had fought for the integration of Birmingham's transportation facilities.[124]

Unfolding before a backdrop of racial tensions, which a white supremacist board of commissioners did little to resolve, the case is another example of the degree to which the defendants were willing to advocate for airport segregation, though increasingly it was a losing legal battle. Unfazed by the *Coke v. Atlanta* decision, Dobbs Houses' local legal team—similar to the company's attorneys in Memphis and Interstate Host's legal counsel in New Orleans—invoked questionable defenses: that the Fourteenth Amendment did not apply to the case because the restaurant operation was privately owned; and that racial segregation in eating establishments in Birmingham was "carried out by custom and voluntary choice and without compulsion by the people in accordance with their own desires and social practices." The behavior of people, even if collective, the defendants' brief pointed out, did not constitute state action, and was therefore constitutional. Among a long list of other arguments, the sixth line of defense stands out, as it was an effort to vilify the plaintiffs. In particular, Fred Shuttlesworth was framed as "a convicted felon" and "known criminal" who did not deserve service.[125] The criminal record referred to by the defendants' attorneys reflected Shuttlesworth's convictions for trespassing, which he had incurred as a participant in local direct-action protest activities. Disregarding these constructions of black masculinity and the slanted legal basis on which the defendants rested their case, the judge ruled for the plaintiffs, and the defendants did not appeal.[126] In "A Southerner Speaks," his regular column for the *Pittsburgh Courier*, Shuttlesworth commented on the outcome of his case: "Thus, one more irrational barrier has fallen in the Magic City, and upon my return there soon, I shall eat a whole—and I would think, very wholesome meal—in the airport, under the very sign, 'It's so nice to have you in Birmingham.'"[127]

Coming in quick succession, the 1962 federal district court decisions left little doubt that the spatial characteristics of airport terminals in the South were changing. The U.S. Supreme Court, with its intervention in *Bailey v. Patterson* and *Turner v. Memphis*, validated the lower court's conceptualization of airports as integrated spaces. With this shift in legal discourse that redefined the relationship between race and space, airport terminals as a building type were about to disappear from the physical landscapes of segregation. The redefinition of airports as integrated facilities had geopolitical implications because it validated the participation of African Americans in the new culture of air mobility. By bringing lawsuits in the federal courts, African Americans sought this validation. On the one hand, they did so as consumers demanding access to spaces for the consumption of food and other services. As air travelers, as a matter of principle, they wanted to access all of the services the air travel experience entailed in and beyond the cabin. On the other hand, they demanded their rightful access to the spaces of air travel as citizens of the United States whose rights included equal access to all areas of public life. As such, the fight for integrated transportation facilities was part of the larger struggle over the renegotiation of racial identities in the postwar period.

CHAPTER 5

Changing the Law of the Land

Regulatory and Statutory Reform

Direct action protest was not only flanked by efforts to challenge airport segregation in the courts. With an urgency that increased in the late 1950s and early 1960s, civil rights activists also tried to put pressure on the federal government and its regulatory agencies. They identified statutory and regulatory reform as tools in the fight against racial discrimination at Jim Crow airports. Civil rights leaders demanded the enforcement of existing provisions and also called for changing the rules of airport administration. There were varying opinions on which statutory grounds were best employed to attack discriminatory practices in airport terminal facilities. Attention focused on the Federal Airport Act and the CAA's authority to regulate access to airport terminals according to the Federal Aviation Act. Actors in the struggle over the reform of laws and regulations were Congress and the administrator of the CAA, which in 1958 was reorganized as the FAA. The perspective will thus shift to explore the role of the legislature and federal regulators in the planning and administration of aviation's built environment. Shifting the focus away from the air travel experience and protest activities at airport terminals means investigating how officials—both elected and appointed—in the nation's capital envisioned passenger terminals to function as spaces of travel. Such an investigation sheds light on the significance of federal and state forces as agents in the creation and dismantlement of the racialized spaces of aviation.

The CAA had taken action before, in 1948, when its administrator ordered the desegregation of National Airport in Washington, D.C. Although dealing with airports that were under municipal control presented challenges that were not present in integrating a federally owned facility, legal experts in the civil rights community and the CAA contemplated a number of ways to tackle the issue. In a 1955 memorandum the NAACP's Washington bureau counsel, Francis Pohlhaus, spelled out the legal grounds on which he thought the federal government could press action against discriminatory practices. In one scenario, he recognized language in the Civil Aeronautics Act (1938) as lending itself to the prohibition of segregation.[1] One particular provision of the Act, which prohibited air carriers from subjecting any person to unjust discrimination, undue or unreasonable prejudice, or disadvantage, could be interpreted along the same lines as nearly identical passages in the Interstate Commerce Act. Because the Interstate Commerce Act applied to terminal facilities, Pohlhaus suggested that provisions in the Civil Aeronautics Act be construed accordingly. Since the latter Act also provided that air carriers were required to make available facilities in connection with the air transportation services they offered, he maintained that federal regulations applied to the administration of these facilities although they were in most instances operated not by air carriers but by local authorities. He insisted: "Those who operate these facilities should be considered acting directly as air carriers or indirectly in their stead and should be required to operate in accordance with all provisions of the Civil Aeronautics Act." The counsel was aware of the broad nature of the term "air carrier." He nonetheless saw potential in enforcing the Civil Aeronautics Act's provisions.[2]

Pohlhaus recognized the enforcement of provisions in the Federal Airport Act as an alternative way of tackling the issue of discrimination at Jim Crow airports. The Federal Airport Act, passed by Congress in 1946, was designed as a tool for aeronautical development across the United States.[3] It invested the CAA with powers to furnish "technical advice in connection with airport site selection, planning, design and construction and in developing maintenance and operating practices for airports."[4] In order to do so, the agency was called upon to prepare and annually revise a National Airport Plan. The plan was to specify the location and types of development considered necessary "to provide a system of public airports adequate to anticipate and meet the needs of civil aeronautics."[5] The CAA was also authorized to provide financial assistance to local airport authorities for the construction of public airports. Airport authorities, the majority of which were municipal agencies, could apply for grant funding made available through the FAAP. Besides financially supporting land acquisitions, the program subsidized the construction of infrastructural features such as runways, towers, fire stations, and terminal facilities.[6] Designed as a grant-in-aid program that required a 50 percent local contribution, FAAP received an appropriation of $500 million for an initial period of seven years.[7] Public agencies sponsoring airport improvement projects were required to prepare detailed project applications including construction plans, which had to be in accordance with the CAA's guidelines concerning, for instance, airport location, airport layout, drainage, lighting, and the safety of approaches.

As part of their application, they also had to make a written pledge that the airport to which the project related would "be available for public use on fair and reasonable terms and without unjust discrimination."[8] This wording left open how broadly the term "unjust discrimination" was defined and whether it, in fact, encompassed racial discrimination. The grant agreements, which were executed between the CAA and local airport authorities, also remained silent on the term's meaning.

By 1955, almost a billion dollars had been dispensed, and hundreds of airports across the country (including Alaska and Hawaii) had received subsidies through FAAP. As a region poor in infrastructure, the South particularly benefited from the rewards of the program, which encouraged the modernization and expansion of existing facilities and enabled the construction of new airports.[9] The airports in Atlanta, Greenville, Jackson, Memphis, Montgomery, New Orleans, and Tallahassee were all built with financial support from the federal government. Many cities applied for funding more than once, spacing their funding requests in accordance with the works projects scheduled for a specific budget year.[10] Some had done so more eagerly than others, reacting on the one hand to increasing consumer demand for air travel that was reflected in rising passenger numbers; on the other hand, many city leaders recognized the business opportunities offered by a city well situated in transportation networks.[11]

Looking at the emerging landscapes of southern aviation, observers like Pohlhaus could not help but realize that federal subsidies had been or were being used for the construction of segregated airports—leading them to conclude that the CAA subscribed to the "separate but equal" doctrine in its dispensation of funds even after the Supreme Court had declared it unconstitutional.[12] The CAA's funding practices were also problematic in light of the fact that appropriations were apportioned among states in accordance with population-area formulas. African Americans counted toward the number of people living in each population area, but in many places they were barred from equal access to terminals built with FAAP money.[13] To put a stop to the misappropriation of federal funds, Pohlhaus saw much potential in encouraging the CAA's administrator to enforce compliance with the antidiscrimination provision of the Federal Airport Act. As developments over the course of the next few years showed, this proved to be the more viable of the two regulatory control scenarios he explored. Representative Charles Diggs, who requested a copy of the counsel's memorandum, agreed with Pohlhaus's assessment.[14] Supporting the efforts of the NAACP, he pressed the CAA to investigate uses of funds and patterns of discrimination, which his 1955 airport survey was bringing to light. He also called on the agency to enforce and if necessary amend existing regulations.[15]

Confronted with such criticism, the agency launched a study of its grant appropriations in the fall of 1955 that confirmed widespread misuse of federal funds by local airport management. In reaction, the CAA's newly appointed administrator, Charles J. Lowen, issued a new directive on airport building policy.[16] It was designed to curb the construction of segregated features in terminal buildings subsidized by the FAAP. The directive provided: "No Federal-Aid Airport Program funds will be made available for the development of separate facilities or space in an airport building when such facilities or space are designed for use now or in the future for separate racial groups."[17] Its detailed language lent specificity to the Federal Airport Act's vague discrimination clause, which now precisely spelled out its applicability to racial discrimination. The ensuing explanatory text provided new guidelines for parts of the FAAP application process. To enforce compliance with the new policy, airport managers were henceforth required to state in writing whether or not their facilities would be available to all patrons without regard to race. Those who did not plan to abide by the new regulation were called upon to explain their position and to describe the areas intended for racially exclusive use. These noncompliant airports had to face sanctions. Future funding requests would be denied if they pertained to terminal building sections where duplicate spaces existed and were slated for design updates and improvement or where duplicate facilities were in the process of being constructed. If, for instance, "separate sanitary facilities are provided for segregated use, all areas involving sanitary facilities will be excluded [from participation in the program]." In contrast, integrated terminal spaces, or airport facilities such as runways, aprons, and towers, would continue to qualify for federal support.[18]

Instead of completely interrupting the flow of money going toward building projects at Jim Crow airports, and instead of excluding from eligibility any building project at passenger terminals designed to include duplicate features, the new directive narrowly cut funding for construction of terminal areas intended to be used as waiting rooms, dining rooms, and restrooms.[19] It was an effort to impose penalties on noncompliant, white supremacist airport authorities without temporarily halting the construction of airports in southern cities or bringing it to a complete stop. Thereby (although it enforced nondiscrimination rules in the skies), the CAA avoided the issue of standing up for civil rights on the ground—that is, the terminal grounds from which air travelers embarked. Rather than take a forceful stand that would have ended federal support of discriminatory local practices and forced integration by withdrawing subsidies, the agency opted for a measure that tightened the rules without slowing down the construction of an aviation infrastructure that was seen as a key element in the modernization of the South.

Situating the agency in a complicated middle ground, the new policy met with mixed reactions. It was welcomed by those in the federal government who championed the enforcement of antidiscrimination laws in all areas of American public life and recognized the federal government's responsibility for doing so. Diggs called it a "laudable step" but also expressed his hopes that the CAA had "further intentions."[20] Yet, the new policy also met with criticism. Neither southern Democrats nor the civil rights community were happy with the measure, albeit for different reasons. U.S. Senator Thomas Wofford, a Democrat from Greenville, South Carolina, who a few years later represented the defendants in *Henry v. Greenville Airport Commission* as a proponent of the status quo, was so incensed by the measure that he threatened to block the confirmation of Lowen's nomination in the Senate.[21] In a hearing before the Senate Committee on Interstate and Foreign Commerce, Wofford accused the administrator of overstepping his discretionary authority, "going further than the Supreme Court has ever gone."[22] In his efforts to lay into Lowen, he was assisted by Sam Ervin, a Democrat from North Carolina. Ervin framed Lowen's action as an attempt at legislating, which he considered going well beyond the administrator's job description as a representative of the executive branch. From Ervin's perspective, the Lowen policy memorandum was an unlawful act.[23]

To the NAACP, on the other hand, the directive failed to reach its mark. Pohlhaus voiced the organization's disappointment in a letter to Lowen's successor, James Pyle, in which he regretted a missed opportunity to prohibit discrimination.[24] "The policy," he wrote, "provides an opportunity for local airport officials to continue this illegal practice. It makes possible the creation of pockets of segregated facilities surrounded by Federally-financed areas of major construction."[25] In avoiding a more drastic approach, Pohlhaus's remarks suggest, the CAA exemplified the federal government's lax stance on civil rights. Recognizing the agency's unwillingness to execute its authority in broader terms based on existing statutes, proponents of airport integration called for an amendment to the Federal Airport Act, which would redefine the rules for the distribution of federal financial aid to airports.[26]

The debate about amending the Federal Airport Act was accelerated in the spring of 1960, when Jacob Javits, a liberal Republican from New York, took up the issue of federally funded airport construction in the Senate.[27] Concerned about the moral implications of segregation's continued toleration by Congress, and frustrated with the ambiguous policies of the FAA (into which the CAA had been reorganized), Javits recognized the Act's upcoming extension as an opportunity to change its funding rules. In May 1960, he introduced an amendment to the appropriations bill for fiscal year 1961 that would have prohibited the disbursement of any FAAP payments to airport terminal building projects where segregated facilities were in the process of being constructed.[28] Highlighting the Eisenhower administration's efforts to end segregation practices in government programs, Javits called on his colleagues to move in the same direction. In his remarks on the Senate floor, he reminded them that, following Lowen's 1956 directive, no federal funds were to go toward the construction of segregated facilities. Since then, however, $600,000 had been spent on passenger facilities in Birmingham, Montgomery, Meridian, Natchez, and Tallahassee, all of which were organized along racially discriminatory lines. Local authorities had complied with FAA requirements by using local money instead of federal funds to build duplicate service facilities. Still, Javits was greatly concerned: "The fact that local funds and not Federal funds are actually used to build such segregated facilities within the federally aided airport building is absolutely no reason for avoiding our national policy against segregation." Inaction, he warned, would continue to implicate the federal government in the creation of racially exclusive transportation landscapes. "Therefore, allowing local authorities in Southern States to build what amounts to segregated 'oases' inside buildings constructed with hundreds of thousands of Federal Government aid looks like tacit approval of a procedure we would not countenance directly."[29] Certainly, to the average air traveler it did appear to suggest approval of these practices.

During the hearing on the amendment before the Senate Subcommittee on Appropriations for Independent Offices, the NAACP came out the most strongly in support of Javits's view. Clarence Mitchell, the director of its Washington Bureau, urged senators to approve the amendment. By continuing to provide money to Jim Crow airports like Montgomery, he said, the "FAA seems to have made a conscious effort to avoid following its own stated policy." Mitchell reminded the committee: "Segregation practices in airports are among the most picayune and annoying types of harassment a traveler must face." As long as Congress and the executive branch permitted "segregation to be established and extended in airports, we shall continue to expose the most peaceful colored or white citizen to physical attack or a jail sentence just because he goes into a washroom set aside for a different racial group." In Mitchell's testimony, race and class provided the subtext for his argument, and it is worth reflecting on his use of the word "picayune" for a moment. To discriminate against black air travelers—mostly middle-class blacks dressed in carefully chosen outfits, such as Gwendolyn Jenkins, Robert

Jenkins, and Ralph Washington—by relegating them to the spatial margins of new, modernist terminals seemed to strike him as petty and small-minded. As a small, albeit growing group ready to join the mainstream of consumers, these travelers sought physical and social mobility, but their presence in the spaces of aviation lay beyond the focus of southern white resistance: interracial education and miscegenation. In these terminal environments, class similarities could most easily be construed to invalidate prevailing notions of racial otherness. Congress, Mitchell pleaded, should not lose any time but seek solutions to the problem.[30]

During the debate about the amendment in the Senate a month later, Javits reiterated his concerns. In his eyes, existing statutes and regulations forbade the spatial organization of terminals according to race. He also found ammunition in *Henry v. Greenville Airport Commission* and *Turner v. Memphis*, in which the Supreme Court had declared the segregation of airport terminal facilities unconstitutional. Given the existing legal framework, Javits criticized the FAA's continued investment in segregated facilities and Congress's complacency, which made it a party "to a violation of the law and a violation of the Constitution." Javits pointed out that, in making a new appropriation without changing the rules, "we would be advancing money which a Government agency is affirmatively using to help . . . an illegal establishment of segregated facilities."[31] The senator added a last point to the justification of his legislative initiative when he put U.S. apartheid into international perspective. While he reiterated his general respect for "the convictions of the men and women who take the very opposite view of this situation from mine," their worldview struck him as increasingly anachronistic. How could the South abide by its local laws and customs when the world around it was increasingly defined by global movements of people? Segregation not only made the region look bad but also was an embarrassment for the entire country.[32] Javits's motion to amend the Federal Airport Act found some support, especially from Hugh Scott (R-Penn.) and Paul Douglas (D-Ill.). Scott warned against ignoring the Cold War context: "We should not give propaganda material to those who are hostile to what we are proud of in the American way of life."[33] But in the end, the amendment was moved to the table by Warren Magnuson (D-Wash.), chair of the Senate Appropriations Committee's Subcommittee on Independent Offices. Although he favored the purpose of the amendment, he reiterated the subcommittee's misgivings over how new program rules could be applied to existing grant agreements. Magnuson and other critics feared a wave of lawsuits against the FAA by airports that would see their grant agreements violated by a sudden withdrawal of federal funds. Sympathetic to the issue, he envisioned legislation that would affect the future planning and design of airport projects.[34]

Although his amendment flopped, Javits's congressional activities did have repercussions in the FAA. A few months after the debates in Congress (in October 1960), the agency issued a new regulation. The new directive redefined the types of airport construction projects eligible for FAAP subsidies starting with the new budget year. It limited eligibility to projects related to airport safety operations.[35] The regulation did what critics of the FAAP had long hoped for: it withdrew federal support for the construction of segregated passenger facilities. In fact, it withdrew federal support for the construction of airport terminal buildings altogether. What is quite noteworthy is that the directive's language remained completely silent on the issue of race. The FAA pretended that race was not the issue. Instead, the new regulation signaled a broader shift of airport funding priorities away from a holistic approach and toward a strategy that focused on technical operations and safety features. The FAA's 1961 Annual Report only briefly touched upon this shift, downplaying its significance. Rather than indicating even vaguely the agency's involvement in civil rights matters, the report highlighted budget concerns as the driving force behind policy changes.[36] The FAA had received funding requests in the amount of more than $150 million. "In selecting projects from these many requests, Federal aid was necessarily limited to airports having the highest national priority in accordance with revised planning criteria, programming standards, and policies in which the element of safety was a prime consideration."[37] The new directive did, however, significantly change the playing field. Like the legal landscapes of aviation, its regulatory landscapes were shifting. This shift led to the redefinition of the FAA's role as an agent in the creation of the entry points to and destinations of the air travel experience. The FAA would still issue building guidelines, design brochures, safety manuals, and so on, but it would no longer be immediately involved in shaping the terminal buildings by providing federal subsidies.[38] If local governments wanted to keep drawing the color line in passenger terminals, they would have to buy their own crayons.

This development left unresolved the issue of withholding federal funding from airports where racial discrimination was in the process of being given built expression in terminal architecture. The new regulation was also more than a step away from making airports that discriminated against African American patrons entirely ineligible for FAAP grants. To resolve the first issue, Senator Javits reintroduced his amendment in 1962. In his efforts to convince his colleagues of the necessity to break existing grant agreements in order to stop building activity, Javits repeated his catalogue of arguments. He sounded more hopeful that his colleagues would be responsive this time, as he felt a growing inclination to push civil rights in the Senate. His measure would have mostly affected the airports in Birmingham, Tallahassee, and Montgomery. Birmingham had yet to receive three-quarters of a $916,025 grant. Tallahassee's grant in the amount of $977,800 had been almost paid in full with the exception of $140,000. Montgomery was granted half a million dollars, of which 10 percent remained unpaid.[39]

Again, his initiative was tabled. Javits's fellow senators were mostly sympathetic to his cause, but they deemed the measure inappropriate. Michael Mansfield (D-Mont.) voiced his concerns over an amendment that to him clearly had legislative character: "It effects a change in existing contractual relationships between the United States and a very small number of airport sponsors." If such a change had to be made, in his eyes the only viable route, and one that he was ready to support, was to amend the Federal Airport Act. A. S. Mike Monroney (D-Okla.), the chairman of the Senate Committee on Commerce's Aviation Subcommittee, concurred.[40] He moreover voiced his discomfort with the idea of breaching contracts to which the United States government was a party. To him, the residual amount of money under consideration (about $850,000) did not justify such a drastic step, especially at a time when FAA eligibility rules had changed. The debate concluded with the remarks of Norris Cotton (R-N.H.), the ranking minority member of the Aviation Subcommittee—the committee that had written the Federal Airport Act in 1946. He shared the concern over breaches of federal contracts, which would not serve a moral purpose. Acknowledging the need for action, however, he drew attention to an amendment to the Federal Airport Act, which his subcommittee was about to report. If passed by Congress, the question of segregation would not arise again in the matter of airport aid.[41]

Patterned on the FAA's earlier directive, the amendment to the Federal Airport Act was to codify the new rules for federal support of airport construction. The flow of federal aid would be discontinued except for buildings related to safety.[42] Like the directive, the amendment did not aim at tackling segregation wholeheartedly, as Javits observed during its debate in the Senate.[43] Jim Crow airports would no longer receive grants to construct terminals, but they could continue to count on the federal government's investment in such structures as towers, weather stations, and runways.[44] Although both houses of Congress passed the amendment in September 1961, hearings in the respective subcommittees confirmed the nature of airport construction as a partisan issue.[45] In particular, members from the South dreaded federal intervention in what they considered states' rights and issues of local concern.

Deliberations about the airport amendment carried particular weight because they coincided with the possible extension of the Federal Airport Act. The extension was to provide for continued federal assistance ($375 million) in creating and improving aviation's built environment over the next five years.

Hearings before the House Subcommittee on Transportation and Aeronautics and the Senate Aviation Subcommittee featured a lineup of industry representatives, public officials, and policy makers, the majority of who came out strongly in favor of extending the Federal Airport Act. Alan Boyd, the chairman of the Civil Aeronautics Board (CAB), stressed the necessity to expand capacities on the ground given the recent paradigm shift in aviation technology. Jet airliners, the new type of aircraft, not only required longer runways, he pointed out; their larger seating capacity, coupled with an expected increase in air traffic, also required improved and enlarged terminal facilities.[46] The new FAA administrator Najeeb Halaby—a former pilot, lawyer, business executive, and government adviser—framed airport construction as a continuing national endeavor.[47] Airport development was of such national importance that it required involvement of the federal government rather than exclusive reliance on local communities. Taking those in attendance through familiar and reformulated provisions of the Federal Airport Act, including the airport amendment, Halaby avoided the issue of race.[48] The amendment's language provided no clues that it was written to target segregated airports. Halaby's comments did nothing to draw senators' attention to the subject of racial discrimination. Prompted by Senate Subcommittee Chairman Monroney's observation that the new bill was the first not to permit financial aid to terminal buildings, Halaby stressed safety as a budget priority: "We have the problem of doing the most with what is made available. We want the maximum airport safety and efficiency per 'buck.'" Such items as "comfort and enjoyment of the airport" would have to come second.[49] For most African American air travelers, "comfort and enjoyment" stood in stark contrast to what defined their airport experience. Rather than provide for the construction of integrated facilities, the federal government would quit subsidizing the construction of passenger terminals and service facilities altogether. This would, of course, affect all passengers, black and white. The Senate Subcommittee endorsed this approach, which, rather than address the issue of Jim Crow airport construction, avoided it altogether. As announced by Norris Cotton, it reported the amendment to the bill on August 1, 1961.[50]

Halaby caught more heat in the House Subcommittee, where Chairman John Bell Williams (D-Miss.) was one of the FAA's high-caliber critics. Unhappy with the amendment to the Federal Airport Act, Williams hoped to derail the FAA's activities by agitating against the Act's five-year extension. He was seconded by John Jarman (D-Okla.), who shared Williams's suspicion of federal agencies like the FAA, whose grant-in-aid programs he denounced as "backdoor financing" devoid of congressional oversight.[51] As a representative from Mississippi, Williams came from one of the most segregated states in the country.[52] He also came from a state that had very much profited from federal programs yet at the same time insisted on the state's right to shape its cultural landscapes according to local preferences.[53] Williams was very much aware of the airport building amendment's original purpose as a civil rights measure. He also followed the intensifying cooperation between the FAA and the Department of Justice in their efforts to desegregate southern airports.[54] This cooperation led to the conflict that was brewing between the FAA and the city of Jackson over the eligibility of airport construction projects for FAAP funding. Disregarding the many voices in favor of long-term appropriations provisions, including Atlanta Mayor William Hartsfield, Williams led his subcommittee to vote out the bill.[55] The final bill—a hard-fought-over compromise between the House and the Senate—provided for the extension of the Federal Airport Act. But it considerably shortened the extension period. Instead of the five years Halaby had lobbied for, he only got three.[56] The Act as finally amended retained the appropriations rules favored by the FAA and the new rules for construction of airport buildings. It was a clear indication of how far American lawmakers were willing to go in shaping the contours of aviation's built environment. Their focus had shifted from addressing issues of safety, convenience, and comfort in air travel to one that prioritized safety concerns.

Passage of the amendment was preceded by intense debates of its merits within the FAA, where Administrator Halaby also looked to the Justice Department, now headed by Robert Kennedy, to address the matter of airport segregation. In a March 1961 letter to Kennedy, Halaby revealed both his reserve and his desire to move forward on desegregation. He expressed concern over the usefulness of the Federal Airport Act, and specifically the FAAP, as an appropriate tool in the government's fight for airport integration. Halaby conceded that provisions of the Act had to be enforced when violations of grant agreements occurred, as they had at Moisant Airport in New Orleans "where the airport authority had made, and thereafter breached, a specific commitment not to engage in racial segregation."[57] But to use the Act to deny funding altogether struck him as problematic; he was also critical of federal lawsuits against airport authorities, which would rest on the nondiscrimination provisions of grant agreements. Both measures, he predicted correctly, imperiled southern congressional support for upcoming extensions of the Federal Airport Act.

Pondering these issues, Halaby was in essence wondering to which degree grant-in-aid programs could be used to attain objectives not specified in the authorizing laws. His remarks suggest that he was reluctant to press for civil rights through the Federal Airport Act, for its aid program served another "primary mission, which is to further air safety and reduce hazards in the flying environment." Without it, he pointed out, much-needed progress toward safer airports would be halted. "Many southern cities," he added, "would forgo the benefits of the federal airport program . . . if the price imposed for receiving grants were mandatory discontinuance of racial segregation practices."[58] Thus, he concluded, damage to airport safety would be significant if legal action was not cautiously pursued and—he seemed to suggest—if civil rights were given priority over airport security matters.

To avoid the impression that the FAA was reluctant to press a civil rights agenda, Halaby pointed to legal action based on *Boynton v. Virginia* as a viable alternative scenario, "whereby air safety and civil liberties can both be effectively served at the same time."[59] The case, which was decided by the Supreme Court in late 1960, directly addressed segregation in terminal facilities requiring bus carriers to make them available to their interstate passengers without racial discrimination.[60] Although the Interstate Commerce Act, on which the case rested, only applied to surface transportation and therefore could not be construed to integrate air terminal facilities, an evaluation of the case prepared by the FAA's counsel pointed to similar language regarding nondiscriminatory access to facilities in the Federal Aviation Act.[61] The Act's provisions lend themselves to address airport segregation practices and serve as the legal basis for lawsuits against local airport authorities. Halaby strongly favored this approach: "It would meet the problem head-on . . . and pose the issue of racial segregation at airports directly." It would not, however, have a negative impact on future extensions of the Federal Airport Act.[62]

The Justice Department shared the FAA's assessment that more than one strategy should be employed to end airport segregation as soon as possible. It also recognized legal action as a viable alternative to regulatory and statutory reform. The months following Halaby's letter to the attorney general saw intense exchanges over these strategies between FAA lawyers and the Justice Department, specifically Burke Marshall, the assistant attorney for civil rights. Although the Kennedy administration did not immediately tackle racial discrimination with the enthusiasm many civil rights advocates had hoped for following John F. Kennedy's presidential campaign, the fight against airport segregation gained some momentum in the spring of 1961.[63]

A sense of urgency with regard to ending Jim Crow practices in aviation seeps through the pages of a report Halaby submitted to the White House in late May. Driven by Halaby's conviction that his agency had been on the issue for quite some time, the report walked the president through the steps the FAA had taken toward the integration of airports beginning with the 1956 Policy Memorandum. To set the tone, the report began with an outline of the basic principle that guided FAA policy, "the obvious necessity of striking a sound balance between civil rights aspects and considerations of public safety." It re-iterated the administrator's concerns regarding the significance of grant-in-aid programs like FAAP as a means of coercion in causes that lay beyond what he saw as his agency's core mission of building an air transportation infrastruc-ture. Like Halaby's previous statements, the report downplayed the consumer perspective, although it was concerned with guaranteeing the constitutional rights of a specific part of the consumer spectrum, African American air trav-elers. By way of conclusion, the report informed the president of immediate plans to press action against Moisant Airport in New Orleans for violations of a FAAP grant agreement.[64] A few weeks later, the Department of Justice came through with filing antisegregation lawsuits against the airports in Montgom-ery and New Orleans. The following year the attorney general would move against the airports in Birmingham and Shreveport.[65]

By the early summer of 1961 then, the executive branch was getting more serious about enforcing civil rights at American airports. The FAA and the Justice Department thus reacted to criticisms of an increasing number of mostly liberal congressional voices and those in the civil rights community who accused it of inaction.[66] Their activities unfolded before the backdrop of the Freedom Rides, which produced a civil rights emergency in transporta-tion not previously known. The Freedom Rides also affected the landscapes of air transportation, as demonstrated by the "Fly-Ins" into Municipal Airport in Jackson, Mississippi (analyzed in chapter 3).

Pressing charges against the four Jim Crow airports in the South, the FAA and the Department of Justice had purposely not included Jackson Municipal Airport because *Bailey v. Patterson*—the private lawsuit against the airport—was pending in the courts. If decided in the plaintiff's favor, it would integrate the airport. In 1962, the airport was indeed court-ordered to end segregation at its old terminal facility. It had, however, only half-heartedly abided by the order, if at all.[67] As more details about the situation in Jackson transpired in 1963, the FAA could not but get involved, for it seemed as if FAAP grant money had gone and was going into the construction of a new passenger terminal. This would have constituted a misappropriation of funds. The plans for the new jet age terminal included Jim Crow features such as separate restrooms, waiting rooms, and eating facilities. When Charles Diggs went to Jackson to investigate the matter and found segregated spaces, he sent a telegram to FAA administrator Halaby:

> Confirmation of segregated and discriminatory rest room and water fountain facilities at Jackson, Mississippi, airport demands immediate correction. What about airport restaurant? Insist also upon explanation of why your agency approved them in the first instance, since such designs were amply evidenced in the original plans and in interpretive communications you received on this subject. I am amazed that despite your own regulations against such practices, you succumbed to the desires of the local community and certain congressional pressure.[68]

One of those sources of congressional pressure no doubt was House Subcommittee Chairman Williams. Why and how did airport authorities in Jackson perpetuate airport segregation when it was slowly disappearing elsewhere? Was Mississippi's state capital immune to shifts in the geopolitics of race?

Mississippi had long struck civil rights activists as one of the most white-supremacist states in the country. It was also one of the most economically backward. Racism and poverty had never mixed well in the state's history. At midcentury, they continued to make Mississippi an inhospitable environment for African Americans, although blacks formed about 42 percent of the population.[69] The annual reports of the Justice Department's Civil Rights Division regularly portrayed Mississippi as a state fully in the grip of a white supremacist ruling elite. The systematic discrimination of African Americans included denial of voting rights, limited freedoms of expression and movement, and complete segregation of buildings and services.[70] Moreover, violence was rampant, as a report by the Mississippi Advisory Committee to the U.S. Commission on Civil Rights made abundantly clear.[71] The Commission on Civil Rights was established in 1957 under the Civil Rights Act to investigate the civil rights situation in the United States and to make policy recommendations designed to tackle discrimination, particularly in the South.[72] A special report by the Commission on Civil Rights issued a few months after the Advisory Committee's report pointed out that "the open and flagrant violation of constitutional guarantees in Mississippi has precipitated serious conflict which, on several occasions, has reached the point of crisis." Each week brought fresh evidence of the danger of a complete breakdown of law and order. Despite the efforts to prosecute violations of federal laws, "the pattern of unlawful activity shows no sign of abating." The Commission concluded that only further steps by the federal government could "arrest the subversion of the Constitution in Mississippi."[73]

The report's analysis covered the problematic state of affairs at the airport in Jackson. The airport example was used to illustrate how massive economic assistance through a number of federal programs had continued despite Mississippi's disregard for civil rights. The commission's chairman, John Hannah, took the report as an opportunity to remind the executive branch of its constitutional obligation to make certain all citizens without distinction benefited from the expenditure of federal funds. The FAA had failed to take such cognizance when it granted over two million dollars in FAAP money for the construction of a new airport without questioning local plans to build a segregated passenger terminal. In order to send a strong signal to local and state governments, the commission recommended that President Kennedy withhold all federal funds "until the State of Mississippi demonstrates its compliance with the Constitution and laws of the United States."[74]

The report caused much critical commentary. Most observers agreed that cutting Mississippi off from federal support was counterproductive. It would increase the state's parochialism and backwardness at a time when modernization was recognized as a remedy against white supremacy. Drawing parallels to the United States' foreign aid, *New York Times* journalist James Reston commented: "Maybe the commission is right, that persuasion has failed and only punitive power will prevail. But maybe not. It could be in the end that we need an Alliance for Progress in Mississippi . . . more interdependence, more 'partnership,' and more 'technical assistance.'"[75] The Kennedy administration reacted with wariness. The president had yet to overcome his lack of enthusiasm for federal intervention in the South, although his administration had been forced to take action on a number of occasions, the Freedom Rides included.[76] But the recommendations of the Civil Rights Commission met with a frosty reaction mostly because, as Nick Bryant has shown, its relationship to the Kennedy administration had grown increasingly antagonistic. Although Burke Marshall and others in the Justice Department's Civil Rights Division agreed in principle that Mississippi was a problem, some of the report's observations and recommendations struck them as blown out of proportion.[77] In the FAA, the commission's assessment triggered concern.

In response to an information request by the commission concerning Jim Crow facilities at Jackson Municipal Airport, the FAA had provided grant-agreement data for the years following 1957. This data confirmed the security-related character of the building projects subsidized with FAAP money.[78] The dataset was originally compiled for a review of the flow of federal aid to the state of Mississippi ordered by President Kennedy after the riots in Oxford in 1962, when an angry mob demonstrated against James Meredith's enrollment at the University of Mississippi.[79] The FAA had also sent staff to Jackson to investigate airport facilities. They were "to compare the final construction layout of the building with the building plans to ascertain whether construction had been in accordance with the plans" originally submitted with the funding application.[80] This was a somewhat curious undertaking, as the original plans clearly spelled out the intention to provide duplicate facilities. The mission's purpose then was to ascertain whether Jim Crow laws would most likely be enforced or not—a speculative endeavor at a time when the airport was not yet open to the public.

Pending the outcome of the field investigation in Jackson, the FAA considered withholding the grant payment apportioned to pay for construction projects scheduled for 1963–1964.[81] This was done in light of the most recent statutory amendments to the Federal Airport Act, not in reaction to the federal funding moratorium proposed by the Civil Rights Commission. As he made clear in a memorandum to President Kennedy written two days after the publication of the commission's report, Administrator Halaby was shocked and frustrated with its findings and recommendations. He deplored the way in which, in his view, it incorrectly portrayed his agency's activities. He conceded that in the early days of the FAAP, southern airports had received grants whether they intended to build segregated facilities or not. Since 1955, however, a number of regulatory and statutory reforms had aimed at narrowing "the grounds on which questions might be raised about segregation in airport terminal buildings." Halaby also pointed out that over the years FAAP grants to Jackson had only funded the construction of safety-related airport buildings, not passenger facilities. Because the FAA had never completely stopped subsidizing Jim Crow airports, the developments in Jackson were beyond the FAA's control: FAAP money paid for land purchases, runway construction, instrument landing systems, a weather bureau, and an air traffic control tower. The passenger terminal, in contrast, was built with local funds. It included duplicate sets of restrooms, water fountains, and dining spaces, an arrangement that according to Halaby "lend itself to segregation." Whether spatial patterns translated into discriminatory practices would become evident after the terminal's opening. Evidence collected at the old passenger terminal in connection with *Bailey v. Patterson* revealed the existence of a similar spatial layout (which the Freedom Flyers Gwendolyn Jenkins, Robert Jenkins, and Ralph Washington had brought to national attention). But investigators had also noticed the lack of color line enforcement: "The unanswered question today therefore . . . is whether the City intends to require and practice segregation after the airport terminal building opens."[82]

Much to Halaby's regret, the debate triggered by the Civil Rights Commission led discussions about effectively abolishing airport segregation back to an issue he had consistently worked hard to avoid: the use of the FAAP as a tool in the struggle for civil rights. He reiterated his position that grant-in-aid programs should not be used to achieve goals not specified in the authorizing laws. Halaby realized that the FAAP was a geopolitical and geo-economic tool. By funding the installation of a transportation infrastructure for the air age, it paved the (air)way for unprecedented movement of people and goods across regions and markets, which would transform the nation. But the FAA's administrator rejected its use as a tool in the geopolitics of race. As a regulator with an almost unique power to shape the contours of landscapes of aviation, Halaby opted for an interpretation of his responsibilities that avoided confrontations over the construction of whiteness and blackness. Instead of using the FAA's power aggressively to open the spaces of air travel to travelers of all racial backgrounds, Halaby favored litigation as a route toward racial integration. Any other strategy would lead to the termination of the FAAP by Congress, where debates about the Javits Amendment and the program's extension had shown how far its members were willing to go. Halaby self-confidently countered the Civil Rights Commission's criticism that certain government agencies lacked a desire to eliminate segregation. As far as the FAA was concerned, nothing was further from the truth, "for all of our actions have been designed to achieve the greatest progress attainable in light of conditions prevailing from time to time when the Agency is called on to act."[83] Although some of the agency's past actions cast doubt on this statement, the FAA proceeded to contain the situation in Jackson.

Unwilling to apply the general provisions of the Federal Airport Act or to cut federal aid money coming through the FAAP, the FAA devised a new sanctioning approach aimed at prohibiting racial discrimination. This time, the federal agency changed provisions in its grant agreement in an effort to close the last loophole that allowed airports to deny responsibility for the maintenance of segregated facilities. The approach seemed especially useful in the Jackson case, for the FAA had essentially known about the city's plan to build duplicate facilities from the start. It issued grant agreements for earlier phases of construction condoning the racial discrimination that would most probably ensue. The FAA thus downplayed consumer rights of access to passenger facilities in an effort to prioritize safety. Rather than sue the airport for grant agreement violations, the FAA required the airport management in Jackson to accept a revised grant agreement for its 1963–1964 building projects. The revised agreement was to include equal access provisions, which the old version did not. A rejection of the newly worded grant agreement by Jackson authorities would entail the suspension of federal subsidies. The measure was thus an indirect way of cutting aid for any airport that did not comply—or rather, was not going to comply—with the government's and the Federal District Court's directives of providing unrestricted access to its airport terminal for all air travelers.

The struggle over the new language in the grant agreement that ensued between the FAA and Jackson's airport management showed how much southern authorities resisted federal intervention in their attempts to maintain the status quo. Upon being notified by Acting Assistant Administrator Paul Boatman that a new clause would be added to the existing grant agreement, which the FAA expected the city to accept, Jackson's mayor Allen Thompson announced the city would rather forsake federal funding.[84] As Michael O'Brien has shown, Thompson was a mayor with strong ties to the local business community and had an interest in the city's economic prosperity. He recognized the importance of connecting Jackson's transportation infrastructure to the rest of the country and was largely responsible for the creation and modernization of the airport.[85] It would be wrong to regard him as a moderate voice in his dealings with the local civil rights movement, which was active in Jackson under the leadership of Medgar Evers. But he struck the NAACP as someone who understood "there must be a realistic facing up to the need to desegregate."[86] His response to the FAA's demand displayed an anger that appeared to be driven more by a rejection of federal authority than Jim Crowism. He accused the agency of changing the rules in midgame and of not coming through with prospective funding "unless we gave the government the right to hire and fire and generally run the airport. We replied they could keep their money. We've got the money in the bank to pay for the addition."[87] The rejection of grant aid would have removed the airport from federal oversight completely. In an effort to avoid this scenario, the FAA embarked on several rounds of negotiations over grant-agreement language that eventually led to a compromise with airport authorities.

At issue was the wording of Clause 5 of the FAA's grant agreements, which set forth the Federal Airport Act's requirements for fair use of airport terminal space on a nondiscriminatory basis. Strengthening those portions of the original clause that framed an airport sponsor's responsibility for granting unrestricted access to and use of airport facilities, the FAA's initial revision of Clause 5 was worded:

> The sponsor shall operate and maintain the airport as provided in the Project Application incorporated herein and specifically covenants and agrees, in accordance with its Assurance 4 in Part III of said Project Application, that in the operation of the entire airport and all facilities thereof which are under the control of the sponsor, neither it nor any persons or organizations occupying

space or facilities thereon will discriminate against any person or class of persons by reason of race, color, creed or national origin.[88]

Accepting responsibility for the actions of third parties doing business at the airport—a legal issue resolved in *Brooks v. Tallahassee*—Mayor Thompson and airport manager Thomas Turner took issue with their corporate responsibility for the "entire airport," seemingly in fear of being made liable for infractions that occurred at airport facilities under the control of the federal government (e.g., the tower as a site of air traffic control). They were also unhappy about the fact that Jackson was about to become the only airport in the country to which the new grant agreement language barring racial discrimination applied. Were the new clause to become standard, they signaled, Jackson would be willing to accept the FAA's new terms.[89]

Inside the FAA, regulators struggled to situate Thompson and Turner's reaction in the context of local and state politics in Jackson. They understood that in the heated debate about the Civil Rights Commission's recommendation for Mississippi, in which Governor Ross Barnett took a defiant stand, it made little political sense for the mayor of the state's capital to position himself as an accommodationist.[90] Drawing into consideration these realities, the FAA gave Jackson officials assurances that a revised Clause 5 would not apply to the Jackson airport exclusively. Rather, it would become the standard clause in all future grant agreements. The agency also agreed to specify the term "airport." The final version of Clause 5 issued in early May 1963 required airport authorities to guarantee "that in its [the airport's] operation and the operation of all facilities on the airport, neither it nor any person or organization occupying space or facilities thereon will discriminate against any person or class of person by reason of race, color, creed or national origin in the use of any of the public facilities on the airport."[91]

This compromise ended the conflict between the FAA and the Jackson airport management, the last to erupt openly before the government's lawsuits against Montgomery, Birmingham, New Orleans, and Shreveport were decided. The new passenger terminal, which opened its doors to the public on July 1, 1963, was an integrated facility. Airport manager Turner struck a conciliatory note when he thanked Administrator Halaby for sending his deputy to the dedication ceremony. Jackson, he assured Halaby, was making substantial progress and was about to become "the real Crossroads of the South for the air traveller."[92] Halaby lauded Jackson's effort as an example "for the world to follow." He also encouraged the airport to weigh its future options realistically. Always a little more concerned about airport infrastructure than civil rights, he expressed his hope that the Jackson airport commission would "as the weather cools see your best interest in accepting our grant offers for $1.2 million which we believe you need."[93]

The FAA's confrontation with Jackson airport authorities had several consequences. Besides permanently changing the language of future grant agreements, it changed conditions on the ground in Jackson. The new jet-age airport was an integrated building, where duplicate facilities were eliminated or repurposed. For civil rights activists in the city, the outcome was a cause for celebration in a difficult environment where erasing the color line was a tough challenge. The new language subsequently became the standard in FAAP project applications, closing the last loophole white supremacists had used in their attempts to shape the landscapes of aviation according to their worldview. At the same time, the FAA's activity once again met with criticism from members of Congress—mostly southern Democrats—who expressed their disapproval with renewed opposition to the next upcoming extension of the Federal Airport Act.

Once again, opposition formed itself in the House and was led by John Bell Williams, the representative from Mississippi. Whereas the Senate Committee on Commerce reported a bill that by and large accommodated the requests of the FAA for the next three years and was easily passed by the Senate in August 1963, the chairman of the House Subcommittee on Transportation and Aeronautics agitated for amendments designed to rein in the powers of the FAA.[94] One amendment addressed the consistency of airport development plans and project applications, barring the administrator from making any changes retroactively.[95] It was an obvious attempt to undo the recent changes made to the FAAP's sponsor's assurances and grant agreements. The amendment found supporters, but its potential impact was expected to be negligible. Not only was the number of airports where segregated facilities were in the process of being constructed rather small, but these airports were also targets of lawsuits filed by the Justice Department. Existing plans for the construction of segregated passenger terminals were therefore unlikely to be translated into actual buildings. A second amendment was more troublesome from the FAA's perspective. It suggested imposing limits on the executive branch's powers to carry out provisions of the Federal Airport Act.[96]

In a letter to Williams, Administrator Halaby once again called on the chairman not to confound the issues of airport development and civil rights. He pointed out that the changes his agency had made reflected the changing legal landscapes with regard to the constitutionality of airport segregation. Regulatory reform, statutory adjustments, and recent jurisdiction had opened terminal doors to African American passengers, irreversibly so. Halaby also underlined the acceptance the new grant agreement had ultimately found in

Jackson and other cities. He implored Williams "to help settle these issues within the executive session of the House Commerce Committee, rather than taking the civil airports bill to the Floor of the House in a form that I am fearful will involve it deeply in other issues." His agency, he stressed, was not "seeking social reform through the civil airports bill." These kinds of reforms were being pursued in other legislative proposals, namely the legislation that would become the 1964 Civil Rights Act. Halaby underlined his hopes "that this technical bill will not be crushed in the forces of this greater controversy."[97]

The administrator's hopes that the amendment would not be sent to the House floor were disappointed and left the FAA scrambling for support. The agency turned to such allies as John Dingell (D-Mich.), Frank Moss (D-Utah), and Abner Sibal (R-Conn.), who had shown their support of the agency's civil rights policies before. At the same time, the FAA tried to determine the constitutionality of the amendment. Its passage would not only involve Congress in micromanagement of the FAAP; it would significantly affect the balance of power between the legislative and the executive branches of government, precluding the president from fully exercising his duties and authority. Legal experts feared the broader implications it would have, possibly involving Congress in the management of other federal programs.[98] In a memorandum to President Johnson, who had been in office for just about a week, Halaby explained what was at stake for the FAA: "Congressman Williams has indicated that any FAA efforts to encourage opposition to his amendment on the floor of the House will kill any further aviation legislation in his Subcommittee." He moreover voiced his confidence that even if the bill ran its natural course the president would have ways of containing its significance (e.g. by adding disclaimers) before signing it.[99] Also, as far as the FAA enforcement of the anti-discrimination provision of the Federal Airport Act was concerned, the amendment would not have an impact for it confirmed the agency's authority to carry "out a provision of law specifically set forth in the Federal Airport Act."[100] Thus, the executive branch would be able to continue to push for airport desegregation in the future.

It turned out that the amendment did not find a majority in the House, and the Federal Airport Act was extended without it.[101] The extension of the Act allowed the FAA to continue its investment in and support of airport construction. It did so without unraveling the FAA's antidiscrimination policies, which had tightened over previous years in a complicated struggle to combine the federal government's civil rights agenda with the agency's focus on building infrastructure and improving security. While proponents of a segregated South like Williams were unwilling to give up their white supremacist ideology in favor of a more integrated worldview that acknowledged the equality of Americans of all racial backgrounds, the political climate in Congress was shifting. It ultimately found expression in the Civil Rights Act of 1964.[102]

Although geographical distance separated them from the facilities African American air travelers hoped to use without being treated as second-class citizens, legislators and regulators defined the frameworks for federally subsidized construction of airport terminals. Leaving the individual designs to architects and planners, the FAA's staff and members of Congress defined which types of spaces would be eligible for federal support. Over the course of a few years, regulatory and statutory reform led to much stricter rules concerning the eligibility of airport construction projects, which closed the loopholes that had previously allowed the local representatives of white supremacy to integrate passenger terminals into the southern landscapes of segregation. As forces in the struggle over the desegregation of airports, regulators and legislators thus played a crucial role in the geopolitics of race. The process of erasing the color line from statutes and regulations that applied to airports brought to light the divisive nature of airport construction. It posed regulators against legislators, the opposition against the administration, and the federal government against representatives of the states. Analyzing the changing rules for federal support of airport construction not only exposes the degree to which the federal government was implicated in the perpetuation of segregation but also serves to show how it worked toward integration. The last actor to be explored in the struggle for the desegregation of American airports is the Department of Justice.

CHAPTER 6

Back in the Courts

Federal Antisegregation Lawsuits

Government activities on integration involved not only the FAA and Congress but also the Department of Justice. Besides assisting the FAA with legal advice in changing the agency's policy regulations, the Justice Department also played a role itself in the struggle for integration of airports. In part it was responding to outside pressure, which reached crisis levels during the Freedom Rides in 1961. At the same time, the Justice Department's activities—in particular those of the Civil Rights Division—were a reflection of its changing responsibilities. They also reflected the growing conviction of officials, such as Attorney General Robert F. Kennedy, that the administration had to become more involved in abolishing segregated travel facilities.[1] As important as the FAA's regulatory reforms and Congress's legislative initiatives were, they left in place racially exclusive spatial regimes that were maintained by local airport authorities. As Robert Dixon has pointed out, the reforms had no effect on the practices of Jim Crow at existing terminal facilities—constructed with or without federal funds—or at terminal buildings to be constructed in the future with local funds.[2]

To challenge these Jim Crow practices, the Department of Justice recognized that federal lawsuits against airport authorities were an effective tool. In selecting airports to press charges against, it closely cooperated with the FAA, which could and did request action from the Justice Department. By the early 1960s, aviation's built environment was in the process of changing. A number of airports by then had integrated voluntarily (like Nashville and Knoxville) in reaction to persuasive efforts by local civil rights groups or representatives of the Civil Rights Division; others, like Tampa, had refrained from building segregated facilities with grant money provided by the FAAP.[3] In a number of other cities, individual private lawsuits against airport authorities had either brought victories for the plaintiffs (e.g., *Coke v. Atlanta*) or proceedings were pending. Jackson was about to be forced into compliance with federal regulations by FAA pressure. This left a number of cities where local authorities were so immune to calls for change from local activists, the FAA, and other antisegregation forces that the Department of Justice initiated legal action against them in 1961 and 1962. These cities—including Montgomery, Birmingham, New Orleans, and Shreveport—can be considered as bastions of airport segregation.[4]

The substantive federal standards on which these lawsuits rested were established in the 1960 *Boynton v. Virginia* case. In *Boynton*, the Supreme Court upheld an interstate carrier's obligation to make terminal facilities available to all passengers on a nondiscriminatory basis, even if those facilities were operated by a lessee. The Court construed these services to include lunch counters and restaurants, thereby overriding state regulation of these facilities.[5] In light of this interpretation, which applied to bus transportation regulated by the Motor Carrier Act, segregated airport terminal facilities also seemed illegal. The Federal Aviation Act, after all, included nondiscriminatory language similar to provisions in the Motor Carrier Act. Lacking the power to enforce the Fourteenth Amendment beyond voting rights, the Justice Department was convinced "it had both statutory and direct constitutional power to file suits to safeguard interstate commerce."[6] The Justice Department also based its actions on its powers to enforce provisions of the Federal Aviation Act if called upon to do so by the FAA or the CAB.[7] These provisions included those designed to guarantee equal access to terminal facilities. Answering to Administrator Najeeb Halaby's request, the Department of Justice filed a complaint against Moisant International Airport in New Orleans on June 26, 1961. Then it moved against Dannelly Field Airport in Montgomery the following month.[8]

Moisant International Airport was a segregated facility from its inception in 1946, when it opened to replace Shushan (Lakefront) Airport, which had outgrown its capacity as New Orleans' main airport.[9] Like the city of Atlanta, New Orleans abstained from building a passenger terminal that in any way echoed the elegance of its older facility. The main terminal at Shushan was a perfectly symmetrical, two-story art deco building above whose main entrance the tragic figure of Icarus was carved into stone. On the inside, it was lavishly decorated with murals and friezes, creating an out-of-the-ordinary environment for an out-of-the-ordinary travel experience. In contrast, the passenger terminal at Moisant International was a simple, almost primitive structure, a hangar-type building repurposed to house passenger services. It reflected a postwar desire to increase passenger capacity quickly and at low cost. Its factory ambience was reinforced by its unfinished interior, featuring pipes, light installations, and air conditioners. Airline ticket counters, insurance sales terminals, concession stands, waiting areas, and dining facilities were arranged in a large rectangle, and in the center stood a giant globe. The globe underlined the airport's growing significance as an international gateway. Moisant International became the major southern hub for flights to Latin America—a fact that was reflected in its publicity slogan, "Air Hub of the Americas."[10]

A 1952 photograph of the terminal's main floor features only white airport patrons and airline employees with the exception of an African American shoeshine boy.[11] No black airport patrons are visible in the image, which reflected the relatively small numbers of African American air travelers. Even more, it reflected the relegation of blacks to areas of the terminals set aside for people of color, which lay on the building's margins not visible in the photograph.[12] The passenger terminal featured duplicate facilities to comply with city ordinances that mandated the racial segregation of public accommodations and all other areas of urban life. Long gone were the days when New Orleans could claim exceptionality as far as race relations were concerned.[13] Like other airports across the South, Moisant International was a stop on the itineraries of African American air travelers. Their frustration with the racially discriminatory practices blacks were subjected to at Moisant International is well documented.

In May 1956, Fay O. Wilson and Rubye Wiggins, two national officers of the Chi Eta Phi Sorority, a professional association for black nurses, contacted the CAA, Delta and American airlines, and Moisant International's airport manager to report an incident that had occurred the previous Thanksgiving.[14] Having arrived in New Orleans from Los Angeles, the two women and two other officers of the association went to the airport restaurant to have breakfast during their layover. They were on their way to attend an executive board meeting in Tuskegee. In their letter of complaint Wilson and Wiggins recounted how a waitress led them to one end of the dining room, where she "began to adjust a wooden screen, of about seven to eight feet in height, which seemed to serve the purpose of screening a table or tables. She directed us behind this screen." The only black patrons in the restaurant at the time, the women concluded that "we were offered these tables behind said screen solely because of our race." The malleable partition was designed to make the four women invisible to the other patrons eating at the restaurant, a practice that the women recognized as "a policy of discrimination and segregation."[15] Refusing to be segregated, the women left the restaurant. They later reported the incident not only to the above-named airlines and agencies but also to the local chapter of the NAACP.[16]

Travelers also complained about the ground transportation services available to blacks. Throughout the 1950s, African Americans were routinely denied limousine service by the operators of the local Yellow Cab service (Toye Brothers). Their referral to the black-owned Morrison Cabs company often resulted in inconveniences. Morrison Cabs had a much smaller fleet of cars and no permanent presence at the airport. For Mrs. J. T. Kennedy, the lack of accessible limousine service meant having to wait for about forty-five minutes for a cab to come and pick her up (she missed her train). She was also confronted with a hefty surcharge, which more than doubled her fare. Mrs. Clarence Redmond and a number of others, who filed complaints with the NAACP, had similar experiences.[17] Closter Current, the NAACP's Director of Branches, to whose attention the issue had come during a visit to New Orleans in 1955, called on the New Orleans Branch to fight against segregated ground transportation: "In view of the fact that the same passengers who rode in the limousine were fellow passengers on the plane and upon disembarking these same passengers ride in limousines with Negroes in other cities, its seems incomprehensible that this situation should obtain any longer."[18]

After New Orleans opened a new passenger terminal in 1960—a facility appropriate for the jet age—little changed in spite of the complaints. When B. H. Nelson from Washington, D.C., and his wife missed a connection to Baton Rouge not long after the terminal's dedication, they went to the coffee shop and presented meal vouchers their airline had issued to them, only to be denied service. Nelson framed his experience in no uncertain terms: "I feel that the discrimination experienced above is illegal both because of my rights as an American citizen and because the new airport in New Orleans was constructed largely with Federal funds."[19] Discrimination in his eyes was not only an unfair treatment of consumers but also an illegal denial of citizenship rights. In an effort to "ease racial segregation" at Moisant International, the airport management integrated the coffee shop the following summer.[20] African Americans could now eat there. However, the new policy did not affect the International Room, the airport's fancy restaurant. The International Room continued to reject African American patrons, who included local civil rights lawyer Alexander P. Tureaud; the NAACP Legal Defense Fund lawyer Constance Baker Motley, who traveled to New Orleans frequently to appear before the U.S. Court of Appeals (for the Fifth Circuit); and the plaintiffs in *Adams v. City of New Orleans*.[21]

The city's Aviation Board had embarked on the project of expanding its airport capacity in the mid-1950s. As the importance of New Orleans as a regional transportation hub was growing, building a new airport struck municipal leaders as an appropriate response. The new facility sat immediately adjacent to the old one. By the time it opened its doors to air travelers from the United States and abroad, millions of dollars had been invested. The terminal alone had cost 2.2 million dollars. Fifty percent of this investment had come from FAAP, the FAA's grant-in-aid program.[22] Whereas the older terminal was constructed completely with local funds, federal money had not only paid for the construction of safety-related features at the expanded Moisant International Airport; it was also used to cover the construction of the segregated terminal. How was that possible? Had not the regulations of the FAA made such a scenario impossible? In a letter to Representative Charles Diggs, who inquired about the matter in early March 1957, CAA administrator James Pyle explained that in order to comply with the agency's new antisegregation regulation, issued the year before, airport authorities in New Orleans had provided the necessary paperwork.[23] Not only had they stated in writing that the buildings to be constructed were for the use of airline operations, airline employees, and the general public on a nonsegregated basis: "The project sponsor has further advised that no funds granted under this project will be utilized in providing duplicate facilities for separate use by persons based on their racial group."[24] The New Orleans grant application had included plans and specifications of all airport buildings, which upon review by the CAA had been approved. The agency, Pyle stressed, had come to the conclusion that, based on their written assurances and architectural plans, airport authorities were not going to build a segregated passengers facility at Moisant International. However, that was exactly what they did. When the terminal opened to the public in 1960, it became obvious that the city of New Orleans had violated the conditions of its grant agreement and misappropriated FAAP money. It had not kept its promise to grant equal access to airport facilities without regard to the racial backgrounds of air travelers and other airport patrons. The city of New Orleans had essentially duped federal regulators.[25]

Looking at the original plans for the passenger terminal, the question arises how FAA officials could have overlooked the color line that was written across these plans. The plans were drawn by Leigh Fisher and Associates in 1954, one of the biggest airport planning firms in the country.[26] Although the specifications were silent on the racial makeup of the clientele expected to use the airport, the floor plans clearly show duplicate facilities. The arrangement of the waiting areas as two separate lounges lent itself to segregated use. More obvious indicators of a racially segregated facility were the restrooms, duplicate sets of which were to be located in different parts of the terminal.[27] Although this early version of the terminal building was replaced in 1956 with plans drawn up by the architecture firm of Goldstein, Parham, & Labouisse, duplicate features remained a defining characteristic of the terminal design.

Again, the restrooms were the most obvious indicator of the intention to make some terminal areas available on a racially exclusive basis. Separate sets of restrooms would be located on the arrivals and departures levels of the terminals. It is impossible to draw conclusions about the dining room and other eating facilities from looking at the floor plans. The planners and architects refrained from labeling these terminal areas as reserved for a select clientele.[28]

Segregated floor plans notwithstanding, the airport's architecture presented a noteworthy alternative to some of the rather generic airport designs discussed in earlier chapters.[29] The city of New Orleans made an effort to stand out. As a local architecture firm, Goldstein, Parham, & Labouisse knew how to interlace modernist architecture with the city's racial hierarchies.[30] They created a building that was proudly introduced as "the city's air-age front door and welcome mat" in the annual report of the Mayor's Office.[31] The terminal was a three-story building. Its outstanding feature was a large rectangular dome, the front and back ends of which were decorated with glass installations. The dome, whose parabolic shape was vaguely reminiscent of the airport's old passenger facility, housed the terminal's main lobby. Rows of seats, arranged in zigzag patterns, lent structure to the vast space. At the front, passengers entered the building through the main entrance. The back end provided access to one of the two concourses. To either side of the main lobby, service areas were located. Air travelers entering the building found the dining facilities—the International Room, the coffee shop, and the bar and lounge—on the left-hand side. To the right was the ticket lobby, a long, wide corridor with counters. The terminal lacked any figurative expressions of local identity. Yet, the building's color scheme rooted its modernism in a specific place. The frames holding glass in the dome's windows, some of the panels decorating the façade, and other parts of the terminal were finished in yellow and blue—the Big Easy's colors—creating a smooth contrast to the otherwise white surfaces. Even more than the building's modernist agenda, the discriminatory rules regulating use of its service areas reflected the terminal's rootedness in the racialized spatial context of New Orleans.

It was this form of racial discrimination that the Justice Department aimed to attack with legal action filed in June 1961. On an earlier occasion in the fall of 1960, the Justice Department had been urged by the NAACP to act along these lines, but the Eisenhower administration shied away from federal litigation during the last few months of its term.[32] Instead, the FAA and the new staff at the Justice Department began to work on the issue within the first 100 days of the Kennedy administration. Efforts to formulate a joint strategy were driven by a desire to contain the situation in New Orleans. The city had undoubtedly acted contrary to its own assurances that it would not engage in racial segregation at the new terminal. The case against the city therefore was "the strongest case of this kind we have had to date," Administrator Halaby opined in a letter to Attorney General Kennedy.[33] Halaby also informed Kennedy about the backing he had received from Senator Mike Monroney (D-Okla.) and Representative Oren Harris (D-Ark.), who did not consider a lawsuit against New Orleans an impediment to debate about the extension of the Federal Airport Act, which was before Congress.[34] They were less enthusiastic about a lawsuit against Montgomery, where a segregated terminal was in the process of being constructed without the misappropriation of FAAP funds. Although Halaby shared the congressmen's misgivings, the FAA and the Justice Department moved ahead, resting the cases not only on the Federal Airport Act but also on jurisdiction from *Boynton v. Virginia*.[35]

The Justice Department's suit came about a year after two private suits were filed against the airport. *Adams v. City of New Orleans* and *Harris v. City of New Orleans*, which were consolidated into one case, were pending in the courts at the time the department moved ahead. Decided in 1963, the consolidated cases eventually rendered moot the federal suit. Given that the case files for *USA v. City of New Orleans* are missing, it is interesting to see how the *Adams* case was handled in the courts.

Thomas P. Harris and a group consisting of William R. Adams, Henry E. Braden III, and Samuel L. Gandy filed complaints in May 1960 to enjoin the airport authorities and the restaurant lessee from discriminating against black airport patrons.[36] The defendants included the city of New Orleans, the New Orleans Aviation Board, and Interstate Hosts Inc., the airport's restaurant concessionaire.[37] Harris and Adams were represented by seasoned NAACP lawyers. The LDF's Jack Greenberg, who came to town for the court hearings, entrusted local lawyer Alexander P. Tureaud with the bulk of the case work. Tureaud had served as attorney for the local NAACP for decades. After graduating from Howard University in 1925, he returned to his hometown New Orleans to practice law. At the time, he was one of only four black lawyers admitted to the bar in Louisiana. By the 1960s, Tureaud had become "Mr. Civil Rights of Louisiana." He had filed most of the civil rights litigation in the state. His efforts led to the abolition of voting rights restrictions and the desegregation of schools, higher education, and public transportation.[38] With regard to the discrimination of black air travelers, Greenberg and Tureaud were convinced that airport segregation was increasingly becoming a nonlitigable issue. They found a sympathetic court in that of U.S. District Judge Herbert W. Christenberry.[39] The defendants, who were represented by local attorneys and Interstate Hosts' general counsel, struggled to build a strong case in their efforts to prove the continued validity of airport segregation.

Although the defendants were aware of the recent rulings in the *Coke* and *Henry* cases, they contested the notion that the operation of airport eating facilities had to be considered government action under all circumstances.[40] They also contested the claim that Interstate Hosts practiced segregation. Herman L. Barnett,[41] the attorney for the company, argued that eating facilities at Moisant International Airport did essentially provide integrated service: the snack bar was not an exclusively white space, and—a year into the proceedings—the coffee shop also began serving African American patrons. To get "the finest of food and drink," Barnett pointed out during a court hearing in July 1961, "nobody goes outside of the building; nobody has to go to another place." Any food service a passenger would want, he suggested, was provided by these two food outlets. As establishments providing "a service in the ordinary run of commerce," they had to respect the different racial backgrounds of potential customers.[42] In contrast, the defendants framed the International Room as "a luxury accommodation for eating purposes and not a necessary facility in interstate commerce."[43] Rather than providing necessary essentials, it catered "to a specialized clientele."[44] It was portrayed as a private business, free of the constraints government agencies were bound by in providing service on a nondiscriminatory basis. As such, the defendants pointed out, it competed against other private restaurants in the New Orleans area, none of which offered integrated facilities or services. Integration, they insisted, would severely hurt the restaurant, for the number of future black clients would not only be "infinitesimal."[45] In addition, they said, white customers would stop coming. This line of argument used the status quo, the existence of racially exclusionary landscapes, to promote its perpetuation. The defendants in New Orleans pushed their agenda with a tenacity and boldness equal to that of their colleagues in Atlanta and Greenville. They ignored the shifting legal climate in the United States, attempting to bend the law to fit their worldview.

However, this shifting climate shaped the outcome of the case as much as the personality of Judge Christenberry. Christenberry was open to hearing a civil rights case. The court in *Henry v. Greenville* had openly displayed its white supremacist leanings, frequently assisting defendants in diminishing plaintiffs and ridiculing the infringement of rights they had suffered. Christenberry positioned himself differently in the contentious debate over the issue of desegregation. His openness expressed itself in how he handled the case and conducted the proceedings. He was responsive to the plaintiffs' concerns and put pressure on the defendants to firmly settle questions of fact and questions of law. Could a governmental agency or a city, he asked Barnett, operate a place such as the International Room and say that it was "so luxurious that only a certain class of citizens are entitled to use it?"[46] Hardly, his question suggested. If one could not call the International Room's practice of "making reservations and admitting whom they wish" segregation, as Barnett proposed, the judge asked: "What else could you call it?"[47] Separating people spatially according to their racial backgrounds was exactly what the term signified, the judge's further comments implied, no matter how hard Barnett tried to frame access to the International Room as a class issue.

Christenberry made clear that he considered settled the case's "decisive question" whether Interstate Hosts' actions constituted "state action" in his opinion delivered on August 2, 1962. The growing number of precedents, he wrote, firmly established the obligation of any lessee of public property to comply with the prescription of the Fourteenth Amendment. He cited the jurisdiction of *Burton v. Wilmington Parking Authority*, which was reaffirmed in *Turner v. Memphis*. "These authorities leave little doubt that plaintiffs in the case before this Court are entitled to injunctive relief as a matter of law."[48] A panel of the Court of Appeals for the Fifth Circuit concurred. In a per curiam decree, it dismissed the defendants' appeal because the Supreme Court had "settled beyond question that no State may require racial segregation of interstate or intrastate transportation facilities." The question was no longer open; it was foreclosed as a litigable issue.[49] The decision integrated Moisant International Airport and abolished segregation at the facility before the government's case against the airport could be brought to a conclusion. Rendering the Justice Department's case moot, the question whether the government's case rested on a sound legal basis had to be answered in the second case, the suit against the airport authorities in Montgomery.

Thus *United States v. City of Montgomery* turned out to be the leading case in the Department of Justice's efforts to tackle airport segregation. It was filed on July 26, 1961, two months after the Freedom Riders had protested against segregated bus terminals in Montgomery and the city had exploded with violence.[50] "We have taken this case to court," Attorney General Kennedy commented on the actions of his department, "only after being unable to work out a voluntary solution with local authorities."[51] To observers this came as no surprise. Montgomery had the reputation of being the most segregated city in the country, where violations of segregation laws often triggered violence sanctioned by local authorities. To protect the Freedom Riders from their attackers, the Kennedy administration had sent federal marshals to the city and imposed martial law.[52] Even after the riots ended, Martin Luther King Jr. implored Kennedy to keep the federal troops in place as "a perpetual reign of terror still exists in Montgomery," and local police offered little protection to African Americans.[53] Federal involvement in the city, while welcomed by local representatives of the civil rights movement, had met with strong resistance on local and state government levels. Governor John Patterson feuded with the attorney general over the federal government's authority to protect the Freedom Riders and had demanded withdrawal of the National Guard.[54] This new move by the Justice Department, which targeted the state capital's airport, did little to quell the governor's anger. Intent on warding off federal action, his administration offered state resources to the city of Montgomery as assistance in dealing with the federal lawsuit.[55]

Since its opening as a commercial enterprise in 1946, Montgomery's municipal airport, Dannelly Field, had been a Jim Crow facility.[56] Whereas the color line was not firmly drawn during the first few years of the airport's existence, when passenger facilities had a makeshift quality and the number of African American passengers served per year was small, the terminal building that opened its doors in 1958 undeniably featured duplicate facilities and Jim Crow signs. They are visible in photographs from the period, which plaintiffs produced as an exhibit to establish the material existence of a segregated structure.[57] The photographs show a modern facility whose architectural design resembled the passenger terminals in Greenville and Tallahassee. The two-story building contained a humble, midcentury modern interior. Its architects had produced a functional environment, albeit one that lacked the kind of jet-age enthusiasm expressed by the terminal in New Orleans. Built into the terminal's modernism were duplicate features that included separate waiting rooms, labeled "White Waiting" and "Entrance Colored Waiting," by illuminated signs; separate dining facilities, like the whites-only Sky Ranch Restaurant; and separate restrooms. Signs reading "White Men" and "White Women," or "Colored Men" and "Colored Women," directed airport patrons to the toilets reserved for their use. Whereas these signs were metal plates with embossed characters put into place with screws, below each sign a sticker added "May Use This" to the racialized directions. The material differences between the plates and the stickers suggest that the stickers were added some time after the plates. They demonstrate an effort to visualize a relaxation of Jim Crow policies at the airport, implemented some time before the Justice Department's gathering of evidence.

The terminal also provided separate water fountains. One exhibition photograph shows the fountains, an identical set of two sitting next to each other in a small alcove (see fig. 6).[58] Signs reading "Colored" and "White," as well as stickers stating "May Use This," were posted on the wall above the fountains. While all photographs were designed to prove the government's case against the airport, the picture of the water fountains proved the most effective one. It is also the best-composed image. Most of the others are images that give away the circumstances of their creation. They look as if they were taken in a hurry,

FIGURE 6. Segregated drinking fountains at Dannelly Field Airport in Montgomery, Alabama (case files, *United States v. Montgomery*, NARA Atlanta).

in an effort not to draw attention to the photographer. The water fountains, however, are represented in perfect symmetry. In their complete identicalness, they provide unambiguous evidence of the "separate but equal" doctrine Dannelly Field's airport management subscribed to. The exhibition photographs thus effectively make visible the stark contrast between a modern facility, built to function as a gateway to the most modern means of transportation, and the conservative social philosophy, which defined the rules for its use.[59]

Conditions at Dannelly Field had also been the subject of numerous complaints about the airport penned by African American travelers and civil rights advocates. In fact, according to the *Journal and Guide*, Montgomery's Dannelly Field was one of the most-complained-about airports in the country.[60] A few months after the opening of the new terminal in 1958, E. B. Henderson, a member of the NAACP's Virginia State Conference's Board of Directors, communicated with the CAA and Representative Charles Diggs. Concerned about the building's Jim Crow features, Henderson inquired about the possible misuse of FAAP funds for their construction. No federal money was used, he was assured. Diggs on his part added: "This, of course, is not the first time that hardened segregationists have been willing to pay for their unjustifiable follies." He promised to keep an eye on the matter.[61] In the spring of 1960, a group of civil rights leaders from Montgomery, including Solomon Seay Sr. and Ralph Abernathy, appealed to the CAB to order the integration of Dannelly Field. The CAB declined to do so on the grounds that it lacked jurisdiction.[62]

Just a few months prior to the initiation of the Justice Department's lawsuit, L. H. Foster, the president of Tuskegee Institute, a historically black vocational training school, approached Robert Kennedy in an effort to draw his attention to the airport in Montgomery. Forster wrote:

> For several years, I have been seeking help from various Federal agencies to eliminate the substantial inconvenience and humiliation caused airline passengers who use the terminals at Columbus, Georgia and Montgomery, Alabama. Segregation practices and signs are found throughout these airports. . . . We at Tuskegee Institute are greatly inconvenienced and embarrassed for ourselves and for our many visitors. . . . I would appreciate it greatly if your department can eliminate these encumbrances on travel which also injure seriously our image of democracy in America.[63]

Although none of the earlier grievances had led to a change in the terminal's spatial arrangements, at this time Burke Marshall, the head of the Justice Department's Civil Rights Division, promised to look into the matter. Reflecting a more general mood at the department, Marshall assured Foster: "I agree that these practices injure seriously our image of democracy in America."[64] Marshall went on to inform FAA administrator Halaby of Foster's request. Having been involved in a dialogue between the FAA and the Justice Department about the best strategies to provide timely relief for African American travelers, Marshall signaled the department's interest in bringing a suit against the airport in Montgomery.[65]

The Department of Justice's legal action was brought in the United States District Court for the Middle District of Alabama. It rested on the Federal Aviation Act's nondiscrimination provision, which required air carriers to treat their customers equally.[66] The term "air carrier" was broadly construed by the department to include airports and all necessary supportive services to air commerce.[67] The legal action also rested on the authority of the executive branch "to remove and prevent an unlawful and unconstitutional burden upon and interference with interstate and foreign commerce."[68] Defendants in the case were the city of Montgomery; the Board of Commissioners of the city of Montgomery; and Board members Earl D. James, Frank B. Parks, and L. B. Sullivan. They were the bodies and individuals responsible for the management of the airport. They also included Ranch Enterprises, the proprietor of the Sky Ranch airport restaurant that did not serve African American customers.[69] The complaint accused the defendants of failing to provide food service on a racially nondiscriminatory basis "to Negro interstate and foreign passengers whose flights are delayed and who receive food checks or vouchers from the Airlines entitling them to obtain dinner service from the defendants at the expense of the Airlines." It furthermore posited that the defendants were maintaining "in the terminal separate waiting room, water fountain and toilet facilities for members of the white and Negro races." To enforce the segregated use of facilities, the defendants had posted signs in the terminal. In preventing white and black airport patrons from freely choosing between airport service facilities, the initial complaint went on to argue, "the defendants are making, giving and causing undue und unreasonable preference and advantage to some persons, while causing unjust discrimination and undue and unreasonable prejudice and disadvantage to others."[70] To prevent these practices from continuing, the plaintiffs sought injunctive relief asking for a summary judgment. Denying a motion to dismiss by the defendants the court gave the go ahead for the lawsuit to proceed.[71]

The government built a strong case against the illegal existence of separate facilities at Dannelly Field. Jim Crow, it hoped to show, was practiced on an everyday basis, sanctioned by airport authorities. It also hoped to show that African American travelers were adversely affected by discriminatory practices and resisted them as an infraction of their civil liberties. To establish beyond a doubt the existence of segregation as a pervasive system of racial discrimination at Montgomery's aerial gateway, the plaintiffs produced exhibition photographs; in addition, they also introduced a number of affidavits from individuals who had experienced discrimination or seen the airport's facilities at first hand. The best known among them were Juanita and Ralph Abernathy. Ralph Abernathy was the pastor of First Baptist Church in Montgomery. Like Martin Luther King Jr., he had come to national prominence during the Montgomery Bus Boycott in 1956, and he became King's closest collaborator and friend.[72] In 1961 he was serving as the vice president of the SCLC, of which he was the cofounder. Juanita Abernathy was a civil rights activist who joined and supported campaigns in and beyond Montgomery.

In her statement, Juanita Abernathy attested to the existence of duplicate facilities at Dannelly Field, which she had visited the night before giving her testimony: "There are racially segregated facilities at the Dannelly Field terminal building and there are signs that indicate which parts are for Negroes and which parts are for white persons." She continued, "I have observed that there are separate waiting rooms, toilet facilities, dining areas, and drinking fountains for whites and Negroes." She also commented on the signs saying

"May Use This," whose appearance as an explanatory subtext to existing signs had come to her attention in the spring of 1961. To her the new signs made little difference because she could still not "use the white part freely." On occasions when she was not a traveler but had come to the airport to pick up her husband, she attested to having preferred to sit in "the telephone booth across from the ticket counters" because she resented using the segregated facilities.[73]

Ralph Abernathy, who described himself as a frequent traveler who had passed through the airport over seventy-five times in the past three years, related two incidents that had occurred over that period. The first had taken place in the winter of 1958–1959 when he had used the white waiting room as he was waiting for his plane. While browsing through magazines at the waiting room's counter, he related, he had been approached by an airport official who directed him to the waiting area reserved for African Americans. Instead of relocating to that area, Abernathy left the terminal and went to his plane. The second incident was the episode depicted in the introduction to this book. It took place in March 1960, when, while waiting for a flight, Abernathy drank from a water fountain reserved for whites. His refusal to stop using the drinking fountain led to an altercation with the airport manager, which also involved his wife. While Abernathy and the manager quarreled, Juanita also drank from the fountain. Her act of provocation led the manager to call the police and also produced comments from bystanders. Abernathy quoted a limousine driver who had said that rather than call the police he would have taken "a billystick and beat his [Abernathy's] head." In an effort to put these incidents into a broader perspective, Abernathy commented on Dannelly Field's segregation as a familiar phenomenon; there had always been signs. Like his wife he had last seen them the night before giving his affidavit. After the past incidents, he had avoided the airport as much as possible.[74]

The hearing of the witnesses for the prosecution was used as an opportunity to show how white supremacy translated into a management style that allowed airport managers and employees to discriminate against black travelers persistently and systematically. Along the way, the witnesses' depositions brought out the nonchalance and mendacity with which airport management defended segregation, while at the same time often refusing to address its existence directly. An interesting case in point was the testimony of airport director James Couch. At the time of his direct examination, he had served as airport director for five years. He was employed on a permanent contract and not on a limited term, so he expected to stay on the job until his retirement.[75] Asked by government attorney J. Harold Flannery[76] whether it was correct that facilities at Dannelly Field were available on a segregated basis only, Couch replied: "What do you mean by 'segregated basis'?" He admitted the airport had available facilities for black and white travelers, but he refused to describe them as either physically separate or designated as segregated. According to his description, "duplication" sounded like a design choice rather than a signifier of racial difference. "There are some partitions that were built in the building as a matter of design, now, like planter boxes and things which were decorative. Now, so far as signs are concerned, we—I would consider the signs as information, the same as if you would go to the ball park and see 'Box Seats,' 'Reserved Seats,' and 'General Admission,' they are for information." Any physical separators like walls, he added, served a solely structural purpose: "Now, whether this is a physical separation or not in its true essence, I don't know there would be a wall there, just like this wall here, remove it and the ceiling would fall."[77] These statements implied that no fixed spatial order existed. Arrangements presumably reflected functional needs and structural requirements. Couch framed racial segregation as an architectural coincidence, thus downplaying his responsibility for its enforcement.

Quite the opposite was true, as his further remarks suggest. In answer to questions about how he dealt with black passengers who used areas reserved for white patrons, Couch outlined his response, which had changed in recent years. Before the repeal of city ordinances mandating segregation in 1959, Couch had approached the person(s) in question and asked them to leave the terminal. Now that the ordinances had been replaced with Jim Crow instructions from Montgomery's city commissioner, Couch was required to call the police when passengers were in noncompliance with expected behavior. Couch's remarks confirmed that the airport management held onto Jim Crow policies. When asked to explain the rationale behind these policies, Couch portrayed the perpetuation of segregationist spatial and visual practices as a response to the voluntary behavior of airport patrons. He insinuated that de facto segregation reflected regional identity. The proper reading of signs was local knowledge whites shared with blacks (often using violence, which Couch unsurprisingly did not touch on). Couch put it in simple terms when he said: "There are customs in this area and if a person wants to use an information sign like that to go by custom, that is his privilege."[78]

The defendants' strategy was to stress that, although a segregationist regime existed at the airport, its rules of behavior were not enforced. Leading defense lawyer Calvin Whitesell posed a long set of questions designed to present the defendant Couch as a public official who respected the laws;[79] who had previously enforced segregation ordinances as a special police officer; who had learned his lesson during the Freedom Ride riots, after which he had to quit the special police forces; and who now took a nonconfrontational approach to the enforcement of racial segregation. Couch's deposition was meant to demonstrate that, since the riots (when protesters had also come out to the airport), racially discriminatory rules of behavior restricting freedom of movement inside the terminal had not been enforced. Yet Whitesell never inquired why the signs directing passengers to specific spaces in the terminal building were still in place.[80]

City Commissioner Franklin Parks took a different line of defense. Asked whether segregation of the races was practiced at the terminal building by Harold Flannery, he freely admitted: "Oh, yes, sir." Asked further whether that policy was represented by signs designating the waiting rooms, he interrupted Flannery to point out: "Yes, we use those signs, that is custom; we have always had signs; that is to show, direct them where they want to go." He qualified that the "May Use This" signs had been recently added, but unlike airport director Couch he did not emphasize the voluntary nature of any decision to abide by the signs. In reply to the inquiry whether African Americans were served food in the white dining area, the Sky Ranch Restaurant, Parks said that to his knowledge that was not the case. "In fact," he added, "I don't know that we have ever had a request for it, as far as I know, they haven't." By mixing "we" and "they," which elsewhere the defendants avoided in an effort to escape liability for their contractor's actions, Parks indicated in no uncertain terms that he considered segregation still firmly in place.[81] His remarks contradicted the statements of at least one African American witness. In her affidavit Kredelle Petway, the daughter of a black minister from Montgomery, related how she and her family had hoped to eat at the airport restaurant but, instead of receiving service, had been asked to leave.[82] Commissioner Parks either did not know about this incident or he did not care to know about it.

Parks's cross-examination by Calvin Whitesell confirmed Couch's testimony that, in theory, all duplicate facilities were available for the use of African American air travelers as the city did not require its employees to enforce segregation in the airport. Pressed about the continuing existence of the signs that seemed unnecessary in a supposedly integrated building, Parks sounded an explanation similar to Couch's earlier remarks:

Well, let me answer that this way, please sir, in the south, as you know, you live in the south, it has been customary to have them separate all these years. I think, I actually believe the negro would prefer to be to himself. For that reason we have these signs to direct them where to go. If you don't have signs they wouldn't know where to go. They don't want to go in any place if they are going to be in the wrong place, if they think they are going to be in the wrong place, they want to know where to go.[83]

According to this line of argument, blacks preferred segregated facilities, which enabled them to avoid interaction with whites. This was an inversion of white supremacist ideology as the source of segregation. Whitesell pushed Parks even further in that direction when he asked in his final question: "Is it true, based on your life in the south, that if you told the ordinary southern negro that he use the white toilet or one designated 'white' he wouldn't use it?" Parks concurred, saying he did not believe a black person would use it if told to do so.[84]

Whitesell pursued the same line of defense in his cross-examination of Earl James, the president of Montgomery's board of commissioners.[85] After James confirmed the continuing existence of a racially exclusive spatial regime at the airport during his interrogation by Flannery, he was led to testify by Whitesell that with regard to segregation the airport resembled other Montgomery business establishments. Downtown stores practiced segregation at their lunch counters; so did downtown restaurants; even hotels and restaurants run by African American proprietors were segregated. Whitesell and Parks ridiculed black efforts to build an alternative infrastructure that provided African Americans with services they were denied elsewhere; moreover, they painted a picture of Montgomery as a community steadfastly dedicated to Jim Crow. De facto segregation at Dannelly Field, the defendants argued, was just one expression of the way things were being done in the South—by whites and by blacks.[86] According to the defendants, then, segregation was not a set of discriminatory practices that systematically excluded African American consumers from the enjoyment of unrestricted access to air travel facilities; rather, it was presented as a voluntary practice of self-marginalization. Looking at segregation from this perspective allowed the representatives of Montgomery to claim no responsibility for the civil rights infractions black citizens were exposed to at the city's airport.

U.S. District Judge Frank M. Johnson Jr. did not buy into this line of thinking. He granted the motion for summary judgment and ordered "all signs designating the use of said facilities, or any part thereof, on the basis of race or color" to be removed by January 5, 1962.[87] In his opinion, he noted the court's reluctance to be blind to the fact that the separate facilities and signs the defendants erected, constructed, and maintained were designed solely to induce and facilitate discrimination because of race or color. "The defendant's contention that the segregation maintained is on a voluntary basis and is not compelled by them is completely refuted by the undisputed facts in this case." Unless restrained by a court order, the defendants would continue to engage in their unconstitutional acts and practices and give "undue and unreasonable preference and advantage to some persons, while causing unjust discrimina-

tion and undue unreasonable prejudice and disadvantage to others." If allowed
to continue, the defendants' actions would cause irreparable injury to the interests of the free flow of interstate commerce. To prevent this from happen-
ing, the court issued an injunction enjoining the defendants from refusing to
make available to all passengers the facilities at Dannelly Field; from engaging
in (forceful) persuasion to discourage travelers from using terminal facilities;
from denying African American travelers service at the Sky Ranch restaurant;
and from discriminating against anyone "traveling in air transportation and
using, while traveling, the airport facilities at Dannelly Field in Montgomery,
Alabama."[88]

Ruling on the abolition of discrimination at Montgomery's airport, including discrimination at the Sky Ranch restaurant, Judge Johnson reaffirmed the
position that restaurant facilities—even if run by a concessionaire—were a
regular and integral part of interstate and foreign air transportation. Restaurant lessees therefore had to abstain from discriminating against patrons
on account of race or color, an understanding the city of Montgomery had
argued against. Johnson also accepted the Justice Department's broad definition of "air carrier," which included airports and all necessary supportive
services to air commerce. Thus, the defendants were construed as air carriers
who had to abide by the provisions of the Federal Aviation Act, including
those prohibiting discrimination of particular groups of air travelers. Chrono-
logically falling between the decisions handed down in individual private suits
against airports, Johnson's ruling left no loopholes for airport managements
that subscribed to a white supremacist ideology. It was a victory for the Justice Department and became the precedent for other lawsuits filed by the
department.

In granting the injunction, the court set the framework for the integration
of other airport terminal facilities targeted by the Justice Department. Like
the rulings in private individual lawsuits, *United States v. City of Montgomery*
underlined the crucial role of federal judicial intervention in the transformation of the southern landscapes of white supremacy. Whereas some federal
judges reaffirmed the (legal) status quo, others played a central role in "testing
the law as an agent of transformative social change."[89] By the time he ruled
in the Montgomery airport case, Judge Johnson had firmly established his
reputation as a staunch defender of constitutional liberties and civil rights.
He handed down a number of landmark civil rights rulings that contributed
to the dismantlement of the system of segregation in the South, among them
his decision in *Browder v. Gayle* (1956) that integrated public transportation
in Montgomery. Rather than look at Judge Johnson as a liberal judicial activist, David Garrow suggests he be considered an "idealistic but resolutely

non-ideological judicial pragmatist."[90] The transformative social change his pragmatism engendered included the ways in which the contours of the built environment were reshaped. Thus, interpreting the law was a central component of the geopolitics of race. Only if the color line were erased from buildings and the laws would black consumers be guaranteed equal access to air travel in the American South.

Municipal authorities in Montgomery resisted this kind of change, especially because it was initiated by the federal government. In reaction to the desegregation ruling, defense attorney Calvin Whitesell announced that rather than accept the integration of the airport terminal's service facilities, the city would close and destroy them. At the same time that segregation signs were to come down, concrete would be poured down all the toilets; the water supply to the sinks and drinking fountain would be cut off; seats would be taken out of the waiting areas; and last but not least, if black patrons tried to use the Sky Ranch restaurant it would close, too. The city's plan was brought to a halt by Montgomery's business community, whose efforts had led to the construction of the new airport terminal in the first place. Deeply worried about the negative impression the partial destruction of facilities would have on business partners from beyond the region, business leaders successfully implored the city commissioners to leave the building intact. Depicting Whitesell's announcement as misinformation, the city then went ahead and desegregated Dannelly Field Airport (see fig. 7).[91]

The Justice Department's legal actions were flanked and followed by efforts of Assistant Attorney Marshall and his staff at the Civil Rights Division to persuade airports to desegregate on a voluntary basis. In an effort to determine where segregation was still practiced and which airports to target for negotiations, the department initiated a survey to be conducted by the FBI the day after emerging victorious from legal proceedings against the airport in Montgomery in early January 1962. Investigating a total of 165 airports in all southern states between Maryland and Texas, the FBI found civil rights violations at nineteen airports where duplicate facilities still existed and Jim Crow signs were on display. Most of those airports integrated their facilities by the summer of 1962 after experiencing pressure from the Department of Justice.[92] They included the airports in Baton Rouge and Pineville, Louisiana; Fort Smith and Texarkana, Arkansas; Columbus, Georgia; Mobile, Alabama; and six airports in Mississippi: Natchez, Jackson, Meridian, Tupelo, Hattiesburg, and Columbus. Upon announcing the successful conclusion of most of the Civil Rights Division's negotiations, Attorney General Kennedy, to the astonishment of the *Cleveland Call and Post*, predicted that "within a very short time, it will be possible to fly to any airport in the country without seeing

FIGURE 7. A workman removes a restroom sign at Dannelly Field Airport in Montgomery, January 5, 1962, in compliance with the federal court order banning segregation (picture alliance/Associated Press).

'white' and 'colored' signs."[93] With regard to two other airports this forecast seemed premature: the airport management in Shreveport and Birmingham displayed defiant attitudes in hopes of upholding their discriminatory spatial regimes. To force these airports into compliance with federal laws and regulations as well, the Justice Department filed lawsuits in the federal district courts.[94]

The suits against Birmingham and Shreveport were filed on June 19, 1962. The case *United States v. City of Birmingham* pitted the U.S. government against the city of Birmingham, the city's commissioners, and the Dobbs Houses, Inc., restaurant company. The group of defendants was almost identical to the group of defendants civil rights leader Fred Shuttlesworth had initiated action against almost two years earlier.[95] Because the Shuttlesworth case was moving rather slowly, mostly due to the fact that he and his fellow plaintiffs initially represented themselves, the Justice Department reacted to a request by the FAA and pressed charges against Birmingham's airport authorities in the early summer of 1962.[96] Resting on the same substantive basis as the case against Dannelly Field Airport in Montgomery, the Justice Department attempted to establish beyond doubt that Birmingham Municipal Airport subscribed to practices of racial discrimination that affected African American patrons who desired to use the airport restaurant.

The Department of Justice produced evidence to show the systematic nature of service refusals experienced by African American travelers at the Birmingham airport's Dobbs House restaurant. Affidavits illustrated two incidents, both similar in nature to what Shuttlesworth and company had gone through. On March 10, 1962, John T. Patterson, a Wall Street stockbroker with university degrees from Lincoln University and Brooklyn Law School, had come to the restaurant for quick meal. He was on one of his frequent business trips to the South, and Birmingham was a stop on his itinerary. After he had chosen a table and sat down, a waitress informed him that she would not be able to serve him at the table but could have something prepared for him to eat either in the kitchen or as takeout. Patterson's brief conversation with the manager confirmed the restaurant's "whites only" policy. The manager explained that whereas blacks were now able to eat at the Dobbs House restaurant at Atlanta Municipal Airport, serving black restaurant customers in Birmingham was against the law. For Patterson, the incident "was a painful episode in an otherwise successful trip."[97] Barbara Ann Robinson fared no better. She was a Peace Corps volunteer on her way to attend a training program at the University of Oklahoma in Norman. After she had entered the restaurant on March 31, 1962, a waitress had approached and informed her: "You people aren't allowed to sit in here, I can only give you coffee in a paper cup." Declining the offer, Robinson left the restaurant. Recounting her experience, she remarked: "I understood and I believe that I was denied service on account of my race."[98] Like the other black air travelers featured in this story, Patterson and Robinson represented the new class of African American consumers. The were affluent, mobile, and well aware of the denial of their citizenship rights.

The government showed that the racist treatment of African American air travelers was based on a provision in Birmingham's racial ordinances (General Code of 1944).[99] It argued that based on the jurisdiction from previous cases against airports, the discriminatory practices the airport management and its restaurant lessee engaged in were illegal and unconstitutional.[100] Rather than let the proceedings run their course, U.S. District Judge Harlan Grooms ordered the case postponed until the date for the trial of *Shuttlesworth v. Birmingham*.[101] He found that it "encompasses claims similar in most, if not in all, respects to the claims asserted in the case of Shuttlesworth et al. v. Dobbs Houses, Inc. . . . pending in this court."[102] He allowed the Department of Justice to produce more evidence until then. Ruling in favor of the plaintiffs in *Shuttlesworth v. Birmingham*, Judge Grooms produced a similar ruling in *United States v. Birmingham*. He enjoined the city and its lessee Dobbs Houses, Inc., from discriminating against African American customers on July 31, 1962, issuing a decree that became effective immediately.[103]

The Justice Department's action against Shreveport targeted the city's Board of Commissioners and the Superintendent of Airports as the bodies responsible for the airport's management. It was also aimed at the airport restaurant's operator, Dobbs Houses, Inc., and its local manager. The plaintiffs' complaint alleged racial discrimination at the Shreveport airport that relegated African American air travelers to the use of a separate waiting room, restroom, dining room, and drinking facilities.[104] The dining room facilities, in particular, struck the Justice Department as inadequate and designed to humiliate. The suit's stipulation of facts included a detailed description of the eating facilities. It showed that although food prepared in the same kitchen was served in the terminal's three dining areas, the dining room reserved for the use of African American passengers was the least spacious and the most simple in décor. Whereas the main dining room offered "tables with linen and other accouterments [*sic*] of a first class restaurant"—seating a total of ninety-four diners at twenty-eight tables—and the lunch room accommodated thirty people between its counter seating area and booth spaces, the dining area reserved for blacks offered only four seats at a counter and a small booth seating two. It was moreover clearly marked as separate by the sign reading "Dining Room—Colored" that hung over its door.[105] Signs also demarcated the waiting rooms and restrooms as separate spaces for blacks and whites. Construction plans for the terminal indicate that the Shreveport airport had been conceived as a segregated building from its inception. All duplicate facilities such as the waiting rooms, restrooms, water fountains, and eating areas are clearly visible on the architectural drawings although they lack racial qualifiers. Those who read these plans and would later use the terminal facilities were certainly able to understand the intent without these qualifiers.[106]

The plaintiffs asked the court to grant injunctive relief that would prohibit the defendants from continuing their white supremacist regime of discrimination at the airport's terminal facilities. The Justice Department based its suit on the same legal principles that had supported the case in Montgomery. It claimed violations of the nondiscrimination provisions of the Federal Airport Act by the defendants. It also alleged their interference with interstate commerce by "making, giving and causing undue and unreasonable preference and advantage to all persons other than those of the Negro race while causing unjust discrimination and undue and unreasonable prejudice and disadvantage to Negroes."[107] In Shreveport as much as in Montgomery, the defendants stood up for their white supremacist worldview. They contested the government's authority to wage a case against them. Rather than dispute the findings of fact, they also freely admitted to their desire to continue their current practices. A memorandum in support of their motion to dismiss the case spelled out their views: "The defendants . . . have great interest in seeking to encourage the voluntary segregation of the races at the airport. While total togetherness of the races may be desirable to the incumbent governmental administration, we submit that this is not desirable to this community from the standpoint of peace and good order."[108] "Forced integration," the motion went on to state, held inherent dangers and was therefore undesirable.[109]

The defendants wanted instead to continue the use of separate facilities, which, they took pains to illustrate, were truly equal at the airport in Shreveport. Portraying the government as biased and out of touch with local realities, the defendants much like their peers in Montgomery framed themselves as the purveyors of stability and the proponents of a social order that had grown out of the principle of voluntary separation, to which—supposedly—both races subscribed.[110] Convinced of their righteousness, the defendants proudly took a last stand at a time when—according to the affidavit by Justice Department lawyer St. John Barrett—their airport was the last airport in the country that continued to practice segregation.[111] The ruling in favor of the plaintiffs by U.S. District Judge Ben C. Dawkins, which was preceded by a preliminary injunction, did not distract the defendants.[112] Refusing to accept the court-ordered integration of their airport, they appealed the case.[113] However, the Court of Appeals for the Fifth Circuit affirmed the the lower court's decision. A mandate issued on July 10, 1963, finally forced Shreveport's airport managers and Dobbs Houses, Inc., into compliance.[114] It led to the integration of the airport and completed the Justice Department's fight against segregated airport terminal facilities in the American South.

CHAPTER 7

Conclusion

As Don Thomas was about to leave the passenger terminal at Birmingham Municipal Airport on February 17, 1965, he was harassed by a group of young white men. They blocked his passage walking through the lobby and then prevented him from using the exit by pushing against the door. Thomas later reported, "Standing face to face with a glass door separating us, one of them yelled, 'Go, home, boy!'"[1] Once outside the terminal, awaiting the arrival of his ride, the chauffeur of Miles College, he was the only passenger to be asked to step away from the main door and stand in the dark. Thomas, the administrative coordinator of Plans for Progress, a volunteer affirmative action program set up in connection with President Kennedy's Committee on Equal Employment Opportunity, was greatly bothered by the incident.[2] It served to remind him "that the Southern front commands the attention of all concerned government agencies, business and industry, and private citizens," irrespective of desegregation and civil rights legislation.[3]

Thomas's report about the incident, which his boss Hobart Taylor Jr. forwarded to FAA Administrator Najeeb Halaby, led to a prompt investigation of the matter.[4] A government investigator was sent to Birmingham. Although his investigation failed to produce the identities of Thomas's harassers, it confirmed the integrated nature of passenger service facilities at Birmingham Municipal Airport, which had been one of the airports targeted by a federal desegregation suit only a few years earlier.[5] Halaby threatened sanctions—more action in the courts or a cutoff of subsidies from the Federal-aid Airport Program—should further inquiries implicate local airport authorities in the matter.[6]

Thomas's story serves to illustrate the findings of this book. By the mid-1960s, institutionalized racial discrimination at southern airports was no longer an issue. Jim Crow terminals had disappeared from the landscapes of transportation—for good—and the mechanisms for dealing with racial dis-crimination had also changed. Even if Thomas had not received the support of his influential boss to raise concern, the repertoire of strategies and tools to address practices of racism in aviation and to implement change had sig-nificantly changed since the first black air travelers had reported incidents to civil rights organizations and the federal government. These changes occurred before but were validated by the Civil Rights Act of 1964, the landmark piece of legislation that signaled a seismic shift in the legal landscape of postwar America.[7] The story also illustrates the impermeability of white supremacy. Although the process of desegregation reconfigured terminal spaces and integrated services and facilities, the minds of many southerners remained immune to the possibilities of change. The group of three young men in the Thomas incident represented the forces of white resistance who rejected black equality. They verbally reinscribed the color line by addressing Thomas ac-cording to the rules of southern racial etiquette. While the playing field also featured moderate whites who were open to change, diehard white suprem-acists were unwilling to renegotiate race relations and insisted on notions of blackness and whiteness they considered normative.

Two concluding questions merit attention. Why had Jim Crow terminals disappeared from southern landscapes even before passage of the Civil Rights Act? How did the legislation affect aviation and air travel? To explain why the process of airport desegregation was completed by the summer of 1963—a year prior to the passage of the Civil Rights Act—when Shreveport became the last city to integrate its passenger terminal, several factors come to mind. It seems that first of all, the struggle for the continuing segregation of public accommodations increasingly looked like a losing battle. If they wanted to preserve the southern way of life, representatives of the status quo had to focus on other areas of racial interaction. Senator Everett Dirksen, a mod-erate Republican from Illinois who was as suspicious of Title II of the Civil Rights Act[8] as many of his Democratic colleagues from the South, verbalized this realization when he commented halfway through the seventy-five-day filibuster of the bill:

> A colored man and his family set out from Blytheville, Ark., for Jackson, Miss. He says to himself, "Here is a highway I helped pay for through Federal and state taxes. They tax my gas. They tax my tires. They tax my car. This is really my high-way. But if I go any distance and take the kids into a comfort station, I do so at my peril." It has altered my thinking a little. The states and localities are entitled to have the first chance to work it out if they can. If they can't work it out, there has to be some place to go.[9]

He might as well have talked about air travel. Except that localities had worked it out at their airports—voluntarily in some communities, in reaction to pressure from civil rights activists, federal regulators, and the Department of Justice in others. The struggle for airports as integrated service facilities then helped pave the way for the desegregation of all public facilities. It established the legal basis on which Titles II and III of the Civil Rights Act rested. The legal and political debates about the racialization of the public spaces of aviation left their mark on those who participated in the hotly contested, seemingly endless debate over passage of this major piece of civil rights legislation.

It is also worth considering whether the citizenship demands of black air travelers were easier to swallow for segregationists than the demands for black equality in other areas of public life. For not only was the absolute number of black air travelers rather small in comparison to both the large numbers of white airline customers and the number of African Americans who used other means of intrastate and interstate transportation; they also mattered less as a numerical phenomenon than as a social and economic one, whose emergence led to the duplication of airport facilities by default. Moreover, their social class undercut racial difference in modern design environments of midcentury airports—at least to some degree. Both white and black air travelers displayed their class backgrounds when they stepped into passenger terminals, wearing for instance carefully chosen outfits like Gwendolyn Jackson and her Freedom Flyer collaborators did. For the black men and women featured in this story, the ability to buy an airline ticket was a marker of their upper-middle-class status and their agency as consumers. As representatives of that status group, their socially disruptive potential was small. H. D. Coke and Martin Luther King Jr. enjoying a passing meal in a terminal restaurant did not present much of a threat to the southern way of life. Segregationists came to realize that. They were much more concerned about issues like interracial schools, interracial sex, and African American political participation. Another reason, then, why airport terminal segregation disappeared even before the 1964 Civil Rights Act was its relatively low priority among Jim Crow supporters. Emotionally, legally, and practically, the airport terminal was one of the weakest bastions of southern white resistance.[10]

However, to say that Jim Crow terminals were a low priority for Jim Crow supporters is not to downplay the finding that their desegregation was a slow process that left many civil rights activists frustrated. The struggle was condensed into a period of about twenty years, which compares favorably with efforts to integrate other public facilities. But it presented those who challenged the status quo with some of the same difficulties and frustrations their fellow activists experienced in other areas of engagement. It also led to some surprising victories. Did the struggle for desegregation produce subregional patterns? Were Jim Crow terminals expunged from the landscapes of transportation in one region before they disappeared in another? The findings show that airport segregation was largely a southern phenomenon. Airport authorities in most deep southern and many border-state cities implemented segregation laws at some point during the mid-1940s and the 1960s. But the struggle for airport desegregation did not follow a border states versus Deep South pattern such as the one that emerged in the fight for the integration of schools.[11] Although deep southern cities like Birmingham, Montgomery, Shreveport, and New Orleans emerged as the most resilient in the efforts to resist terminal integration (or any other form of integration)—which ultimately led the Justice Department to move against them—so did Memphis. Unlike Knoxville and Nashville, which abandoned terminal segregation in 1954, the city of Memphis and its airport authority fought a protracted legal battle against Jesse Turner to fend off his class action lawsuit over equal access to airport service facilities, which lasted until 1962. Some facilities were softer targets, due more to the dynamics of local race relations than to their location in a particular subregion of the South.

Finally, how did the Civil Rights Act affect aviation and air travel? What changed in the aftermath of its passage? The bill's provisions required FAA regulators and airport authorities to act, but it affected black air travelers only indirectly in that the bill reiterated their rights as citizens and consumers. The FAA did not have to translate the Act's Titles II and III into new regulations, and policies for the racial integration they required had become a reality at the nation's airports by 1964. The FAA did, however, have to deal with Title VI (nondiscrimination requirements in federally assisted programs) and Title VII (equal employment opportunity). Nondiscrimination requirements in federally assisted programs applied to the FAA's Federal-aid Airport Program. The program had always been defined by the Federal Airport Act's provisions against unjust discrimination, and grant agreements over the years had been tightened to prevent the racial discrimination of patrons by local airport authorities. Still, the FAA was required to amend its regulations further in order to comply with the new legislative directive that forbade discrimination on the ground of race, color, or national origin under any program or activity that received federal financial assistance. The new regulation required airport operators who had received federal assistance to provide equal access to waiting rooms, sightseeing areas, and sanitary and other facilities; and to give assurance that their tenants operated businesses like restaurants on a nondiscriminatory basis. The new regulation also provided the tools to deal with incidents of noncompliance.[12] It thus reiterated the rights of black air travelers that previous regulatory and legislative activity and court decisions had firmly established.

Title VII's equal employment opportunity provisions also called for a review of nondiscrimination requirements in the FAA. Regulators identified three areas to which the new legislative directive applied: FAA employment, FAA procurement, and FAA-administered federal assistance (FAAP). Hiring procedures within the agency began to focus on diversity in the aftermath of Executive Order 10925, which prohibited discrimination because of race, creed, color, or national origin and promoted the employment of qualified persons within the federal government and those on government contracts.[13] The agency had also set up programs for assuring compliance with nondiscrimination policies on all levels of personnel management and processes for dealing with complaints of discrimination.[14] Further research is necessary to find out whether these were actually implemented and how diverse an agency the FAA had become by the mid-1960s. A 1965 civil rights policy paper prepared by the agency's general counsel, Nathaniel Goodrich, indicates some room for improvement. It recommended that "in the future special attention be given to making sure that qualified non-white persons are considered for promotion and special Agency training programs." It also suggested to target "schools or training institutions which are known to be attended by non-white persons" (i.e., historically black schools and colleges) in future human resources recruitment.[15] Next to the FAA, its procurement contractors were required to practice nondiscrimination in hiring and dealing with their employees. And last but not least, recipients of FAAP subsidies (local airport authorities) were expected to offer equal employment opportunities. They also had to ensure that the subcontractors they hired in airport construction projects did not discriminate in employment—an ambitious scenario that presented challenges in oversight and enforcement. The FAA mostly reverted to reporting cases of discrimination to the Equal Employment Opportunities Commission—the executive body set up to enforce the provisions of Title VII.[16]

For African American air travelers, the Civil Rights Act reaffirmed their right to be mobile. Nondiscriminatory access to public facilities at the nation's airports redefined the air travel experience for all black travelers who passed through spaces of aviation in the American South. In the process of desegregation, the region's aerial gateways were transformed into integrated environments that served as steppingstones to an integrated journey from one city to another. All along, aircraft cabins continued to exist as spaces where class superseded race as a signifier of social difference (and legroom). Airline customers used their purchasing power to buy first-class or economy-class tickets—whichever their paychecks or expense accounts yielded. But white air travelers and black air travelers would sit together once they had boarded their flight.[17] But air travel continued to be the most expensive way of traveling, and for many Americans—both black and white—traveling by airplane would remain a distant dream for years to come. Not until after deregulation in 1978, when ticket prices began to fall dramatically, would more lower-middle-class and working-class Americans be able to travel by air. But even for those African Americans who had to stay grounded, airport terminals became more hospitable environments where a curious visitor could go to the observation desk, stop by the restrooms, and grab a sandwich on the way out.

The story of this book—the emergence of Jim Crow airports and the process of desegregation—enables us to understand how the negotiation of spatial arrangements played into the construction of racial identities in the postwar period. In construing terminal facilities as spaces essentially reserved for the use of whites, southern white supremacists—with financial help from the federal government—transposed ideas of forced confinement and immobility to a new spatial context. They did so in an effort to marginalize the place of African Americans in southern cultural landscapes and in the landscapes of transportation. Black air travelers resisted these efforts to define access to the public spaces of air travel and constrict their rights as citizens. At the same time, they claimed their right to participate as equals in the burgeoning postwar consumer society in which travel—and air travel in particular—played an increasingly big role. To be American consumers and air travelers meant to participate in a modernist lifestyle and to fashion modernist subjectivities that could no longer be considered a privilege of the white middle class. Acts of resistance by individual travelers, as well as efforts of civil rights organizations and their allies, led to the integration of Jim Crow airports and—especially if considered in conjunction with the integration of other public facilities—to a spatial reconfiguration of America based on equality.

The city of Birmingham, at whose airport Don Thomas encountered the ghosts of the past embodied by three white teenagers in the opening episode, came to terms with its past in 2008. That year, the Birmingham Airport Authority board of directors approved renaming the airport to Birmingham-Shuttlesworth International Airport.[18] This was done in order to honor the legacy of the city's prominent civil rights leader Fred Shuttlesworth, whose fight against segregation in Birmingham included his efforts to integrate the airport.[19] In the course of his protracted legal battle against the airport, Shuttlesworth in June 1962 remarked on his inability to eat at the airport: "To be denied the opportunity to use the restaurant there on the same basis as white persons is a gross inconvenience in the course of my interstate travels."[20] A month later, the inconvenience was removed by court order. Forty-six years later, the renaming of the airport not only signaled the continuing relevance of Shuttlesworth's civil rights leadership—it also underlined the significance of airports as sites of conflict in the renegotiation of race relations in postwar America.

NOTES

Notes to Chapter 1

1. Affidavit of Ralph Abernathy, 20 October 1961, *United States v. City of Montgomery*, Civil Case Files (CCF), Box 73, U.S. District Court for the Middle District of Alabama, Northern Division, Records of District Courts of the United States, Record Group 21, National Archives and Records Administration (NARA)—Southeast Region (Atlanta).

2. Congressman Charles C. Diggs (D-Mich.), who investigated the racial politics of aviation in the 1950s and 1960s, came to this conclusion. Diggs expressed his appreciation in a letter to the presidents of various airlines. Charles Diggs to airline presidents, 4 June 1958, Series 7, Civil Rights, Box 42, Folder 1, Charles Diggs Collection, Manuscript Division, Moorland-Spingarn Research Center, Howard University. Legal historian Robert G. Dixon agrees in "Civil Rights in Air Transportation and Government Initiative," *Virginia Law Review* 49 (1963): 205–231, 205.

3. C. Vann Woodward, *The Strange Career of Jim Crow* (New York: 1955; rpt., Oxford University Press, 2002), 117.

4. *City of Shreveport v. United States*, 316 F.2d 928 (1963).

5. See Catherine Barnes, *Journey from Jim Crow: The Desegregation of Southern Transit* (New York: Columbia University Press, 1983); Williamjames Hull Hoffer, *Plessy v. Ferguson: Race and Inequality in Jim Crow America* (Lawrence: University Press of Kansas, 2012); David J. Garrow, ed., *The Montgomery Bus Boycott and the Women Who Started It: The Memoir of Jo Ann Gibson Robinson* (Knoxville: University of Tennessee Press, 1987); Derek C. Catsam, *Freedom's Main Line: The Journey of Reconciliation and the Freedom Rides* (Lexington: University Press of Kentucky, 2009); Raymond Arsenault, *Freedom Riders: 1961 and the Struggle for Racial Justice* (New York: Oxford University Press, 2006); Blair L. M. Kelley, *Right to Ride: Streetcar Boycotts and African American Citizenship in the Era of Plessy v. Ferguson* (Chapel Hill: University of North Carolina Press, 2010).

6. Robert Horonjeff and Francis X. McKelvey, *Planning and Design of Airports* (New York: McGraw-Hill, 1994), 3–4. See also Roger E. Bilstein, "Travel by Air: The American Context," *Archiv für Sozialgeschichte* 33 (1993): 275–288, 286.

7. See Anke Ortlepp, "Cultures of Air Travel in Postwar America," Habilitation, University of Munich, unpublished paper, 2009; Joseph J. Corn, *The Winged Gospel: America's Romance with Aviation* (Baltimore: Johns Hopkins University Press, 2002); Daniel L. Rust, *Flying across America: The Airline Passenger Experience* (Norman: University of Oklahoma Press, 2009); Janet R. Daly Bednarek with Michael H. Bednarek, *Dreams of Flight: General Aviation in the United States* (College Station: University of Texas Press, 2003).

8. See Lizabeth Cohen, *A Consumers' Republic: The Politics of Mass Consumption in Postwar America* (New York: Vintage, 2003); Stephanie Capparell, *The Real Pepsi Challenge: The Inspirational Story of Breaking the Color Barrier in American Business* (New

York: Free Press, 2007); Ted Ownby, *American Dreams in Mississippi: Consumers, Poverty and Culture, 1830–1998* (Chapel Hill: University of North Carolina Press, 1999); Marcus Alexis, "Some Negro-White Differences in Consumption," *American Journal of Economics and Sociology* 21.1 (1962): 11–28; Marcus Alexis, "Patterns of Black Consumption 1935–1960," *Journal of Black Studies* 1.1 (1970): 55–74. Whereas my own work is the first to probe African American consumption of air travel, the role of African Americans in aviation, particularly military aviation, has received more attention; see Von Hardesty and Dominick A. Pisano, *Black Wings: The American Black in Aviation* (Washington, D.C.: Smithsonian Institution Press, 1984), Neal V. Loving, *Loving's Love: A Black American's Experience in Aviation* (Washington, D.C.: Smithsonian Institution Press, 1994), as well as the literature on the Tuskegee Airmen.

9. Kelley, *Right to Ride*, 9, 10. Also see Jennifer Roback, "The Political Economy of Segregation: The Case of Segregated Streetcars," *Journal of Economic History* 46.4 (1986): 893–917. Roback argues that laws segregating streetcars were "binding constraints and not simply the codification of customary practice" (893). Streetcar companies were not creators of these laws and often opposed them as inconveniences that disrupted what was largely an integrated business. It seems that the growing political pressures from forces favoring segregation rather than shifting attitudes of streetcar companies led to the introduction of these laws.

10. Grace Hale, *Making Whiteness: The Culture of Segregation in the South, 1890–1940* (New York: Vintage, 1998).

11. Catsam, *Freedom's Main Line*.

12. Hale, *Making Whiteness*, 128; Barnes, *Journey from Jim Crow*. Also see Grace Hale, "'For Colored' and 'For White': Segregating Consumption in the South," *Jumpin' Jim Crow: Southern Politics from Civil War to Civil Rights*, ed. Jane Dailey, Glenda E. Gilmore, and Bryant Simon (Princeton: Princeton University Press, 2000), 162–182.

13. Victoria W. Wolcott, *Race, Riots, and Roller Coasters: The Struggle over Segregated Recreation in America* (Philadelphia: University of Pennsylvania Press, 2012), 3.

14. Ownby, *American Dreams in Mississippi*; Pete Daniel, *Lost Revolutions: The South in the 1950s* (Chapel Hill, Washington, D.C.: University of North Carolina Press and Smithsonian Institution Press, 2000); Paul R. Mullins, *Race and Affluence: An Archaeology of African America and Consumer Culture* (New York: Kluwer Academic, 1999).

15. See Ortlepp, "Cultures of Air Travel."

16. Aniko Bodroghkozy, *Equal Time: Television and the Civil Rights Movement* (Urbana: University of Illinois Press, 2012), 7.

17. David R. Goldfield, *Region, Race, and Cities: Interpreting the Urban South* (Baton Rouge: Louisiana State University Press, 1997); David R. Goldfield, *Cotton Fields and Skyscrapers: Southern City and Region, 1607–1980* (Baton Rouge: Louisiana State University Press, 1982); Hale, *The Making of Whiteness*; Elizabeth Abel, *Signs of the Times: The Visual Politics of Jim Crow* (Berkeley: University of California Press, 2010); Karen K. Thomas, *Deluxe Jim Crow: Civil Rights and American Health Policy, 1935–1954* (Athens: University of Georgia Press, 2011).

18. Jason M. Ward, *Defending White Democracy: The Making of a Segregationist Movement and the Remaking of Racial Politics, 1936–1965* (Chapel Hill: University of North Carolina Press, 2011), 93.

19. Jason Ward, *Defending White Democracy*, 4; Jason Sokol, *There Goes My Everything: White Southerners in the Age of Civil Rights, 1945–1975* (New York: Knopf, 2006);

Clive Webb, ed., *Massive Resistance: Southern Opposition to the Second Reconstruction* (New York: Oxford University Press, 2005).

20. David A. Nichols, *A Matter of Justice: Eisenhower and the Beginning of the Civil Rights Revolution* (New York: Simon & Schuster, 2007); Michael R. Gardner, *Harry Truman and Civil Rights: Moral Courage and Political Risks* (Carbondale: Southern Illinois University Press, 2002); William E. Juhnke, "President Truman's Committee on Civil Rights: The Interaction of Politics, Protest, and Presidential Advisory Commission," *Presidential Studies Quarterly* 19.3 (1989): 593–610; Nick Bryant, *The Bystander: John F. Kennedy and the Struggle for Black Equality* (New York: Basic Books, 2006); Robert E. Gilbert, "John F. Kennedy and Civil Rights for Black Americans," *Presidential Studies Quarterly* 12.3 (1982): 386–399; Michael J. Klarman, *From Jim Crow to Civil Rights: The Supreme Court and the Struggle for Racial Equality* (New York: Oxford University Press, 2004).

21. Dianne Harris, "Race, Space, and the Destabilization of Practice," *Landscape Journal* 26 (2007): 1–9, 2.

22. Ibid., 4.

23. See ibid.; Richard H. Schein, ed., *Landscape and Race in the United States* (New York: Routledge, 2006); Thomas J. Surgue, "Jim Crow's Last Stand: The Struggle to Integrate Levittown," in *Second Suburb: Levittown, Pennsylvania*, ed. Dianne Harris (Pittsburgh: University of Pittsburgh Press, 2010), 175–199; Andrew W. Kahrl, *The Land Was Ours: African American Beaches from Jim Crow to the Sunbelt South* (Cambridge: Harvard University Press, 2012); Grey Gundaker, ed., *Keep Your Head to the Sky: Interpreting African American Home Ground* (Charlottesville: University Press of Virginia, 1998); Robert R. Weyeneth, "The Architecture of Racial Segregation: The Challenges of Preserving the Problematical Past," *Public Historian* 27 (Fall 2005): 11–44.

24. Dianne Harris, *Little White Houses: How the Postwar Home Constructed Race in America* (Minneapolis: University of Minnesota Press, 2013); Dianne Harris, *Second Suburb: Levittown, Pennsylvania* (Pittsburgh: University of Pittsburgh Press, 2010); Richard H. Schein, ed., *Landscape and Race in the United States* (New York: Routledge, 2006).

25. David Delaney, *Race, Place, and the Law, 1836–1948* (Austin: University of Texas Press, 1998), 22, 23.

26. Kenneth W. Mack, *Representing the Race: The Creation of the Civil Rights Lawyer* (Cambridge: Harvard University Press, 2012), 6.

Notes to Chapter 2

1. For a timeline of black codes and Jim Crow laws, see http://www.blackpast.org /primary/jim-crow-laws-tennessee-1866-1955. See also Murray, *States' Laws on Race and Color*, 439–440.

2. Florida Laws 1887, c. 3743, §§ 1, 2.

3. Barnes traces the emergence of Jim Crow transit in *Journey from Jim Crow*, 1–19. Vann Woodward summarizes the codification of racial segregation in *The Strange Career of Jim Crow*, 97–102.

4. Charles Chestnutt, *The Marrow of Tradition* (1921; rpt., Ann Arbor: University of Michigan Press, 1969), 57.

5. W. E. B. Du Bois, *The Souls of Black Folk* (1903; rpt., New York: Penguin, 1989), 93–94. See also *Darkwater: Voices from behind the Veil* (1921; rpt., New York: Schocken Books, 1969), 229–230; *Dusk of Dawn: An Essay toward an Autobiography of a Race*

Concept (New York: Harcourt, Brace, 1940), 153: "But what is this group: and how do you differentiate it; and how can you call it 'black' when you admit it is not black? I recognize it quite easily and with full legal sanction; the black man is a person who must ride 'Jim Crow' in Georgia."

6. Hale, *The Making of Whiteness*, 50.

7. For regulations on buses see Murray, *States' Laws on Race and Color*; Stetson Kennedy, *Jim Crow Guide: The Way It Was* (Boca Raton: Florida Atlantic University Press, 1990). Rosa Parks details her experience in *Rosa Parks: My Story* (New York: Dial Books, 1992). See also Jeanne Theoharis, *The Rebellious Life of Mrs. Rosa Parks* (Boston: Beacon Press, 2013).

8. The suit had been brought by Irene Morgan, who on a journey from Virginia was forced to sit in the back of the bus although she was an interstate passenger on her way to Baltimore. *Morgan v. Virginia* 328 U.S. 373 (1946).

9. Kennedy, *Jim Crow Guide*, 188.

10. The Civil Aeronautics Act of 1938 (52 Stat. 973) established the CAA as the federal agency in charge of regulating aviation. In 1958, the act was replaced by the Federal Aviation Act (72 Stat. 732), which reorganized the CAA into the Federal Aviation Agency. See Donald R. Whitnah, *Safer Skyways: Federal Control of Aviation, 1926–1966* (Ames: Iowa State University Press, 1966); John W. Gelder, "Air Law: The Federal Aviation Act of 1958," *Michigan Law Review* 57.8 (June 1959): 1214–1227. The agency and its policies will be discussed in more detail in chapter 5.

11. An exception was the case of Ella Fitzgerald, who was denied her seat in first class on a Pan American flight from Honolulu, Hawaii, to Sydney, Australia, in 1955. The singer successfully sued the airline. Her case confirmed the right of equal access to airline service, *Fitzgerald v. Pan American World Airways* 229 F.2d 499 (1956).

12. For the early history of American airport development, see Janet R. Daly Bednarek, *America's Airports: Airfield Development, 1918–1947* (College Station: Texas A&M University Press, 2001); Geza Szurvoy, *The American Airport* (St. Paul: MBI Publishing, 2003); Charles Froesch and Walther Prokosch, *Airport Planning* (New York: John Wiley & Sons, 1946).

13. After the end of World War II, the need for a second airport in the national capital region became apparent. To meet the growing demand for capacity, Congress passed the Washington Airport Act of 1950 to enable the construction of Dulles Airport in Chantilly, Virginia. Dulles Airport opened in 1962. See Bednarek, *America's Airports*, 114–118; and website of the Metropolitan Washington Airports Authority: http://www .metwashairports.com/dulles/661.htm.

14. For images of National Airport in the 1940s, see the Horydczak Photograph Collection at the Library of Congress.

15. Code of Virginia (1950), Sec. 1796a. A proprietor's failure to do so resulted in fines between $100 and $500. Murray, *States' Laws on Race and Color*, 480.

16. Letter from Harold Young to National CIC Committee to Abolish Discrimination, 25 September 1945, Box II: B 218, Folder 3, National Association for the Advancement of Colored People (NAACP) Records, Manuscript Division, Library of Congress (LOC).

17. For a reevaluation of the civil rights record of the Truman administration, see Michael R. Gardner, *Harry Truman and Civil Rights: Moral Courage and Political Risks* (Carbondale: Southern Illinois University Press, 2002). On Truman and civil rights, also see William E. Juhnke, "President Truman's Committee on Civil Rights: The Interaction

of Politics, Protest, and Presidential Advisory Commission," *Presidential Studies Quarterly* 19.3 (1989): 593–610. Monroe Billington, "Civil Rights, President Truman and the South," *Journal of Negro History* 58.2 (1973): 127–139; Harvard Sitkoff, "Harry Truman and the Election of 1948: The Coming of Age of Civil Rights in American Politics," *Journal of Southern History* 37.4 (1971): 597–616.

18. Mamie Davies filed a complaint with American Airlines after her experience. Letter from Mamie E. Davis to P. S. Damon, 8 August 1946, Box II: B 218, Folder 3, NAACP Records, LOC.

19. Code of Virginia, 1950, Transportation, Air Carriers §56–196: "Waiting rooms and other public facilities.—The [State Corporation] Commission may require the establishment of separate waiting rooms at stations or depots [of aircraft carriers] for the white and colored races by the operators of such stations and depots," quoted in Murray, *States' Laws on Race and Color*, 481.

20. For the history of Norfolk Municipal Airport, see http://www.norfolkairport.com/mission-history.

21. Baltimore *Afro-American*, 12 May 1951, 19; Letter from Walter White to branches, 7 May 1953, Box II: A 233, Folder 4, NAACP Records, LOC. According to White the "white" and "colored" restrooms for men and women were replaced by restrooms for male and female airports patrons and male and female airport employees, all four of which were used on an integrated basis.

22. Norfolk *Journal and Guide*, 5 May 1951, 14.

23. See Forrest R. White, *Pride and Prejudice: School Desegregation and Urban Renewal in Norfolk, 1950–1959* (Westport: Praeger, 1992); Earl Lewis, *In Their Own Interests: Race, Class, and Power in Twentieth-Century Norfolk, Virginia* (Berkeley: University of California Press, 1991).

24. Yiorgos Anagnostou, *Contours of White Ethnicity: Popular Ethnography and the Making of Usable Pasts in Greek America* (Athens: Ohio University Press, 2009), 93, 136–139, 233–234n10.

25. David R. Roediger, *Working toward Whiteness: How America's Immigrants Became White: The Strange Journey from Ellis Island to the Suburbs* (New York: Basic Books, 2005), 332. For interethnic cooperation see Dan Georgakas, *My Detroit: Growing Up Greek and American in Motor City* (New York: Pella, 2006). For the changing conceptualizations of Europeans as white or nonwhite, see Matthew Frye Jacobson, *Whiteness of a Different Color: European Immigrants and the Alchemy of Race* (Cambridge, Mass.: Harvard University Press, 1998); Nell Irvin Painter, *The History of White People* (New York: W. W. Norton, 2010); and Gary Gerstle, *American Crucible: Race and Nation in the Twentieth Century* (Princeton: Princeton University Press, 2001).

26. Norfolk *Journal and Guide*, 24 January 1953, C1.

27. Code of Virginia, 1950, §18–327. Murray, *States' Laws on Race and Color*, 480.

28. Grace Hale and Elizabeth Abel have argued that it was the very nature of arbitrariness that provided white supremacy with its longevity. As and when the necessity arose, white power brokers could redraw the color line without fundamentally questioning notions of whiteness and blackness. See Hale, *Making Whiteness*; and Abel, *Signs of the Times*.

29. Norfolk *Journal and Guide*, 7 February 1953, 14.

30. Katherine Beckett and Steve Herbert, *Banished: The New Social Control in Urban America* (New York: Oxford University Press, 2010) 13.

31. See Daniel, *Lost Revolutions*; Ward, *Defending White Democracy*, 93–109; Goldfield, *Region, Race and Cities*, 37–68; James C. Cobb, *The South and America since World War II* (New York: Oxford University Press, 2012), in particular chaps. 2 and 3.

32. Materials concerning Oklahoma City airport incident in Box II: A 233, Folder 4, NAACP Records, LOC.

33. Memorandum from Gloster Current to Robert Carter, 15 December 1954, and Letter from W C. Patton to Clarence Mitchell, 7 October 1955, Box II: A 233, Folder 4, NAACP Records, LOC.

34. *Cleveland Call and Post*, 23 January 1954.

35. *Pittsburgh Courier*, 1 May 1954, 8.

36. Ibid.

37. Walter White served as the NAACP's executive secretary for almost a quarter-century. He was instrumental in planning and overseeing the organization's fight against segregation and disenfranchisement. See Kenneth R. Janken, *Walter White: Mr. NAACP* (Chapel Hill: University of North Carolina Press, 2006); Patricia Sullivan, *Lift Every Voice: The NAACP and the Making of the Civil Rights Movement* (New York: New Press, 2010).

38. Included in the list were branches in Alabama, Florida, Georgia, Kansas, Kentucky, Louisiana, Maryland, Mississippi, North and South Carolina, Oklahoma, Tennessee, Texas, Virginia, and West Virginia. Letter from Walter White to branches, 7 May 1953, Box II: A 233, Folder 4, NAACP Records, LOC.

39. The NAACP Memphis Branch was the strongest branch in the South after Atlanta due to the city's large black middle-class population.

40. For the history of LeMoyne College, see http://www.loc.edu/about-loc/history .asp. Price was the first African American president of the college.

41. For the history of Memphis Municipal Airport, see http://www.mscaa.com/about /history.

42. For images of the airport, see the Tennessee State Library and Archives digital collections. An image is also available in the Images of Tennessee collection on Wikimedia Commons.

43. Kennedy, *Jim Crow Guide*, 206.

44. Letter from J. F. Estes and Utillus Phillips to Walter White, 25 June 1953, Box II: A 233, Folder 4, NAACP Records, LOC. The letter also includes the line "Come back anytime, Phillips."

45. For a discussion of forms of American racism and the ideological origins of white supremacy, see Painter, *The History of White People*; Alden T. Vaughan, *Roots of American Racism: Essays on the Colonial Experience* (New York: Oxford University Press, 1995); Reginald Horsman, *Race and Manifest Destiny: The Origins of American Racial Anglo-Saxonism* (Cambridge: Harvard University Press, 1981).

46. Houston International Airport opened an expanded terminal facility the previous year. In 1950, Pan Am began offering nonstop service to Mexico City using Houston as a hub for connecting flights to and from the East and West Coast. See Geza Szurvoy, *The American Airport* (St. Paul: MBI Publishing, 2003), 119.

47. *New York Times*, 24 August 1955, 4.

48. Transcript of the ABC radio program "Edward P. Morgan and the News," 24 August 1955, Box II: A 233, Folder 4, NAACP Records, LOC. The NAACP files show that for years the local Houston branch had been very active in its attempts to integrate the air-

port. Stetson Kennedy recounts an anecdote that serves to prove Morgan's point: in order to travel freely and be treated as white, Jesse W. Routte, an Afro-Caribbean from Jamaica, often wore a turban and imitated a Swedish accent. In most places he was treated respectfully as a "visiting dignitary"; *Jim Crow Guide*, 53.

49. *New York Times*, 24 August 1955; *Washington Post*, 25 August 1955, 53; Baltimore *Afro-American*, 3 September 1955, 6.

50. Dwight D. Eisenhower's civil rights policy has undergone a reevaluation in recent years. See Nichols, *A Matter of Justice*. The impression remains, however, that he was not an adamant proponent of civil rights. Whereas he endorsed the desegregation of the District of Columbia, he never came out in full support of *Brown v. Board of Education*. See David A Nichols, "'The Showpiece of Our Nation': Dwight D. Eisenhower and the Desegregation of the District of Columbia," *Washington History* 16.2 (2004–2005): 44–65; and Michael S. Mayer, "With Much Deliberation and Some Speed: Eisenhower and the *Brown* Decision," *Journal of Southern History* 52.1 (1986): 43–76.

51. See Kimberley L. Phillips, *War! What Is It Good for?: Black Freedom Struggles and the U.S. Military from World War II to Iraq* (Chapel Hill: University of North Carolina Press, 2012); Lawrence P. Scott and William M. Womack Sr., *Double V: The Civil Rights Struggle of the Tuskegee Airmen* (East Lansing: Michigan State University Press, 1994); and Lee Finkle, "The Conservative Aims of Militant Rhetoric: Black Protest during World War II," *Journal of American History* 60.3 (1973): 692–713.

52. For an excellent analysis of the Cold War, communism, and civil rights, see Mary L. Dudziak, *Cold War, Civil Rights: Race and the Image of American Democracy* (Princeton: Princeton University Press, 2000).

53. Transcript of the ABC radio program "Edward P. Morgan and the News," 24 August 1955, Box II: A 233, Folder 4, NAACP Records, LOC.

54. *New York Times*, 24 August 1955, 4.

55. Charles C. Diggs Jr. represented a majority black district in Detroit (MI-13). He was Michigan's first African American representative. He would later become the founder and first chairman of the Congressional Black Caucus. See Carolyn P. DuBose, *The Untold Story of Charles Diggs: The Public Figure, the Private Man* (Arlington: Barton Publishing House, 1998).

56. Diggs also investigated the discriminatory hiring practices of U.S. commercial airlines. For airline hiring practices, see Jennifer Vantoch, *The Jet Sex: Airline Stewardesses and the Making of an American Icon* (Philadelphia: University of Pennsylvania Press, 2013), chap. 3.

57. Letter from Charles C. Diggs to Ralph Damon (TWA) and other airline presidents, 12 May 1955, Series 7, Civil Rights, Box 42, Folder 7, Charles Diggs Collection, Howard University.

58. Letter from Charles C. Diggs to Ralph Damon (TWA) and other airline presidents, 12 May 1955, Series 7, Civil Rights, Box 42, Folder 7, Charles Diggs Collection, Howard University.

59. Abel, *Signs of the Times*, 123–159.

60. Letter from Charles C. Diggs to Ralph Damon (TWA) and other airline presidents, 12 May 1955, Series 7, Civil Rights, Box 42, Folder 7, Charles Diggs Collection, Howard University.

61. Letter from S. G. Tipton to Charles C. Diggs, 2 August 1955, Series 7, Civil Rights, Box 42, brown folder, Charles Diggs Collection, Howard University.

62. Letter from T. A. Armstrong to Charles C. Diggs, 20 May 1955, Series 7, Civil Rights, Box 42, brown folder, Charles Diggs Collection, Howard University.

63. Letter from C. R. Smith to Charles C. Diggs, 24 May 1955, Series 7, Civil Rights, Box 42, Folder 7, Charles Diggs Collection, Howard University.

64. Letter from C. E. Woolman to Charles C. Diggs, 26 May 1955, Series 7, Civil Rights, Box 42, Folder 7, Charles Diggs Collection, Howard University.

65. See Chanelle N. Rose, *The Struggle for Black Freedom in Miami: Civil Rights and America's Tourist Paradise, 1896–1968* (Baton Rouge: Louisiana State University Press, 2015); Raymond A. Mohl, *South of the South: Jewish Activists and the Civil Rights Movement in Miami, 1945–1960* (Gainesville: University Press of Florida, 2004); and Marvin Dunn, *Black Miami in the Twentieth Century* (Gainesville: University Press of Florida, 1997).

66. Letter from G. T. Baker to Charles C. Diggs, 20 May 1955, Series 7, Civil Rights, Box 42, brown folder, Charles Diggs Collection, Howard University. For the history of the airlines mentioned in this paragraph, turn to Geza Szurvoy, *Classic American Airlines* (Osceola: Motorbooks International, 2000); Don Bedwell, *Silverbird: The American Airlines Story* (Sandpoint: Airways International, 1999); Sidney F. Davis, *Delta Air Lines: Debunking the Myth* (Atlanta: Peachtree, 1988).

67. Letter from Charles C. Diggs to airport manager, 21 July 1955, Series 7, Civil Rights, Box 42, Folder 2, Charles Diggs Collection, Howard University.

68. One also has to keep in mind that the information provided may not be correct. As in the case of Montgomery, Alabama, the data provided does not match other sources.

69. Survey reply Greater Cincinnati Airport, Byron R. Dickey, airport manager, 28 July 1955, Box 42, Folder 2, Charles Diggs Collection, Howard University.

70. Survey reply Municipal Airport Cumberland, Md., Warren R. Mullenax, airport manager, no date, Box 42, Folder 2, Charles Diggs Collection, Howard University.

71. Survey reply Municipal Airport Gainesville, no date, Box 42, Folder 2, Charles Diggs Collection, Howard University.

72. Survey reply Dade County Port Authority, Miami, Fla., J. Mark Wilcox, General Counsel, 25 July 1955, Box 42, Folder 2, Charles Diggs Collection, Howard University.

73. An example is Lafayette Airport; see survey reply Lafayette Airport Commission, Lafayette, La., Sheldon Blue, Director of Aviation, 22 August 1955, Box 42, Folder 2, Charles Diggs Collection, Howard University.

74. Ralph Abernathy, *And the Walls Came Tumbling Down: An Autobiography* (New York: Harper & Row, 1989), 483.

75. Survey reply Sarasota-Bradenton Airport, Manager, no date, Box 42, Folder 2, Charles Diggs Collection, Howard University.

76. Survey reply Mobile Municipal Airport, Springhill, Ala., O. N. Barney, 4 October 1955, Box 42, Folder 2, Charles Diggs Collection Howard University.

77. Survey reply City of Jacksonville, E. E. Bentley, Manager of Airports, 26 August 1955, Box 42, Folder 2, Charles Diggs Collection, Howard University.

78. Survey reply Broward County International Airport, Fort Lauderdale, Fla., L. E. Wagener, Manager, August 1, 1955, Box 42, Folder 2, Charles Diggs Collection, Howard University.

79. Survey reply Memorial Field, Hot Springs, Ark., Ralph C. Disheroon, airport manager, Box 42, Folder 2, Charles Diggs Collection, Howard University.

80. Belafonte and Poitier discuss air travel–related experiences in their autobiographies: Harry Belafonte with Michael Shnayerson, *My Song: A Memoir of Art, Race, and Defiance* (New York: Vintage, 2011); and Sidney Poitier, *The Measure of a Man: A Memoir* (New York: Simon & Schuster, 2000).

81. The scholarly literature remains silent on the issue of black air mobility. Neither studies interested in the development of the aviation industry nor works dealing with the changing contours of consumer society deal with the growing numbers of African American air travelers. Paul Edwards's *The Southern Urban Negro as a Consumer* (New York: Negro University Press, 1932) is useful but fails to cover the postwar period. In describing the above trend, I am therefore relying on my own research in a large body of materials ranging from the corporate records of airlines to autobiographies.

82. For all quotations see TWA advertisements published in *Ebony* magazine in 1964.

83. American Airlines advertisement, *Ebony* (1963). For Dorothy Height and the activities of the National Council of Negro Women, see Dorothy I. Height, *Open Wide the Freedom Gates: A Memoir* (New York: PublicAffairs, 2003); and Tracey A. Fitzgerald, *The National Council of Negro Women and the Feminist Movement, 1935–1975* (Washington, D.C.: Georgetown University Press, 1985).

84. Abernathy, *When the Walls Came Tumbling Down*, 195.

85. A number of biographies trace King's life and his constant traveling: see David Garrow, *Bearing the Cross: Martin Luther King, Jr., and the Southern Christian Leadership Conference* (New York: W. Morrow, 1986); Harvard Sitkoff, *King: Pilgrimage to the Mountaintop* (New York: Hill and Wang, 2008); and Taylor Branch's biographical trilogy (with Simon and Schuster): *Parting the Waters: America in the King Years, 1954–63* (1988); *Pillar of Fire: America in the King Years, 1963–65* (1998); *At Canaan's Edge: America in the King Years, 1965–68* (2006).

86. I borrow the term from Joseph Corn, *The Winged Gospel: America's Romance with Aviation* (Baltimore: Johns Hopkins University Press, 1983). Corn uses the terms "winged gospel" and "gospel of aviation" to describe Americans' hopes, dreams, and expectations at the dawn of the air age. Flight, he argues, became almost like a religious cause. Americans assumed that airplanes would positively affect human affairs and bring perfection on a global scale. The visions and prophecies aviation engendered are more commonly associated with religion.

87. "Unfulfilled Hopes, Sermon Outline," Montgomery, Alabama, 5 April 1959, *Martin Luther King, Jr., Papers*, vol. 6: *Advocate of the Social Gospel (Sept 1948–March 1963)*, ed. Claiborne Carson (Berkeley: University of California Press, 2000), 363.

88. See, e.g., James Farmer, *Lay Bare the Heart: An Autobiography of the Civil Rights Movement* (New York: Arbor House, 1985), 270, 272, 285–288; John Lewis, *Walking with the Wind: A Memoir of the Movement* (New York: Simon & Schuster, 1998), 144, 239; Roy Wilkins, *Standing Fast: The Autobiography of Roy Wilkins* (New York: Viking Press, 1982), 326, 341; Andrew Young, *An Easy Burden: The Civil Rights Movement and the Transformation of America* (New York: HarperCollins, 1996), 249, 459, 466; James Baldwin, *The Fire Next Time* (New York: Dial, 1963), 69–70; John D'Emilio, *Lost Prophet: The Life and Times of Bayard Rustin* (New York: Free Press, 2003), 242, 270, 354, 383; Barbara Ransby, *Ella Baker and the Black Freedom Movement: A Radical Democratic Vision* (Chapel Hill: University of North Carolina Press, 2003), 180, 226; Dennis C. Dickerson, *Whitney M. Young, Jr.: Militant Mediator* (Lexington: University Press of Kentucky, 1998), 56, 210.

89. Heavy case loads and frequent travel are among the subjects covered in Constance Baker Motley's autobiography *Equal Justice under Law* (New York: Farrar, Straus and Giroux, 1998); and in Juan Williams, *Thurgood Marshall: American Revolutionary* (New York: Times Books, 1998).

90. See Bodroghkozy, *Equal Time*; Gene Roberts and Hank Klibanoff, *The Race Beat: The Press, the Civil Rights Struggle, and the Awakening of a Nation* (New York: Knopf, 2006).

91. Letter from O. L. Sherrill to Charles C. Diggs, 25 October 1955, Series 7, Civil Rights, Box 42, Folder 5, Charles Diggs Collection, Howard University.

92. See Barnes, *Journey from Jim Crow*, 86–107; *Sarah Keys v. Carolina Coach Company*, 64 MCC 769 (1955).

93. Letter from Roy Wilkins to branches, 8 May 1957, Folder 8 "Discr. Transp. General 1956–59," Box III: A 111, NAACP Records, LOC. The attached questionnaire listed questions addressing conditions in railroad travel, interstate and municipal bus transportation, restaurant facilities, and airports.

94. Joint action by the mayor and city council ended segregation at the Sky Chef Airport Restaurant in Knoxville, Tennessee, on January 14, 1954. Nashville followed suit on May 21, 1954, in an explicit effort to adopt a uniform spatial policy at both airports; see Baltimore *Afro-American,* 23 January 1954; *Pittsburgh Courier,* 23 January 1954; Nashville City Council Resolution No. 54–1532, Folder 4 "Discrimination Airports 1952–55," Box II: A 233, NAACP Records, (LOC). Reporter James N. Rhea confirmed in 1957 that "not even the toilet, that most segregated of all Southern facilities, was separate" at Berry Field in Nashville, "We Went South: October 1957," *Reporting Civil Rights, Part I: American Journalism 1941–1963* (New York: Library of America, 2003), 389.

95. Letter from Chester I. Lewis to Mayor Andy Bremyer, 28 February 1959, Folder 12 "Discrimination Airports 1959–63," Box III: A 107, NAACP Records, LOC. A press release in the same folder announced the integration of the airport's Hangar Café in mid-March 1959. The restaurant's integration was the result of negotiations between McPherson's mayor Andrew Bremyer and the NAACP branch in Wichita, Kansas, which was chaired by Chester Lewis.

96. Charleston *Evening Post,* 24 September 1960.

97. Lillian Welch Voorhees, who began teaching at Fisk University in 1943 and became the founding chairperson of the Department of Speech and Dramatics, was also a civil rights activist. She was particularly interested in ending discrimination in accommodation. She protested against the treatment she and her friends received in Baton Rouge, writing to the airlines serving the airport and reporting the incident to the NAACP. See letter from Lillian W. Voorhees to General Manager of Southern Airways, 18 May 1963 and other materials in Folder 9, "Transp. Interstate Travel 1956–65," Box III: A 111, NAACP Records, LOC.

98. Abel, *Signs of the Times*, 5.

99. The description of the segregated terminal facilities at Dannelly Field is based on photographs produced as exhibits by the Department of Justice in a federal lawsuit against Montgomery's airport authorities. The photographs were probably taken in the spring of 1961. Exhibit photographs, case files, *United States v. City of Montgomery.* For more on the lawsuit, see chapter 6.

100. *New York Times,* 4 June 1961, E8.

Notes to Chapter 3

1. See James Tracy, *Direct Action: Radical Pacifism from the Union Eight to the Chicago Seven* (Chicago: University of Chicago Press, 1996); D'Emilio, *Lost Prophet*; Barbara Allen, "Martin Luther King's Civil Disobedience and the American Covenant Tradition," *Publius* 30 (2000): 71–113; Clayborne Carson, *In Struggle: SNCC and the Black Awakening of the 1960s* (Cambridge: Harvard University Press, 1995); August Meier and Elliott Rudwick, *CORE: A Study in the Civil Rights Movement, 1942–1968* (New York: Oxford University Press, 1973).

2. Gunnar Myrdal, *An American Dilemma: The Negro Problem and Modern Democracy* (New York: Harper, 1944), 635.

3. See Barnes, *Journey from Jim Crow*; Garrow, *Montgomery Bus Boycott*; Catsam, *Freedom's Main Line*; Arsenault, *Freedom Riders*. Segregation was also challenged in the courts. For the landmark case concerning interstate bus transportation, see the Interstate Commerce Commission's decision: *Sarah Keys v. Carolina Coach Company*, 64 MCC 769 (1955).

4. *Browder v. Gayle*, 142 F. Supp. 707 (M.D. Ala.).

5. As there was fallout from the incidents, particularly in Birmingham and Montgomery, the Department of Justice filed charges against the Ku Klux Klan to enjoin the Klan from committing acts of violence that involved local law enforcement members. *United States v. United States Klans, et al.*, Civil 1718–N, 1961–1965.

6. *Sarah Keys v. Carolina Coach Company*, 64 MCC 769 (1955). See Arsenault, *Freedom Riders*.

7. Members of the City Council were initially concerned that a refurbished hangar would adversely reflect on Atlanta's image as a symbol of the new, modern South. They were convinced otherwise by the chairman of the aviation committee. See Betsy Braden and Paul Hagan, *A Dream Takes Flight: Hartsfield Atlanta International Airport and Aviation in Atlanta* (Atlanta: Atlanta Historical Society; Athens: University of Georgia Press, 1989), 114.

8. No business history of Dobbs Houses, Inc., is available. For some basic information refer to http://www.dobbsmanagement.com/portfolio.html. Dobbs Houses, Inc., also owned the airport restaurants in Birmingham, Memphis, and Shreveport, which became targets of lawsuits. See chapters 4 and 6.

9. Joel Chandler Harris, *Uncle Remus and His Legends of the Old Plantation* (London: David Bogue, 1881).

10. *Jet*, 17 March 1955, 33.

11. See Braden and Hagan, *A Dream Takes Flight*.

12. Henderson Travel Agency was the first black travel agency in Atlanta and the fifth in the nation. It was established and owned by Freddye Scarborough Henderson. Henderson travel specialized in organizing tour packages, particularly to Africa. See Casper L. Jordan, "Freddye Scarborough Henderson," *Notable Black American Women*, book 2, ed. Jesse C. Smith (Detroit: Gale Research, 1996), 284–287.

13. Sidney Poitier, *The Measure of a Man: A Memoir* (New York: Simon & Schuster, 2000), 94–96.

14. Letter from Martin Luther King Jr. to Sylvester S. Robinson, 3 October 1956, *Martin Luther King, Jr., Papers*, vol. 3: *Birth of the New Age (Dec 1955–Dec 1956)*, ed. Claiborne Carson (Berkeley: University of California Press, 1997), 391–393.

15. Testimony of Martin Luther King Sr., court hearing, 8 December 1959, transcript, *Coke v. City of Atlanta*, CCF, Sept. 23, 1938–Nov. 9, 1962, Case Nos. 2491–2504, Box 280, U.S. District Court for the Western District of South Carolina, Atlanta Division, Records of the District Courts of the United States, RG 21, NARA Atlanta, 52–66.

16. For an analysis of *Coke v. Atlanta* (1960) see chapter 5.

17. See Virginia H. Hein, "The Image of 'A City Too Busy to Hate': Atlanta in the 1960's," *Phylon* 33.3 (1972): 205–221.

18. Tomiko Brown-Nagin, *Courage to Dissent: Atlanta and the Long History of the Civil Rights Movement* (New York: Oxford University Press, 2011). See also Winston A. Grady-Willis, *Challenging U.S. Apartheid: Atlanta and Black Struggles for Human Rights, 1960–1977* (Durham: Duke University Press, 2006).

19. Goshen College is a Mennonite liberal arts college in Goshen, Indiana.

20. For a history of the Southern Christian Leadership Conference, see Adam Fairclough, *To Redeem the Soul of America: The Southern Christian Leadership Conference and Martin Luther King, Jr.* (Athens: University of Georgia Press, [2001], 1987); Garrow, *Bearing the Cross*; Thomas R. Peake, *Keeping the Dream Alive: A History of the Southern Christian Leadership Conference from King to the Nineteen-Eighties* (New York: Peter Lange, 1987). For the Fellowship of Reconciliation, see Paul R. Dekar, *Creating the Beloved Community: A Journey with the Fellowship of Reconciliation* (Telford: Casadia Publishing House, 2005).

21. Tobin Miller Shearer, *Daily Demonstrators: The Civil Rights Movement in Mennonite Homes and Sanctuaries* (Baltimore: Johns Hopkins University Press, 2010).

22. *Cleveland Call and Post*, 8 August 1959, 1C.

23. *CORE-lator*, Summer 1959, 2, reel 49, Congress of Racial Equality Records, 1941–1967, microfilm at Manuscript Division, LOC.

24. "CORE Attacks Segregation in Atlanta, Ga. Airport," *Cleveland Call and Post*, 8 August 1959, 1C.

25. Peter F. Lau, *Democracy Rising: South Carolina and the Fight for Black Equality since 1965* (Lexington: University Press of Kentucky, 2006), 156.

26. The activities of the local NAACP chapter reached back to the 1940s. The Greenville CORE chapter was founded sometime between 1957 and 1959. Membership seems to have at times overlapped or migrated between the two organizations, which created some amount of tension but did not prevent their cooperation. Ibid., 218–219. Also see Stephen O'Neill, "Memory, History, and the Desegregation of Greenville, South Carolina," *Toward the Meeting of the Waters: South Carolina during the Twentieth Century*, ed. Winfried B. Moore, Jr. and Orville V. Burton (Columbia: University of South Carolina Press, 2008), 286–299.

27. *Henry v. Greenville Airport Commission* (1961) will be discussed in chapter 4.

28. For a history of the airport, see http://www.greenvilledowntownairport.com /History.html.

29. For images of the airport, see ibid. and the Coxe Collection of photographs at the Greenville Historical Society. The slogan is quoted from O'Neill, "Memory, History, and the Desegregation of Greenville, South Carolina," 288.

30. Most textile mills segregated their labor force by gender and race before the passage of the Civil Rights Act in 1964. For studies that investigate mill culture in Greenville and its neighboring town Spartanburg see Ray Belcher, *Greenville County, South Carolina: From Cotton Fields to Textile Center of the World* (Charleston: History Press, 2006),

and Betsy W. Teter, ed., *Textile Town: Spartanburg County, South Carolina* (Spartanburg: Hub City Writers Project, 2002).

31. Jackie Robinson was the first African American to play in the all-white National Baseball League. In 1947 he joined the Brooklyn Dodgers as their first baseman in his first season. He would move to second base in the next season and play for the team as one of its most successful players until his retirement in 1956. See Arnold Rampersad, *Jackie Robinson: A Biography* (New York: Knopf, 1997); Jules Tygiel, *Baseball's Great Experiment: Jackie Robinson and His Legacy* (New York: Oxford University Press, 2008); Jackie Robinson, *I Never Had It Made: An Autobiography of Jackie Robinson* (New York: Harper Perennial, 2003).

32. The day before, Richard McClain, the NAACP's chief accountant, and John Brooks, the organization's voter registration director, who had also attended the conference, were refused service in the airport's "Redwood Dining Room." They retreated to the waiting area, which they were allowed to use. Richard McClain filed a report about the incident: Richard W. McClain to Robert L. Carter, 27 October 1959, Folder 12 "Discrimination Airports 1959–63," Box III: A 107, NAACP Records, LOC.

33. Memorandum from Gloster B. Current to Robert L. Carter, 28 October 1959, Folder 12 "Discrimination Airports 1959–63," Box III: A 107, NAACP Records, LOC. Richard W. McClain to Robert L. Carter, 27 October 1959, Folder 12 "Discrimination Airports 1959–63," Box III: A 107, NAACP Records, LOC.

34. *New York Times*, 2 January 1960, 4. The NAACP and CORE had a difficult relationship in Greenville. This did not prevent them from cooperating, however. See Lau, *Democracy Rising*.

35. James T. McCain, "State Wide Protest at Jimcrow Airport," *CORE-lator*, January 1960 (Brotherhood Month), 1–2, reel 49, CORE Records, 1941–1967, LOC.

36. William Arms Fisher, *America the Beautiful*, lyrics by Katharine Lee Bates (Boston: Oliver Ditson Company, 1917).

37. *Cleveland Call and Post*, 16 January 1960, 1_C; *Chicago Daily Defender*, 5 January 1960, 5.

38. *Cleveland Call and Post*, 16 January 1960, 1_C.

39. *New York Times*, 2 January 1960, 4; *Washington Post*, 3 January 1960, B 14.

40. *Cleveland Call and Post*, 16 January 1960, 1_C.

41. Only mentioning the prayer pilgrimage in passing, Derek Catsam agrees that it came as a shock to Greenville's white establishment, which like the rest of the state was largely unfamiliar "with challenges to the Jim Crow system of seating and service," *Freedom's Main Line*, 121.

42. The Ku Klux Klan was a key component of the forces of massive resistance across the South; see, e.g., David Cunningham, *Klansville, U.S.A.: The Rise and Fall of the Civil Rights Era Ku Klux Klan* (New York: Oxford University Press, 2013). See also Neil R. McMillen, *The Citizens' Council: Organized Resistance to the Second Reconstruction, 1954–64* (Urbana: University of Illinois Press, 1994).

43. James T. McCain, "State Wide Protest at Jimcrow Airport," *CORE-lator*, January 1960 (Brotherhood Month), 1–2, reel 49, CORE Records, 1941–1967, LOC.

44. O'Neill, "Memory, History, and the Desegregation of Greenville, South Carolina," 290; *Cleveland Call and Post*, 16 January 1960, 1_C.

45. Catsam, *Freedom's Main Line*, 8.

46. Barnes, *Journey from Jim Crow*, 86–107.

47. The Supreme Court made clear that it considered the availability of dining and other services an integral part of transportation service, even if they were delivered not by the carrier but by private contractors. *Boynton v. Virginia*, 364 U.S. 454 (1960).

48. For an in-depth analysis of the Freedom Rides see Catsam, *Freedom's Main Line*; and Arsenault, *Freedom Riders*. Nick Bryant explores the role of the Kennedy administration in *The Bystander: John F. Kennedy and the Struggle for Black Equality* (New York: Basic Books, 2006).

49. *Boston Globe*, 8 June 1961, 10.

50. C. Vann Woodward, *Origins of the New South* (Baton Rouge: Louisiana State University Press, 1951), 151.

51. For the activities of the civil rights movement in Mississippi and the forms of resistance it encountered see John Dittmer, *Local People: The Struggle for Civil Rights in Mississippi* (Urbana: University of Illinois Press, 1994); Charles M. Payne, *I've Got the Light of Freedom: The Organizing Tradition and the Mississippi Freedom Struggle* (Berkeley: University of California Press, 1995); James P. Marshall, *Student Activism and Civil Rights in Mississippi: Protest Politics and the Struggle for Racial Justice, 1960–1965* (Baton Rouge: Louisiana State University Press, 2013); Ted Ownby, ed., *The Civil Rights Movement in Mississippi* (Jackson: University Press of Mississippi, 2013); Neil R. McMillen, *The Citizens' Council: Organized Resistance to the Second Reconstruction, 1954–64* (Urbana: University of Illinois Press, 1994).

52. See Jackson Municipal Airport Authority's website: http://jmaa.com/jmaa-history/. Mississippi Heritage Trust also provides some information about the terminal building: http://www.mississippiheritage.com/list01.html#4.

53. In 1963, Hawkins Field, which was located north of downtown, was abandoned and a new airport (Allen C. Thompson Field) opened east of the city.

54. Letter from Department of Commerce, Civil Aeronautics Administration, Office of the Administration to Charles C. Diggs, 7 June 1956, Series 7, Civil Rights, Box 42, Folder 4, Charles Diggs Collection, Howard University.

55. For an explanation of duplication and other spatial strategies of white supremacy, see Weyeneth, "The Architecture of Racial Segregation," 15–18.

56. The first group of Freedom Riders arrived on May 24, 1961. See Catsam, *Freedom's Main Line*, 248, and Arsenault, *Freedom Riders*, 183–213.

57. For biographical information see the Civil Rights Digital Library (http://crdl.usg .edu/people/j/jenkins_gwendolyn_c_1940/?Welcome); the roster of Freedom Riders on the interactive website connected to the American Experience (PBS) program "Freedom Riders" (http://www.pbs.org/wgbh/americanexperience/freedomriders/people/roster/); and Eric Etheridge, *Breach of Peace: Portraits of the 1961 Mississippi Freedom Riders* (New York: Atlas and Co., 2008). The volume also contains mug shots from the Mississippi State Sovereignty Commission files and short interviews conducted with surviving riders. Unfortunately, the interviewees do not include the Freedom Flyers.

58. *Daily Jackson News* and other newspapers.

59. On the visual and discursive construction of the "civil rights subject," see Bodroghkozy, *Equal Time*. For more images of the airport protest see the digital archive of the Associated Press at http://www.apimages.com.

60. Abel, *Signs of the Times*, 140.

61. Sutton would later represent Malcolm X. Obituary, *New York Times*, 28 December 2009.

62. Arsenault, *Freedom Riders*, 218.

63. For members of the group refer to the roster of riders at: http://www.pbs.org/wgbh /americanexperience/freedomriders/people/roster/. The roster also mentions a fourth group of riders, about whom no information was to be obtained.

64. This book will return to Jackson Municipal Airport in chapter 5 to analyze the FAA's conflict with the airport over the misappropriation of Federal-aid Airport Program grants in 1963. The conflict led to a reform of the grant application process for FAAP funding.

65. The group included eighteen black and white rabbis and ministers: Donald C. Alstork of Saratoga, N.Y.; Robert McAfee Brown, a Presbyterian theologian and professor at Union Theological Seminary; John Collier of Newark; Israel "Si" Dresner, the rabbi of a reformed Jewish congregation in Springfield, N.J., and a well-known Jewish civil rights activist ("most arrested rabbi in America"); Malcom Evans of Brooklyn; Martin Freedman of Patterson, N.J., a protégé of Bayard Rustin; Arthur L. Hardge of New Britain, Conn.; Wayne C. Hartmire of New York; George Leake of Buffalo; Allen Levine of Bradford, Pa.; Petty D. McKinney of Springfield, Mass., a member of the NAACP; Walter Plaut of Temple Emanuel in Great Neck, N.Y. and chairman of the National Conference of Christians and Jews; Henry Proctor of Syracuse; Ralph L. Roy, a longtime CORE member and pastor of Grace Methodist church in New York; Perry A. Smith of Washington, D.C.; and Robert Stone, A. McRaven (Mack) Warner, and Edward White, all of New York. Freedom Rides materials (application letters, correspondence etc.), reel 25, # 116– 118, CORE Records, 1941–1967, LOC.

66. See Arsenault, *Freedom Riders*, 220; Governor Farris Bryant had worked behind the scenes for weeks to ensure that any Freedom Riders who came to North Florida would be served to avoid racial violence and the bad publicity it entailed; see Glenda Alice Rabby, *The Pain and the Promise: The Struggle for Civil Rights in Tallahassee, Florida* (Athens: University of George Press, 1999), 135–136.

67. Savarin was a restaurant franchise like Dobbs Houses with locations at airports across Florida (Ft. Lauderdale, Jacksonville, Miami, Pensacola, St. Petersburg, Tallahassee, and Tampa). It was owned by American News Company and managed by Union News Company, American News Co.'s branch in charge of serving train stations and airports.

68. The *CORE-lator* reported about the negotiations in "Freedom Rides Roll On," *CORE-lator* June 1961, 1, reel 49, CORE Records, 1941–1967, LOC.

69. Rabby, *Pain and the Promise*, 135.

70. See Murray, *States' Laws on Race and Color*; Kahrl, *The Land Was Ours*; Irvin D. S. Winsboro, ed., *Old South, New South, or Down South?: Florida and the Modern Civil Rights Movement* (Morgantown: West Virginia University Press, 2009); Robert P. Ingalls, *Urban Vigilantes in the New South: Tampa, 1882–1936* (Gainesville: University Press of Florida, 1993); David R. Colburn, *Racial Change and Community Crisis: St. Augustine, Florida, 1877–1980* (New York: Columbia University Press, 1985); Abel A. Bartley, *Keeping the Faith: Race, Politics, and Social Development in Jacksonville, Florida, 1940–1970* (Westport: Greenwood Press, 2000).

71. Abernathy, *Walls Came Tumbling Down*, 282.

72. CORE activists Priscilla Stevens and her sister were instrumental in these activities.

73. The list included Gainesville, Miami, Melbourne, St. Petersburg, Tampa, and Sarasota-Bradenton. Airport survey materials, Box 42, Folder 2, Charles Diggs Collection, Howard University.

74. In a report about the sit-in movement in Tallahassee, writer James Baldwin describes the old terminal as "Tallahassee's shambles of an airport." He was struck by the segregated service features, which included a "colored waiting room" and segregated taxi services. On unfamiliar territory as an African American from New York, Baldwin muses about how "a study of Federal directives regarding interstate ravel would have been helpful" in letting him navigate this territory of white supremacy. James Baldwin, "They Can't Turn Back," *Reporting Civil Rights*, Part I (New York: Library of America, 2003), 478–479.

75. Testimony of John Collier, court hearing, 16 September 1961, transcript, *Brooks v. City of Tallahassee*, CCF, Box 175, U.S. District Court for the Northern District of Florida, Tallahassee Division, Records of the District Courts of the United States, RG 21, NARA Atlanta, 77.

76. They had done so ignoring the concerns of Governor LeRoy Collins, a moderate white voice for civil rights. Collins had pointed out that if there was any place where people ought to be able to eat together it was the airport. Rabby, *Pain and the Promise*, 136–137.

77. Quoted from Arsenault, *Freedom Riders*, 222.

78. *Los Angeles Times*, 16 June 1961, 2.

79. Ibid.

80. As the riders waited, Collins was on the phone with Robert Kennedy, hoping the attorney general would help protect their rights (*Washington Post*, 23 June 1961 A7). See *Los Angeles Times*, 16 June 1961, 2; *Chicago Daily Tribune*, 17 June 1961, N11; *Washington Post*, 18 June 1961, A2. State Attorney William Hopkins later testified that he was struck by the group's "sullen" defiance. Testimony of William Hopkins, court hearing, 16 September 1961, transcript, case files, *Brooks v. City of Tallahassee*, 167.

81. Deposition of Frank Stoutemire, court hearing, 16 September 1961, transcript, case files, *Brooks v. City of Tallahassee*, 170–182.

82. Various studies trace the framing of civil rights activists as outside agitators, e.g., Charles W. Eagles, *Outside Agitator: Jon Daniels and the Civil Rights Movement in Alabama* (Chapel Hill: University of North Carolina Press, 1993); Dittmer, *Local People*, chap. 5.

83. *Los Angeles Times*, 18 June 1961, F12.

84. *Washington Post*, 23 June 1961, A7.

85. An interesting detail that came to light during testimony concerns the activities of Attorney General Robert Kennedy during the airport protest. Apparently, if one is to believe a report by the *Washington Post*, Kennedy tried to convince the protesters to call off their sit-in and hunger strike. Moreover, he weighed down on local police officers to delay their arrest. *Washington Post*, 23 June 1961, A7.

86. Cit. from Rabby, *Pain and the Promise*, 137–138. *Tallahassee Democrat*, 23 June 1961.

87. *Dresner v. City of Tallahassee*, 375 U.S. 136 (1963).

88. *Brooks v. City of Tallahassee*, 202 F. Supp. 56 (1961). During the court hearings it transpired that the American News Company did have a policy of nondiscriminatory service, which it abided by at its other airport locations in Miami, Ft. Lauderdale, St. Petersburg, Jacksonville, Pensacola, and Tampa—a fact that the defendants were able to corroborate because they had tested the airport restaurants. It was the city of Tallahassee that had imposed a racial order on the terminal space and required its concessionaire to

abide by it. Testimony of restaurant manager Hubert A. Isdell, court hearing, 16 September 1961, transcript, case files, *Brooks v. City of Tallahassee*, 151–156.

89. Barnes, *Journey from Jim Crow*, 177–180. Attorney General Robert Kennedy had filed the petition asking the ICC to adopt regulations prohibiting segregation in interstate bus travel on May 29, 1961, in an effort to contain the Freedom Rides and their fallout. He hoped that ICC action would "end the legal confusion" and establish new and enforceable rules for bus travel. See Arsenault, *Freedom Riders*, 205.

90. *Carolina Times*, 15 October 1955.

91. For a history of segregation in North Carolina see Betty Jamerson Reed, *School Segregation in Western North Carolina: A History, 1860s–1970s* (Jefferson, N.C.: McFarland, 2011); David S. Cecelski, *Along Freedom Road: Hyde County, North Carolina and the Fate of Black Schools in the South* (Chapel Hill: University of North Carolina Press, 1994); Jeffrey J. Crow, Paul D. Escott, and Flora J. Hatley, *A History of African Americans in North Carolina* (Raleigh: Office of Archives and History, North Carolina Dept. of Cultural Resources, 2011).

92. See Leslie Brown, *Upbuilding Black Durham: Gender, Class, and Black Community Development in the Jim Crow South* (Chapel Hill: University of North Carolina Press, 2008), 14. Also see Jean Bradley Anderson, *A History of Durham County, North Carolina* (Durham: Duke University Press and Historic Preservation Society of Durham, 1990).

93. Bednarek, *America's Airports*, 163–164.

94. *Carolina Times*, 15 October 1955. An online history of Raleigh-Durham Airport is available at: http://www.rdu.com/aboutrdu/history.htm#1950.

95. For images of the airport, see the photographic collections of the North Carolina State Archives at http://www.ncdcr.gov/archives/home.aspx.

96. Weyeneth, "Architecture of Racial Segregation," 15–18.

97. Letter from Walter White to Alexander Kelly, 28 October 1953, Box II: A 233, Folder 4, NAACP Records, LOC.

98. Abel, *Signs of the Times*, 81.

99. Brown, *Upbuilding Black Durham*, 323–324. See also, Sarah Caroline Thuesen, *Greater Than Equal: African American Struggles for Schools and Citizenship in North Carolina, 1919–1965* (Chapel Hill: University of North Carolina Press, 2013).

100. Letter from J. S. Stewart to Charles C. Diggs, 20 October 1955, Series 7, Civil Rights, Box 42, Folder 5, Charles Diggs Collection, Howard University.

101. Norfolk *Journal and Guide*, 15 October 1955, B5.

102. *New York Times*, 12 October 1961, 24.

103. Telegram from John Edwards, Callis Brown, and Billy Thorpe to John F. Kennedy, 9 October 1961, Series 7, Civil Rights, Box 42, Folder 5, Charles Diggs Collection, Howard University.

104. The understanding that the United States was fighting for a civil rights agenda in Europe, which it failed to translate into domestic policy, had inspired the Double-V campaign during World War II. The moral obligation to deliver full benefits of citizenship rights to African Americans continued to be a focus of the civil rights movement in the postwar period, when it pointed to the continuing double-standard of U.S. anticommunist engagements abroad and the lack of civil rights enforcement at home. This double standard, observers often pointed out, besides hurting minorities negatively, affected the United States in its struggle against the Soviet Union. See Scott and Womack, *Double V*; Thomas Borstelmann, *The Cold War and the Color Line: American Race Relations in the*

Global Arena (Cambridge, Mass.: Harvard University Press, 2001); Mary L. Dudziak, *Cold War Civil Rights: Race and the Image of American Democracy* (Princeton: Princeton University Press, 2000); Penny M. Von Eschen, *Race against Empire: Black Americans and Anticolonialism, 1937–1957* (Ithaca: Cornell University Press, 1997).

105. *New York Times,* 12 October 1961, 24.

106. For the role of students in the civil rights movement see Carson, *In Struggle;* Andrew B. Lewis, *The Shadows of Youth: The Remarkable Journey of the Civil Rights Generation* (New York: Hill & Wang, 2009); Ellen Levine, *Freedom's Children: Young Civil Rights Activists Tell Their Own Stories* (New York: Putnam, 1993); Doug McAdam, *Freedom Summer* (New York: Oxford University Press, 1988).

Notes to Chapter 4

1. Delaney, *Race, Place, and the Law.*

2. *Brown v. Board of Education of Topeka,* 347 U.S. 483 (1954).

3. Richard Kluger, *Simple Justice: The History of Brown v. Board of Education and Black America's Struggle for Equality* (New York: Vintage, 2004).

4. For the desegregation of the District of Columbia, see David A Nichols, "'The Showpiece of Our Nation': Dwight D. Eisenhower and the Desegregation of the District of Columbia," *Washington History,* Fall/Winter (2004–2005): 44–65.

5. Correspondence between the NAACP and the Department of Commerce, Box II: B 218, Folder 3, NAACP Records, LOC. Here reference is made in particular to a letter from NAACP Assistant Special Counsel Franklin H. Williams to Secretary of Commerce W. Averell Harriman written on 9 October 1946.

6. For the organization's history and its legal campaigns see Gilbert Jonas, *Freedom's Sword: The NAACP and the Struggle against Racism in America, 1909–1969* (New York: Routledge, 2005). For a critical appraisal of litigation see Brown-Nagin, *Courage to Dissent.*

7. Letter from Harold Young to National CIC Committee to Abolish Discrimination, 25 September 1945, Box II: B 218, Folder 3, NAACP Records, LOC.

8. Assimilative Crimes Act, 18 U.S.C. §13 (a): "Whoever within or upon any of the places now existing or hereafter reserved or acquired as provided in section 7 of this title, or on, above, or below any portion of the territorial sea of the United States not within the jurisdiction of any State, Commonwealth, territory, possession, or district is guilty of any act or omission which, although not made punishable by any enactment of Congress, would be punishable if committed or omitted within the jurisdiction of the State, Territory, Possession, or District in which such place is situated, by the laws thereof in force at the time of such act or omission, shall be guilty of a like offense and subject to a like punishment."

9. "The Federal Assimilative Crimes Act," *Harvard Law Review* 70.4 (February 1957): 685–698.

10. 59 Stat. 552–554, chap. 443.

11. Letter from Franklin H. Williams to Averell Harriman, 9 October 1946, Box II: B 218, Folder 3, NAACP Records, LOC.

12. Letter from Adrian S. Fisher to Franklin H. Williams, 4 March 1947, Folder 3 "Washington Airport 1942–49," Box II: B218, NAACP Records, LOC.

13. Letter from Adrian S. Fisher to Franklin H. Williams, 4 March 1947, Folder 3 "Washington Airport 1942–49," Box II: B218, NAACP Records, LOC. It is not quite clear

whether he did. Following up on Fisher's promise, the NAACP Legal Defense Fund's Special Counsel Thurgood Marshall submitted a statement to the Committee on Civil Rights, in which he sketched the emergence of Jim Crow at National Airport, commented on its unlawfulness, and requested that the matter be brought to the attention of the president. Thurgood Marshall, "To the President's Civil Rights Committee," 21 March 1947, Folder 3 "Washington Airport 1942–49," Box II: B218, NAACP Records, LOC. For the President's Committee on Civil Rights, which was established by executive order by President Truman in 1946, see Michael R. Gardner, *Harry Truman and Civil Rights: Moral Courage and Political Risks* (Carbondale: Southern Illinois University Press, 2002).

14. *New York Times*, 18 November 1947.

15. *Washington Post*, 18 November 1947, 1.

16. Delos Rentzel was appointed administrator of the CAA by President Truman on June 1, 1948. He had a background in radio communications. Before joining the federal government, he served as communications director for American Airlines (since 1941) and advised the army and navy on aviation during World War II. He left the CAA to become chairman of CAB before moving on serve as the Department of Commerce's Under Secretary for Transportation under Truman. Obituary, *New York Times*, 8 September 1991; Donald R. Whitnah, *Safer Skyways: Federal Control of Aviation, 1926–1966* (Ames: Iowa State University Press, 1966).

17. The Washington National Airport Act, passed by Congress in 1940, formed the basis of federal governance at the airport, 54 Stat. 686–688, Chapter 444. The daily operations of the airport followed the General Regulations of the Washington National Airport and were governed by the Administrator of Civil Aeronautics, 14 C.F.R. 1949 570Ff.

18. 13 Fed. Reg. 8736 (1948); 14 C.F.R. § 570.16, 1962.

19. NAACP press release, "White Demands Enforcement of C.A.A. Airport Bias Ban," 30 December 1948, Folder 3 "Washington Airport 1942–1949," Box II: B218, NAACP Records, LOC.

20. *Washington Post*, 29 December 1948.

21. Ibid., 1.

22. *Washington Post*, 29 December 1948, 1. The Alpha Kappa Alpha sorority was incorporated by a group of Howard University students in 1913. Founded as a forum to provide sisterhood and support, the organization has since then become one of the most important and influential power networks for college-educated and professional African American women. It works with local communities in the fields of education, health, family, and business. See Earnestine Green McNealey, *The Pearls of Alpha Kappa Alpha: The History of America's First Black Sorority* (Washington, D.C.: Alpha Kappa Alpha, 2010), and Deborah E. Whaley, *Disciplining Women: Alpha Kappa Alpha, Black Counterpublics, and the Cultural Politics of Black Sororities* (Albany: SUNY Press, 2010).

23. *Washington Post*, 30 December 1948, 1; *Cleveland Call and Post*, 8 January 1949, 1B.

24. Albert V. Bryan was a Truman nominee who was appointed to the Court in 1947. One of his noteworthy decisions in the desegregation context was on the implementation of school desegregation in Fairfax County, Virginia. See Michael J. Klarman, *Brown v. Board of Education and the Civil Rights Movement* (New York: Oxford University Press, 2007), 122.

25. *Air Terminal Services v. Rentzel*, 81 F. Supp. 611 (1949).

26. *Washington Post*, 5 January 1949, 1.

27. Ibid.

28. *New York Times*, 5 January 1949, 4.

29. *Washington Post*, 4 January 1949, 1.

30. Before her retirement, Helen Nash taught at Dunbar High School. The public secondary school was one of Washington, D.C.'s most prestigious schools for African American students. Among its graduates was Charles Hamilton Houston, the NAACP's litigation director, whose law firm represented Nash.

31. The women were represented by the African American law firm Houston, Houston, Hastie and Waddy in Washington, D.C., whose partners included Charles Hamilton Houston, the dean of Howard University Law School. Sadie Tanner Mossell Alexander was the first black woman to receive a PhD (1921, economics) in the United States, to get a law degree from the University of Pennsylvania's Law School, and to join the Pennsylvania Bar Association. Initially a partner in her husband's law firm, she opened her own practice in 1959 specializing in family law. She held a number of prominent national positions, among them a seat on the President's Committee on Civil Rights, to which President Truman appointed her in 1946. Alexander requested the case to be dropped after segregation at the airport was banned by the CAA. Kenneth W. Mack, "A Social History of Everyday Practice: Sadie T. M. Alexander and the Incorporation of Black Women into the American Legal Profession, 1925–60," *Cornell Law Review* 87 (2002): 1405–1474; and Mack, "Sadie Tanner Mossell Alexander," *Notable American Women: A Biographical Dictionary Completing the Twentieth Century*, ed. Susan Ware (Cambridge, Mass.: Harvard University Press, 2004), 18–19.

32. Letter from Charles H. Houston to Edward R. Dudley, 26 January 1948, Folder 3 "Washington Airport 1942–1949," Box II: B218, NAACP Records, LOC.

33. *Nash v. Air Terminal Services, Inc.*, 85 F. Supp. 545 (1949).

34. Dixon, "Civil Rights in Air Transportation," 213–214.

35. *Nash v. Air Terminal Services, Inc.*, 85 F. Supp. 545 (1949).

36. Ibid.

37. Ibid.

38. Baltimore *Afro-American*, 24 December 1949, 7.

39. Barnes, *Journey from Jim Crow*, 139.

40. James A. Crumlin (president, NAACP Kentucky) filed suit in September 1955 against Dobbs Houses, Inc., at the airport in Louisville to challenge discriminatory service patterns. *Martha S. Brisbane v. Greensboro-High Point Airport Authority*, filed in 1957, challenged segregated eating arrangements at the local airport.

41. Affidavit H. D. Coke, 28 November 1958, case files, *Coke v. Atlanta*, RG 21, U.S. District Court, Western District of South Carolina, Civil Case Files, Sept. 23, 1938–Nov. 9, 1962, Case Nos. 2491–2504, Box 280, NARA Atlanta. For the experiences of Sidney Poitier and Martin Luther King Jr. see the previous chapter.

42. Coke gave a detailed description of the incident in his examination and cross-examination during the proceedings on 8 December 1959. See transcript of proceedings, *Coke v. City of Atlanta*.

43. Motion for preliminary injunction, 30 September 1959, case files, *Coke v. City of Atlanta*.

44. See Rawn James Jr., *Root and Branch: Charles Hamilton Houston, Thurgood Marshall, and the Struggle to End Segregation* (New York: Bloomsbury Press, 2010); Juan Williams, *Thurgood Marshall: American Revolutionary* (New York: Broadway Books, 2000); Will Haygood, *Thurgood Marshall and the Supreme Court Nomination That Changed*

America (New York: Knopf, 2015); Jack Greenberg, *Crusaders in the Courts: Legal Battles of the Civil Rights Movement* (New York: Twelve Tables Press, 2004); Maurice C. Daniels, *Saving the Soul of Georgia: Donald L. Hollowell and the Struggle for Civil Rights* (Athens: University of Georgia Press, 2013). For Peter Hall see Fred D. Gray, *Busride to Justice: The Life and Works of Fred D. Gray* (Montgomery: New South Books, 1995).

45. J. Mills Thornton III, *Dividing Lines: Municipal Politics and the Struggle for Civil Rights in Montgomery, Birmingham, and Selma* (Tuscaloosa: University of Alabama Press, 2002), 158–198; Glenn T. Eskew, "'Bombingham': Black Protest in Postwar Birmingham, Alabama," *Historian* 59.2 (1997): 371–390.

46. Coke's examination and cross-examination, 8 December 1959, transcript of proceedings, case files, *Coke v. City of Atlanta*, 31, 50–51.

47. Complaint, 23 December 1958, case files, Coke v. City of Atlanta, 4.

48. Barnes, *Journey from Jim Crow*, 140.

49. Statement following the pretrial hearing on behalf of Dobbs Houses, Inc., 14 October 1959, case files, *Coke v. City of Atlanta*.

50. Ibid.

51. Ibid.

52. Testimony Freddye Henderson, 8 December 1959, transcript of proceedings, case files, *Coke v. City of Atlanta*, 67–76.

53. Testimony Roselle V. Douglas, 8 December 1959, transcript of proceedings, case files, *Coke v. City of Atlanta*, 76–78.

54. Testimony Martin Luther King Sr., 8 December 1959, transcript of proceedings, case files, *Coke v. City of Atlanta*, 50–57.

55. B. D. Murphy was a partner at Powell, Goldstein, Frazer, and Murphy, a prominent law firm in Atlanta since 1909. He was a friend of three-term segregationist Georgia governor Eugene Talmadge and the personal attorney of Talmadge's son Herman, who also served as governor (1948–1955) before moving on to the U.S. Senate. Murphy was a fierce proponent of the status quo. In 1957, he was quoted in the *Atlanta Constitution* as saying: "There will be no integration in schools, in churches, in colleges in my lifetime or yours. No social, political, economic or military power is sufficient to bring it about." Qtd. in Sara Mitchell Parsons, *From Southern Wrongs to Civil Rights: The Memoir of a White Civil Rights Activist* (Tuscaloosa: University of Alabama Press, 2000), 28. He found a like-minded colleague in Newell Edenfield, who at the time of the trial served as president of the Georgia Bar Association.

56. Testimony H. D. Coke, 8 December 1959, transcript of proceedings, case files, *Coke v. City of Atlanta*, 25–26.

57. Ibid., 49.

58. Airport manager B. F. Buttrey freely admitted to having singlehandedly and without consulting with company headquarters introduced segregation at the restaurant. Asked about his reasons for doing so he stated: "Well, I would say there was two reasons, and the two reasons that I have given most to people in talking to them, and I tried to be polite and courteous to all of them; that, first I would tell them that due to this section of the country being segregated we felt like for the protection of the company, and I did not feel like that I was justified in any way that I could jeopardize our company's position as far as doing volume of business by allowing anything else but segregation. Number 2, I have told quite a few of them in talking to them that actually it would be for their protection, too, so that they would not be embarrassed, or have any embarrassing

situation to happen to them." Examination of B. F. Buttrey, 8 December 1959, transcript of proceedings, case files, *Coke v. City of Atlanta*, 90–91.

59. William Boyd Sloan was nominated by President Harry S. Truman to a seat on the United States District Court for the Northern District of Georgia. He received his commission in March 1951. "William Boyd Sloan," United States, Federal Judicial Center, History of the Federal Judiciary, Judges of the United States Courts, *Biographical Directory of Federal Judges*: http://www.fjc.gov/history/home.nsf/page/judges.html.

60. *Coke v. City of Atlanta*, 184 F. Supp. 579 (1960). *Derrington v. Plummer*, 240 F.2d 922 (1956) integrated the Courthouse in Harris County Texas.

61. *Coke v. City of Atlanta*, 184 F. Supp 579 (1960).

62. Decree, 20 January 1960, case files, *Coke v. City of Atlanta*.

63. *Atlanta Daily World*, 7 January 1960, 1.

64. Dixon, "Civil Rights in Air Transportation," 216.

65. *Baltimore Afro-American*, 12 March 1960, 5.

66. WSB-TV newsfilm clip of the Atlanta airport's Dobbs House restaurant following its court-ordered desegregation, Atlanta, Georgia, 1960, *The Civil Rights Digital Library*, http://crdl.usg.edu/export/html/ugabma/wsbn/crdl_ugabma_wsbn_42532.html?Welcome.

67. The suit was filed January 24, 1959.

68. Testimony Richard B. Henry, 14 September 1960, transcript of proceedings, *Henry v. Greenville Airport Commission*, CCF, Sept. 23, 1938–Nov. 9, 1962, Case Nos. 2491–2504, Box 280, U.S. District Court for the Western District of South Carolina, Records of the District Courts of the United States, RG 21, NARA Atlanta, 15–16.

69. Ibid., 16.

70. *Henry v. Greenville Airport Commission*, 175 F. Supp 343 (1959).

71. Lincoln C. Jenkins Jr. was a native Columbian and a graduate of Howard University School of Law. Returning to Columbia after graduation in the late 1940s, he immediately became involved in the struggle for civil rights. In 1951, he partnered with Matthew Perry, another black lawyer, to open the law firm Jenkins & Perry in Columbia. He would later become the general counsel for the state NAACP. See James L. Felder, *Civil Rights in South Carolina: From Peaceful Protests to Groundbreaking Rulings* (Charleston, S.C.: History Press, 2012), 23, 54.

72. Thomas Wofford was a former federal attorney and graduate of Harvard Law School. He had served as the defense attorney in the Willie Earle lynching case (the last in South Carolina) and made no secret of his white supremacist leanings. In April 1956 he was appointed to the U.S. Senate to fill a six-month vacancy caused by the resignation of Strom Thurmond. See Winfred B. Moore Jr. and Orville V. Burton, eds., *Toward the Meeting of the Waters: South Carolina during the Twentieth Century* (Columbia: University of South Carolina Press, 2008); and "Thomas Albert Wofford," *Biographical Dictionary of the U.S. Congress*: http://bioguide.congress.gov/scripts/biodisplay.pl?index=W000666. George Bell Timmerman was nominated in 1941 by Franklin D. Roosevelt. He served on the United States District Court for the Western District of South Carolina and the United States District Court for the Eastern District of South Carolina until his death in 1966. Strom Thurmond biographer's describes Timmerman as being content with the status quo. He resisted the idea "that something was wrong with 'custom and tradition.'" Nadine Cohodas, *Strom Thurmond and the Politics of Southern Change* (New York: Simon & Schuster, 1993), 106.

73. Jack Greenberg, proceedings, 20 July 1959, transcript, case files, *Henry v. Greenville Airport Commission*, 9.

74. George Timmerman intervention, proceedings, 20 July 20, 1959, transcript, case files, *Henry v. Greenville Airport Commission*, 11.

75. Thomas Wofford, proceedings, 20 July 1959, transcript, case files, *Henry v. Greenville Airport Commission*, 23–24, 33–35, 39.

76. *Henry v. Greenville Airport Commission*, 175 F. Supp 343 (1959).

77. Ibid.

78. *Plessy v. Ferguson*, 163 U.S. 537 (1896).

79. See Ward, *Defending White Democracy*; Webb, *Massive Resistance*.

80. See Philipps, *War! What Is It Good for?*

81. This information is based on Richard Henry's testimony, proceedings, 14 September 1960, transcript, case files, *Henry v. Greenville Airport Commission*, 13–15.

82. *Henry v. Greenville Airport Commission*, 279 F.2d 751 (1960).

83. Ibid.

84. Proceedings, 14 September 14, 1960, transcript, case files, *Henry v. Greenville Airport Commission*, 40.

85. Proceedings, 14 September 1960, transcript, case files, *Henry v. Greenville Airport Commission*, 41. Timmerman also targeted the plaintiffs' witnesses with his skepticism. Why had Rev. J. S. Hall, the pastor of Baptist Church, who had last used the airport on July 7, 1960, to take a flight to Charlotte with two colleagues, not made use of his right to use the "colored" waiting room? How was he able to tell the difference between the two waiting areas when he had never actually used the waiting area reserved for blacks?

86. Testimony J. S. Hall, proceedings, 14 September 1960, transcript, case files, *Henry v. Greenville Airport Commission*, 53–54.

87. Order signed by George B. Timmerman, 19 October 1960, case files, *Henry v. Greenville Airport Commission*.

88. *Henry v. Greenville Airport Commission*, 284 F.2d 631 (1960).

89. Order signed by George B. Timmerman, 17 February 1961, case files, *Henry v. Greenville Airport Commission*.

90. Barnes, *Journey from Jim Crow*, 141.

91. See Dixon, "Civil Rights in Air Transportation," 216; *Bailey v. Patterson*, 369 U.S. 31 (1962).

92. See Dixon, "Civil Rights in Air Transportation," 216–217.

93. See chapter 2.

94. Sky Chefs was an airline catering company owned by American Airlines. It started doing business in 1942. It later expanded into serving airport restaurants. Sky Chefs became an independent company and a subsidiary of Onex Food Services in 1986. In 1993, Lufthansa acquired a minority interest in the company forming LSG Sky Chefs, which has since expanded globally. See Don Bedwell, *Silverbird: The American Airlines Story* (Sandpoint: Airways International, 1999).

95. Constance Baker Motley, *Equal Justice under Law* (New York: Farrar, Straus & Giroux, 1998), 144.

96. Complaint, 1 April 1960, *Turner v. City of Memphis*, CCF, Box No. 437 369–R, U.S. District Court for Western District of Tennessee, Western Division, Records of the District Courts of the United States, RG 21, NARA Atlanta.

97. Hearing, 9 November 1960, transcript of proceedings, case files, *Turner v. City of Memphis*.

98. Relevant was in particular Tennessee State Code Section 53-2320: "Restaurant catering to both white and Negro patrons should be arranged so that each race is properly segregated. Segregation will be considered proper where each race shall have separate entrances and separate facilities of every kind necessary to prevent patrons of the different races coming in contact with the other in entering, being served, or at any other time until they leave the premises."

99. Tri-State Bank of Memphis, http://www.tristatebank.com/about-us/history -financial-info/; "Tri-State Bank," The Tennessee Encyclopedia of History and Culture, http://tennesseeencyclopedia.net. For the civil rights movement in Memphis, see Laurie B. Greene, *Battling the Plantation Mentality: Memphis and the Black Freedom Struggle* (Chapel Hill: University of North Carolina Press, 2007), Elizabeth Gritter, *River of Hope: Black Politics and the Memphis Freedom Movement, 1865–1954* (Lexington: University Press of Kentucky, 2014), and Bobby L. Lovett, *The Civil Rights Movement in Tennessee: A Narrative History* (Knoxville: University of Tennessee Press, 2005).

100. Testimony Jesse Turner, hearing, 9 November 1960, transcript of proceedings, case files, *Turner v. City of Memphis*, 8–9.

101. Whereas the integration of the reading rooms took place on a voluntary basis, a court order integrated restrooms and lavatories. *Turner v. Randolph*, 195 F. Supp. 677 (W.D. Tenn. 1961).

102. *Derrington v. Plummer*, 240 F.2d 922 (1956).

103. Hearing on motion for summary judgment, 3 June 1960, transcript of proceedings, case files, *Turner v. City of Memphis*, 8.

104. Frank Gianotti was Memphis's longtime city attorney who served until 1964 when he was relieved of his duties by incoming mayor William Ingram. John Heiskell was a former county attorney general and part of the Shelby County Democratic political machine. See G. Wayne Dowdy, *Crusades for Freedom: Memphis and the Political Transformations of the American South* (Jackson: University of Mississippi Press, 2010), 44.

105. Constance Baker Motley earned her law degree at Columbia Law School in 1946. She joined the LDF after graduation and started her legal career working for Thurgood Marshall. She helped write the legal briefs filed in *Brown v. Board of Education* and later became the fund's associate counsel. She participated in most of the civil rights cases between 1945 and 1965, winning an amazing nine of the ten cases she argued before the Supreme Court. In 1966, she became the first female African American federal judge (U.S. District Court for the Southern District of New York). See Motley, *Equal Justice under Law*; Floris Barnett Cash, "Constance Baker Motley: Lawyer, Politician, Judge," *Notable Black American Women*, book 1, ed. Jessie Carney Smith (Detroit: Gale Research, 1991), 779–782.

106. "Marion Speed Boyd," United States, Federal Judicial Center, History of the Federal Judiciary, Judges of the United States Courts, *Biographical Directory of Federal Judges*: http://www.fjc.gov/history/home.nsf/page/judges.html.

107. Archie Walter "A. W." Willis was a University of Wisconsin Law School graduate. He served as the lead attorney for the Memphis NAACP. In the mid-1950s he opened the first integrated law firm in Memphis. He was active in the battle for school desegregation and served as legal counsel for James Meredith in his fight against the University of Mississippi. In 1964, Willis became the first African American elected to the Tennessee

General Assembly since the 1880s. See Willis's biographical entry in the *Tennessee Encyclopedia of History and Culture*: http://tennesseeencyclopedia.net/entry.php?rec=1517. Russell Sugarmon was a Harvard Law School graduate and a partner at Willis's law firm. He served in the Tennessee House of Representatives from 1967 to 1969; see Dowdy, *Crusades for Freedom*. Benjamin Hooks was a young lawyer ("the catch of Memphis") and later became the executive secretary of the NAACP; see *Ebony*, February 1981, 92. Least is known about H. T. Lockett, who eventually seems to have practiced law in Kentucky.

108. Motley, *Equal Justice under Law*, 144–145.

109. Although lawyers like Sadie T. M. Alexander and Pauli Murray were pioneers in the profession, black women found it more difficult to be accepted. Unlike Motley and Murray, who became civil rights lawyers, Alexander and other black women lawyers only came before family and probate courts. See Mack, *Representing the Race*, chaps. 6 and 9.

110. John D. Martin was also an FDR nominee and Boyd's predecessor in the Federal Court in Memphis. He was nominated to the Sixth Circuit Court of Appeals on August 27, 1940, and received commission a few days later. William E. Miller was nominated to the bench by President Eisenhower in 1955. "John D. Martin" and "William E. Miller," United States, Federal Judicial Center, History of the Federal Judiciary, Judges of the United States Courts, Biographical Directory of Federal Judges: http://www.fjc.gov /history/home.nsf/page/judges.html. The judges were on rather friendly terms with the defense lawyers. Martin repeatedly called Frank Gianotti "brother Gianotti" and "Frank." Proceedings, 9 November 1960, transcript, case files, *Turner v. City of Memphis*, 14–15.

111. 28 U.S.C. § 2101 (f).

112. *Turner v. Memphis*, 369 U.S. 350 (1962).

113. *New York Times*, 27 March 1962, 1.

114. Order, 11 May 1962, case files, *Turner v. City of Memphis*.

115. *New York Times*, 27 March 1962, 1.

116. *New York Times*, 12 April 1960.

117. A few months later, the Department of Justice brought a third case not only aimed at eliminating discriminatory spatial practices but also looking into the city's misappropriation of Federal-aid Airport Program funds for the construction of terminal facilities. *United States v. City of New Orleans*, Civil Action No. 11254. See chapter 6.

118. See chapter 6 for a biographical portrait of A. P. Tureaud.

119. Court hearing for summary judgment, 12 July 1961, transcript of proceedings, *Adams v. City of New Orleans*, CCF 10055–10062, Box 893, U.S. District Court for the Eastern District of Louisiana, New Orleans, Records of the District Courts of the United States, RG 21, NARA Fort Worth, 27.

120. Opposition to plaintiffs' motion for a summary judgment, 11 July 1961, case files, *Adams v. City of New Orleans*.

121. *Adams v. City of New Orleans*, 208 F. Supp. 427 (E.D. LA. 1962).

122. *City of New Orleans v. Adams*, 321 F.2d 493 (1963). The court quotes *Bailey v. Patterson*, 369 U.S. 31 (1962).

123. *Shuttlesworth v. Dobbs Houses, Inc.*, Civil Action No. 9765 July 31, 1962 (N.D. Alabama); *Washington Post*, 18 July 1962, A2. Harlan Hobart Grooms was an Eisenhower nominee who received commission in 1953. "Harlan Hobart Grooms," United States, Federal Judicial Center, History of the Federal Judiciary, Judges of the United States Courts, *Biographical Directory of Federal Judges*, http://www.fjc.gov/history/home.nsf /page/judges.html.

124. Thornton, *Dividing Lines*, Birmingham chapter; Glenn T. Eskew, *But for Birmingham: The Local and National Movements in the Civil Rights Struggle* (Chapel Hill: University of North Carolina Press, 1997); Andrew M. Manis and Marjorie L. White, eds., *Birmingham's Revolutionaries: The Reverend Fred Shuttlesworth and the Alabama Christian Movement for Human Rights* (Macon: Mercer University Press, 2000).

125. Answer to supplemental complaint as amended, 15 June 1962, *Shuttlesworth v. Dobbs Houses, Inc.*, CCF, Box 476, Case Nos. 9758–9769, U.S. District Court for Northern District of Alabama, Southern Division (Birmingham), Records of the District Courts of the United States, RG 21, NARA Forth Worth.

126. Shortly before the conclusion of *Shuttlesworth v. Dobbs Houses*, a group of Birmingham blacks sued the airport motel over racial discrimination. Judge Grooms granted an injunction ordering the integration of the Airway Motel, a judgment that was affirmed by the Fifth Circuit Court of Appeals in February 1964. *Smith v. City of Birmingham*, 226 F. Supp. 838 (1964); *Afro-American*, 21 December 1963, 3; Thornton, *Divided Lines*, 210.

127. *Pittsburgh Courier*, 4 August 1962, 13. Shuttlesworth also commented on the defense's strategy to paint him as a criminal. In defense of segregation, "even the most brilliant lawyer, like Maurice Bishop, will stoop to low-level, below-the-belt antics." Bishop's attempts to portray African Americans as immoral and criminally minded struck Shuttlesworth as a measure of last resort.

Notes to Chapter 5

1. 52 Stat. 973–1030, chapter 601.

2. Memorandum from J. Francis Pohlhaus to Robert Carter concerning the "Segregation and Racial Discrimination in the Operation of Airport Terminal Facilities Restaurants, Limousine Services, etc.," Series 7, Civil Rights, Box 42, Folder 5, Charles Diggs Collection, Howard University; Baltimore *Afro-American*, 11 June 1955, 21.

3. 60 Stat. 170–180, chapter 251.

4. United States Department of Commerce, Civil Aeronautics Administration, *Second Annual Report of the Federal Airport Act 1947* (Washington, D.C.: U.S. Department of Commerce, 1947), 4.

5. Federal Airport Act 60 Stat. 171 § 3(a).

6. Three factors were applied to assess projects. Developments had to contribute to the safety and efficiency of operations and provide facilities for the convenience of airport patrons. *Fourteenth Annual Report of Operations under the Federal Airport Act 1959*, 5.

7. Congress extended the program repeatedly until 1970, when the Federal Airport Act was repealed and replaced by the Airport and Airway Development Act, Public Law 91–258; Bednarek, *America's Airports*, 151–177.

8. Federal Airport Act 60 Stat. 176 § 11(1).

9. Of the $42,750,000 appropriated for the first FAAP year, southern states received 24 percent ($7,498,600). *Second Annual Report of the Federal Airport Act 1947*, 3.

10. *Annual Reports of Operations under the Federal Airport Act* (Washington, D.C.: FAA 1946–1963).

11. Atlanta, for instance, in the postwar years quickly developed into the central air transportation hub of the South, thanks in large part to the boosterist efforts of Atlanta Mayor William Hartsfield. Birmingham, in contrast, fell behind in the 1940s and 1950s,

mostly due to the inactivity of its chamber of commerce, whose members clung to rail to connect the steel town to the rest of the country. Glenn Eskew has pointed out that as air transportation grew in importance, progressive members of the chamber attempted "to wrestle control of the airport away from the city commission through the formation of an airport authority. The fight strained the relationship between the city's political leaders and its service-sector businessmen." Not until 1960 did Birmingham expand its airport to include a new passenger terminal, relying until then on the facilities built in the early 1930s. Braden and Hagan, *A Dream Takes Flight*; Bellury, *Georgia Flight*; Eskew, *But for Birmingham*, 167–168; Don Dodd and Amy Bartlett Dodd, *Deep South Aviation* (Charleston: Arcadia, 1999).

12. Letter from J. Francis Pohlhaus to Charles C. Diggs, 28 July 1955, Series 7, Civil Rights, Box 42, Folder 5, Charles Diggs Collection, Howard University.

13. *Second Annual Report of the Federal Airport Act 1947*, 3.

14. Letter from Charles C. Diggs to J. Francis Pohlhaus, 2 August 1955, Series 7, Civil Rights, Box 42, Folder 5, Charles Diggs Collection, Howard University.

15. "Diggs Seeks to Withhold Financial Funds from Segregated Airports," press release, The Office of Congressman Charles C. Diggs, 28 September 1955, Series 7, Civil Rights, Box 42, Folder 4, Charles Diggs Collection, Howard University.

16. Charles J. Lowen began his term as CAA administrator in December 1955, serving on an interim appointment. His nomination was confirmed the following summer. Lowen served for less than a year until September 1956, when he died of cancer. He was succeeded by James T. Pyle (Dec. 1956–Dec. 1958); Stuart I. Rochester, *Takeoff at Midcentury: Federal Aviation Policy in the Eisenhower Years, 1953–1961* (Washington, D.C.: 1976), 118, 139.

17. "Programming Standard G (3), October 1, 1955," cited in "Airport Policy and Procedure Memorandum No. 41, April 6, 1956," *Race Relations Law Reporter* 1 (1956): 783.

18. Ibid., 784; *Atlanta Daily World*, 14 June 1956, 4; *Chicago Daily Tribune*, 5 May 1956, 14.

19. This approach allowed local communities to use their own funds for the construction of said facilities and rely on federal funds for other projects.

20. Letter of Charles C. Diggs to Civil Aeronautics Administration, 7 June 1956, Series 7, Civil Rights, Box 42, Folder 4, Charles Diggs Collection, Howard University.

21. *Washington Post*, 30 May 1956, 25; *Atlanta Daily World*, 14 June 1956, 4. Wofford only served in the Senate for six months. He was appointed in April 1956 to fill the vacancy caused by the resignation of Strom Thurmond. For biographical information, see "Thomas Albert Wofford," *Biographical Dictionary of the U.S. Congress*: http://bioguide .congress.gov/scripts/biodisplay.pl?index=W000666.

22. United States Congress, Senate, Committee on Interstate and Foreign Commerce, *Hearing on the Nomination of Charles J. Lowen, Jr. to Be Administrator of Civil Aeronautics*, 11 May 1956 (Washington, D.C.: Government Printing Office, 1956), 88.

23. Ibid., 97–103; 112–114. Ervin was critical of the increasing powers that regulatory agencies assumed. At one point in the hearing, he said to the CAA's legal counsel: "If that is the basis you regulate things on, then your field of regulation is unlimited as the universe, isn't it?" (112). For biographical information on Sam Ervin, see "Samuel James Ervin, Jr." *Biographical Dictionary of the U.S. Congress*: http://bioguide.congress.gov /scripts/biodisplay.pl?index=E000211; Karl E. Campbell, *Senator Sam Ervin, Last of the Founding Fathers* (Chapel Hill: University of North Carolina Press, 2007).

24. James T. Pyle had served as Lowen's deputy before he succeeded him as administrator of the CAA. Serving as the agency's chief officer during a period of rapid growth in commercial aviation, he made air safety his top priority. He was also instrumental in merging the CAA and some functions of the CAB into the FAA. At the FAA, he returned to the position of deputy administrator under Elwood R. Quesada. Obituary, *New York Times*, 9 April 1998; Rochester, *Takeoff at Midcentury*, chaps. 6–12.

25. Letter from J. Francis Pohlhaus to James T. Pyle, May 8, 1956, Series 7, Civil Rights, Box 42, Folder 4, Charles Diggs Collection, Howard University.

26. The NAACP was among those weighing the significance of an amendment. Letter from J. Francis Pohlhaus to Roy Wilkins, 3 February 1959, Folder 9, "Airports 1959–62," Box IX: 2, NAACP Records, LOC.

27. During his long career in both houses of Congress, he took up a number of liberal causes, setting himself apart from the mainstream of his party. As a firm believer in social justice, he was a Republican ally of the civil rights movement. Before attacking airport segregation, he had supported anti–poll tax legislation and endorsed a ban on segregation in federally funded housing projects. He also was a supporter of President Johnson's Great Society programs. See "Jacob Javits," *Biographical Dictionary of the U.S. Congress*: http://bioguide.congress.gov/scripts/biodisplay.pl?index=J000064; Jacob Javits and Rafael Steinberg, *Javits: The Autobiography of a Public Man* (Boston: Houghton Mifflin, 1981).

28. The amendment provided: "That no payments shall be made out of appropriations for the liquidation of contract obligations entered into such authority, which provide for the construction of airport terminal buildings containing racially segregated dining or other facilities, whether or not the portions of such building containing such segregated facilities have been constructed without Federal contributions." 106 Cong. Rec. 10108 (1960). Aware of southern Democrats' fundamental opposition to antisegregation amendments, Javits had originally hoped the FAA could be convinced to issue another policy memorandum along these lines. However, the agency was unwilling to take such a step, according to Javits. 106 Cong. Rec. 13764 (1960).

29. 106 Cong. Rec. 10107-10108 (1960). See also news release, Jacob K. Javits, United States Senate, 12 May 1960, Folder 9, "Airports 1959–62," Box IX: 2, NAACP Records, LOC. For an evaluation of the Eisenhower administration's civil rights record, see Nichols, *A Matter of Justice*.

30. Testimony of Clarence Mitchell, Director of Washington Bureau of the National Association for the Advancement of Colored People before the Senate Subcommittee on Appropriations for Independent Offices, 24 May 1960, Folder 9, "Airports 1959–62," Box IX: 2, NAACP Records, LOC.

31. 106 Cong. Rec. 13765 (1960).

32. 106 Cong. Rec. 13766 (1960).

33. Ibid.

34. 106 Cong. Rec. 13767–13769 (1960).

35. It provided: "In order to insure that funds made available under the Federal Airport Act are utilized for items of airport development required in the interest of safety, it will be the policy of the FAA to participate in the cost of construction of only those airport buildings or portions thereof that are required for safety of aircraft operating to, from and in the vicinity of the airport. Accordingly no airport buildings will be considered eligible items of airport development." The directive listed as exceptions build-

ings housing flight services, Air Traffic Control, the Weather Bureau, and fire and crash equipment. Airports and Procedure Memorandum No. 76, 28 October 1960; 14 C.F.R. § 550.24 (i), 1962.

36. Dixon, "Civil Rights in Air Transportation," 213–214.

37. *Sixteenths Annual Report of Operations under the Federal Airport Act 1961*, 5.

38. For building and design guidelines, see, for instance, United States, Civil Aeronautics Administration, *Airport Design* (Washington, D.C.: CAA, 1949); and United States, Civil Aeronautics Administration, *Airport Terminal Buildings* (Washington, D.C.: CAA, 1953).

39. 107 Cong. Rec. 14151 (1961).

40. Monroney had earned the title of "Mr. Aviation" in Congress for his long support of aviation. Richard J. Kent Jr., *Safe, Separated and Soaring: A History of Federal Civil Aviation Policy 1961–1972* (Washington, D.C.: U.S. Department of Transportation, FAA, 1980) 19–20.

41. 107 Cong. Rec. 14152–14153 (1961).

42. Amendment to the Federal Airport Act, 49 U.S.C. § 1112 (b), Supp. III (1962).

43. 107 Cong. Rec. 17964–17968 (1961).

44. Another amendment required that safety facilities, which were originally often situated in terminal buildings, be housed in freestanding towers, in order to underline the point that no federal funding went into terminal structures. 49 U.S.C. § 1110 (5), Supp. III, 1962.

45. 107 Cong. Rec. 17968 (1961).

46. United States, Congress, House of Representatives, *Hearings before a Subcommittee of the Committee on Interstate and Foreign Commerce*, 87th Congress, 1st Session, Federal Airport Aid Extension, H.R. 6580 and 6680 (Washington, D.C.: Government Printing Office, 1961), 5; United States, Congress, Senate, *Hearings before the Aviation Subcommittee of the Committee on Commerce*, 87th Congress, 1st Session, Federal Aid to Airport Program, S. 1703 (Washington, D.C.: Government Printing Office, 1961), 5.

47. Najeeb E. Halaby succeeded Elwood R. Quesada (Nov. 1959–Jan. 1961) and served as the FAA administrator from March 1961 until July 1965. He left the FAA to join Pan Am, whose CEO he became in 1969. See Kent, *Safe, Separated, and Soaring*, chaps. 1–4; Obituary, *New York Times*, 3 July 2003.

48. House of Representatives, *Hearings before a Subcommittee of the Committee on Interstate and Foreign Commerce 1961*, 8–10. Senate, *Hearings before the Aviation Subcommittee of the Committee on Commerce, 1961*, 42.

49. Ibid., 57.

50. United States, Congress, Senate, 87th Congress, 1st Session, *Report No. 654, Amendments to the Federal Airport Act*, 1 August 1961.

51. House of Representatives, *Hearings before a Subcommittee of the Committee on Interstate and Foreign Commerce 1961*, 14, 17. The remarks tie into a political discourse critical of the increasing powers of regulatory agencies in the postwar period. Joanna L. Grisinger explores the development of administrative agencies and their critics in *The Unwieldy American State: Administrative Politics since the New Deal* (New York: Cambridge University Press, 2012).

52. Sandra S. Vance, "The Congressional Career of John Bell Williams, 1947–1967," Ph.D. dissertation, Mississippi State University, 1976; "John Bell Williams," *Biographical Dictionary of the U.S. Congress*: http://bioguide.congress.gov/scripts/biodisplay.pl?index =W000517.

53. See Dennis J. Mitchell, *A New History of Mississippi* (Jackson: University of Mississippi Press, 2014); Cobb, *The South and America since World War II*.

54. Letter from Najeeb E. Halaby to John Bell Williams, 19 July 1961, Folder 5, Box 30, "Segregation," Office of the Administrator, Administrator's Subject/Correspondence File, 1959–1982 (OA/Correspondence), RG 237, Records of the Federal Aviation Administration (FAA Records), National Archives and Records Administration at College Park (NARACP).

55. United States, Congress, House of Representatives, 87th Congress, 1st Session, *Report No. 728, Amendments to the Federal Airport Act*, 18 July 1961; Kent, *Safe, Separated, and Soaring*, 46–50.

56. Public Law 87–255 (75 Stat. 523).

57. Letter from Najeeb E. Halaby to Robert F. Kennedy, 24 March 1961, Folder "Federal Aid Airport Program," Box 28, Office of the Administrator, Administrator's Subject/Correspondence File, 1959–1982 (OA/Correspondence), RG 237, FAA Records, NARACP.

58. Ibid.

59. Ibid.

60. *Boynton v. Virginia*, 364 U.S. 454 (1960).

61. "Notes on *Boynton v. Virginia* as Basis for Federal Legal Action to End Racial Segregation at Airports," March 1961, Folder "Federal Aid Airport Program," Box 28, OA/Correspondence, RG 237, FAA Records, NARACP. The advisory opinion identified Federal Airport Act sections 404(b) (prohibition of discrimination), 401(g) (cancellation of air carrier certificate), and 1007(a) (authority to take legal action to enforce provisions of the Act) as the basis for legal action.

62. Najeeb E. Halaby to Robert F. Kennedy, 24 March 1961, Folder "Federal Aid Airport Program," Box 28, Office of the Administrator, Administrator's Subject/Correspondence File, 1959–1982 (OA/Correspondence), RG 237, FAA Records, NARACP.

63. See Bryant, *The Bystander*; Philip A. Goduti Jr., *Robert F. Kennedy and the Shaping of Civil Rights, 1960–1964* (Jefferson, N.C.: McFarland, 2012); Mark Stern, "John F. Kennedy and Civil Rights: From Congress to the Presidency," *Presidential Studies Quarterly* 19.4 (1989): 797–823.

64. Report on Federal Aviation Agency Actions to Terminate Segregation Practices at Public Airports, 25 May 1961, Folder 5 "Segregation," Box 30, Office of the Administrator, Administrator's Subject/Correspondence File, 1959–1982 (OA/Correspondence), RG 237, FAA Records, NARACP.

65. See chapter 6. Copies of Halaby's letters to Kennedy requesting legal action are located in Folder "5100 Jackson, Miss. Airport," Box 82, Office of the Administrator, Administrator's Subject/Correspondence File, 1959–1982 (OA/Correspondence), RG 237, FAA Records, NARACP.

66. See correspondence between Halaby and members of Congress in Folder 5 "Segregation," Box 28, Office of the Administrator, Administrator's Subject/Correspondence File, 1959–1982 (OA/Correspondence), RG 237, FAA Records, NARACP.

67. Airport authorities were given one week to remove signs from drinking fountains and restrooms. Restaurant proprietor Cicero Carr was given ten days to integrate the restaurant. *Bailey v. Patterson*, 369 U.S. 31 (1962).

68. Telegram from Charles C. Diggs to Director of the Federal Aviation Agency, 18 April 1963, Folder "5100 Jackson, Miss. Airport," Box 82, Office of the Administrator,

Administrator's Subject/Correspondence File, 1959–1982 (OA/Correspondence), RG 237, FAA Records, NARACP.

69. Campell Gibson and Kay Jung, "Historical Census Statistics on Population Totals by Race, 1790 to 1990, and by Hispanic Origin, 1970 to 1990, for the United States, Regions, Divisions, and States," *Working Paper Series No. 56*, United States, Census Bureau, Washington, D.C., September 2013 (http://www.census.gov/population/www/documentation/twps0056/twps0056.html).

70. The Civil Rights Division was created by the enactment of the Civil Rights Act of 1957. It had jurisdiction over and was responsible for the enforcement of all federal statutes relating to civil rights. For the reports see Box 76, Civil Rights Division, Office of the Assistant Attorney General, Subject Files of the Assistant Attorney General Burke Marshall, 1961–1965, Box 30, RG 60, General Records of the Department of Justice, NARACP.

71. United States, Commission on Civil Rights, Mississippi Advisory Committee, *Administration of Justice in Mississippi: A Report to the United States Commission on Civil Rights* (Washington, D.C.: United States Commission on Civil Rights, 1963).

72. For the history of the Civil Rights Commission see John F. Dulles, *The Civil Rights Commission: 1957–1965* (Ann Arbor: Michigan University Press, 1968).

73. Interim Report of the United States Commission on Civil Rights, "5100 Jackson, Miss. Airport," Box 82, Office of the Administrator, Administrator's Subject/Correspondence File, 1959–1982 (OA/Correspondence), RG 237, FAA Records, NARACP. See also Bryant, *The Bystander*, 377–378.

74. Interim Report of the United States Commission on Civil Rights, "5100 Jackson, Miss. Airport," Box 82, Office of the Administrator, Administrator's Subject/Correspondence File, 1959–1982 (OA/Correspondence), RG 237, FAA Records, NARACP. See also United States, Commission on Civil Rights, *Civil Rights: Report of the United States Commission on Civil Rights '63* (Washington, D.C.: United States Commission on Civil Rights, 1963). Both Kennedy brothers had a contentious relationship with the Commission, whose fault-finding reports made for uncomfortable reading. See Bryant, *The Bystander*, 288–290.

75. James Reston, "How to Make Things Worse Than They Are," *New York Times*, 19 April 1963, 42. Also see other editorials in the *New York Times* and the *Washington Post* published on April 19, 1963.

76. Burke Marshall best explains the administration's position on civil rights and federal authority in *Federalism and Civil Rights* (New York: Columbia University Press, 1964).

77. Bryant, *The Bystander*, 290.

78. Jackson was included in the National Airport Plan in 1955; 1956 was the first year it applied for FAAP grants; 1957 was programmed for land acquisition and site preparation. In 1958, site preparation continued and the runway was paved. In 1959, the instrument runway was constructed. In 1960, the taxiways and terminal apron were paved and marked. In 1961, the control tower and Weather Bureau offices were constructed. Runway lights, beacons, and apron floodlights were installed. In 1962, the electrical power plant and electricity and gas distribution systems were built; the sewer system and sewage treatment plant were constructed; and the crash station and maintenance service road were put into place. Before the new airport's opening in 1963, the main gas pipeline was relocated. See *Annual Reports of Operations under the Federal Airport Act* (Washington, D.C.: FAA, 1946–1963).

79. See William Doyle, *An American Insurrection: James Meredith and the Battle at Oxford, Mississippi, 1962* (New York: Anchor Books, 2003).

80. Chester G. Bowers, Memorandum to the Files, 12 April 1963, Folder "5100 Jackson, Miss. Airport," Box 82, Office of the Administrator, Administrator's Subject/Correspondence File, 1959–1982 (OA/Correspondence), RG 237, FAA Records, NARACP. As the original plans for the airport in Jackson are incomplete, it is not entirely clear whether these plans provided for all facilities such as restrooms, water fountains, and the restaurant to be segregated.

81. Ibid.

82. Memorandum from Najeeb E. Halaby to John F. Kennedy, 19 April 1963, Folder "5100 Jackson, Miss. Airport," Box 82, Office of the Administrator, Administrator's Subject/Correspondence File, 1959–1982 (OA/Correspondence), RG 237, FAA Records, NARACP.

83. Ibid.

84. The letter stated: "In order to remove any doubt that might arise from the existence of duplicate public facilities in the new terminal building, and to make clear the intention of the City to give effect of its commitment to the U.S. District Court that heard the Bailey case, the enclosed clause will be made part of any grant agreement offer made in connection with pending project applications. . . . It provides that in the operation of the new airport, the City of Jackson will not, in offering services and facilities to the public, discriminate on account of race, creed or color." Letter from Paul H. Boatman to The Mayor, City of Jackson (Allen C. Thompson), 16 April 1963, Folder "5100 Jackson, Miss. Airport," Box 82, Office of the Administrator, Administrator's Subject/Correspondence File, 1959–1982 (OA/Correspondence), RG 237, FAA Records, NARACP.

85. Michael J. O'Brien, *We Shall Not Be Moved: The Jackson Woolworth's Sit-Ins and the Movement It Inspired* (Jackson: University of Mississippi Press, 2013), 18–19.

86. Letter from Clarence Mitchell to Roy Wilkins, 5 June 1963, Box III: A 322, NAACP Records, LOC.

87. Allen C. Thompson quoted in Associated Press news release, 18 April 1963, Folder "5100 Jackson, Miss. Airport," Box 82, Office of the Administrator, Administrator's Subject/Correspondence File, 1959–1982 (OA/Correspondence), RG 237, FAA Records, NARACP.

88. A copy of revised Clause 5 was attached to the letter from Boatman to Thompson, 16 April 1963, Folder "5100 Jackson, Miss. Airport," Box 82, Office of the Administrator, Administrator's Subject/Correspondence File, 1959–1982 (OA/Correspondence), RG 237, FAA Records, NARACP. For sponsor's assurances prior to revision, see Letter from Najeeb E. Halaby to Robert F. Kennedy, 16 June 1961, case files, *United States v. City of Montgomery*.

89. Memorandum from Chester B. Bowers to Najeeb N. Halaby, 26 April 1963, Folder "5100 Jackson, Miss. Airport," Box 82, Office of the Administrator, Administrator's Subject/Correspondence File, 1959–1982 (OA/Correspondence), RG 237, FAA Records, NARACP.

90. See Dittmer, *Local People*, chapter 9; Memorandum from Nathaniel H. Goodrich to Najeeb E. Halaby, 25 April 1963, Folder "5100 Jackson, Miss. Airport," Box 82, Office of the Administrator, Administrator's Subject/Correspondence File, 1959–1982 (OA/Correspondence), RG 237, FAA Records, NARACP.

91. Revised Clause, Folder "Justice Department 1963," Box 64, Office of the Administrator, Administrator's Subject/Correspondence File, 1959–1982 (OA/Correspondence), RG 237, FAA Records, NARACP. Burke Marshall had hoped to eliminate the phrase "occupying space or facilities thereon" to make it impossible for airport authorities "to turn their backs when local bullyboys undertake to patrol public facilities on a vigilante or volunteer basis." FAA's position was to make sure that above all airport concessionaires did not discriminate against air travelers. General Counsel Goodrich feared the broadly framed "any person and organization" would make the clause objectionable to Southern cities. Memorandum from Nathaniel H. Goodrich to Najeeb E. Halaby, ibid.

92. Letter from T. A. Turner to Najeeb E. Halaby, 25 July 1963, Folder "5100 Jackson, Miss. Airport," Box 82, Office of the Administrator, Administrator's Subject/Correspondence File, 1959–1982 (OA/Correspondence), RG 237, FAA Records, NARACP.

93. Letter from Najeeb E. Halaby to T. A. Turner, 20 August 1963, Folder "5100 Jackson, Miss. Airport," Box 82, Office of the Administrator, Administrator's Subject/Correspondence File, 1959–1982 (OA/Correspondence), RG 237, FAA Records, NARACP.

94. United States, Congress, Senate, 88th Congress, 1st Session, *Report No. 422, Amendments to the Federal Airport Act*, 20 August 1963; 109 Cong. Rec. 15740–15765 (1963). Also see United States, Congress, Senate, *Hearings before the Aviation Subcommittee of the Committee on Commerce*, 88th Congress, 1st Session, Federal Aid to Airport Program, S. 1153 (Washington, D.C.: Government Printing Office, 1963).

95. United States, Congress, House of Representatives, 88th Congress, 1st Session, *Report No. 1002, Amendments to the Federal Airport Act*, 5 December 1963, 5–6.

96. The amendment provided: "Except for the purpose of carrying out a provision of law specifically set forth in this Act or in another Act of Congress, no rule, no regulation, requirement, or restriction, or order heretofore or hereafter issued, established, proclaimed or published by any officer, employee, department, agency, or establishment, in, of or under the executive branch of the Government shall apply to the construction, maintenance, operation, or administration of any airport or project with respect to which funds have been or may be obligated or expended under this Act." United States, Congress, House of Representatives, 88th Congress, 1st Session, *Report No. 1002, Amendments to the Federal Airport Act*, 5 December 1963, 12.

97. Letter from Najeeb E. Halaby to John B. Williams, 13 November 1963, Folder "Justice Department 1963," Box 64, Office of the Administrator, Administrator's Subject/Correspondence File, 1959–1982 (OA/Correspondence), RG 237, FAA Records, NARACP.

98. Legal memorandum, Nathaniel H. Goodrich to Najeeb E. Halaby, 3 December 1963, Folder 5100 Federal Airport Program 1963," Box 81, Office of the Administrator, Administrator's Subject/Correspondence File, 1959–1982 (OA/Correspondence), RG 237, FAA Records, NARACP.

99. Memorandum by Najeeb E. Halaby to Lyndon B. Johnson, 29 November 1963, Folder "5100 Federal Airport Program 1963," Box 81, Office of the Administrator, Administrator's Subject/Correspondence File, 1959–1982 (OA/Correspondence), RG 237, FAA Records, NARACP.

100. United States, Congress, House of Representatives, 88th Congress, 1st Session, *Report No. 1002, Amendments to the Federal Airport Act*, 5 December 1963, 12.

101. As enacted, the bill amending the Federal Airport Act is Public Law 88–280 (78 Stat. 158). Kent, *Safe, Separated and Soaring*, 90.

102. See Clay Risen, *The Bill of the Century: Epic Battle for the Civil Rights Act* (New York: Bloomsbury Press, 2014); Eric Schickler, Kathryn Pearson, and Brian D. Feinstein, "Congressional Parties and Civil Rights Politics from 1933–1972," *Journal of Politics* 72.3 (2010): 672–689.

Notes to Chapter 6

1. Civil Rights Act 1957 (71 Stat. 634). For an in-depth analysis of the activities of the Civil Rights Division see Brian K. Landsberg, *Enforcing Civil Rights: Race Discrimination and the Department of Justice* (Lawrence: University Press of Kansas, 1997).

2. See Dixon, "Civil Rights in Air Transportation," 223.

3. Survey reply Tampa International Airport, W. A. Berlin, airport manager, 26 July 1955, Series 7, Civil Rights, Box 42, Folder 2, Charles Diggs Collection, Howard University.

4. Filing complaints against Birmingham and New Orleans, the Justice Department seconded the individual private lawsuit pending in the courts, which, however, rested on a different statutory basis.

5. *Boynton v. Virginia*, 364 U.S. 454 (1960).

6. Dixon, "Civil Rights in Air Transportation," 224. See also Marshall, *Federalism and Civil Rights*, 52.

7. 49 U.S.C. 1487, Sec. 1007.

8. Letters from Najeeb E. Halaby to Robert F. Kennedy, "5100 Jackson, Miss. Airport," Box 82, Office of the Administrator, Administrator's Subject/Correspondence File, 1959–1982 (OA/Correspondence), RG 237, FAA Records, NARACP.

9. The airport was named after John Moisant, a local aviation pioneer. In 1960 its name changed to New Orleans International Airport. In 2001, it was renamed Louis Armstrong International Airport.

10. The slogan appears on 1954 stationery of the New Orleans Aviation Board. International routes were served by Pan Am, Braniff International, and Taca Airlines, an El Salvadoran airline serving Central American destinations.

11. For photographs of the airport, see the digital photo archive of *The Times-Picayune* at http://www.nola.com/multimedia/photos/.

12. Unfortunately, the sources are silent on the treatment Latin American travelers of different ethnic backgrounds received at the airport. One photograph shows travelers arriving from abroad in the customs area; they look white and are being assisted by African American porters.

13. See Lawrence N. Powell, *The Accidental City: Improvising New Orleans* (Cambridge: Harvard University Press, 2013); Jennifer M. Spear, *Race, Sex, and Social Order in Early New Orleans* (Baltimore: Johns Hopkins University Press, 2009); Arnold R. Hirsch and Joseph Logsdon, ed., *Creole New Orleans: Race and Americanization* (Baton Rouge: Louisiana State University Press, 1992); Dale A. Somers, "Black and White in New Orleans: A Study in Urban Race Relations, 1865–1900," *Journal of Southern History* 40.1 (1974): 19–42.

14. *Atlanta Daily World*, 18 December 1955, 4. Chi Eta Phi Sorority is a professional organization for registered professional nurses and student nurses. It was founded in 1932. See Helen Sullivan Miller, *The History of Chi Eta Phi Sorority, Inc.* (Washington, D.C.: Association for the Study of Negro Life and History, 1968).

15. Letter from Fay O. Wilson and Rubye Wiggins to CAA, 22 May 1956, Series 7, Civil Rights, Box 42, Folder 2, Charles Diggs Collection, Howard University.

16. *Atlanta Daily World*, 18 December 1955, 4.

17. For documentation see Series 7, Civil Rights, Box 42, Folder 7, Charles Diggs Collection, Howard University.

18. Letter from Gloster B. Current to A. (Arthur) J. Chapital, 28 April 1955, Box II: A 233, Folder 4, NAACP Records, LOC.

19. Letter from B. H. Nelson to NAACP, 29 August 1960, Folder 9, "Airports 1959–62," Box IX: 2, NAACP Records, LOC.

20. Baltimore *Afro-American*, 8 July 1961, 3.

21. Ibid.; Affidavit by Constance Baker Motley, 5 July 1961, case files, *Adams v. City of New Orleans.*

22. *Annual Reports of Operations under the Federal Airport Act* (Washington, D.C.: FAA, 1955–1960).

23. "Airport Policy and Procedure Memorandum No. 41, April 6, 1956," *Race Relations Law Reporter* 1 (1956): 783.

24. Letter from James T. Pyle to Charles C. Diggs Jr., 21 March 1957, Series 7, Civil Rights Box 42, Folder 2, Charles Diggs Collection, Howard University.

25. Letter from Najeeb E. Halaby to Robert F. Kennedy, 24 March 1961, Box 28, Office of the Administrator, Administrator's Subject/Correspondence file, 1959–1982, RG 237, FAA Records, NARACP.

26. For a history of the company, see http://www.leighfisher.com/meet-leighfisher /overview.

27. Leigh Fisher & Associates, *Moisant International Airport: Air Trade Study, Airport Master Plan, Terminal Requirements, Schematic Plans, Design Comments for the City of New Orleans Aviation Board* (South Bend, Ind.: Fisher, 1954), 136–138.

28. Goldstein, Parham, & Labouisse, Schematic sketch of Moisant International Airport, 16 February 1959, case files, *Adams v. City of New Orleans.*

29. These designs translated into reality many of the suggestions the FAA made available in its large collection of manuals.

30. The architecture firm was founded by Moise H. Goldstein and his former assistants Frederick D. Parham and F. Monroe Labouisse after World War II. By then Goldstein had submitted a number of successful entries for public works in New Orleans. His partnership with Parham, who for many years served on the city's planning and zoning commission and was thus well connected, led to participation in a number of high-profile building projects, among them New Orleans City Hall, the Public Library, and Moisant International Airport. See Milton G. Scheuermann Jr., "Moise H. Goldstein." In *Know LA: Encyclopedia of Louisiana*, ed. David Johnson, Louisiana Endowment for the Humanities, 2010–. Article published January 12, 2011. http://www.knowla.org/entry/874/.

31. City of New Orleans, *Annual Report of the Mayor 1959–1960* (New Orleans: City of New Orleans, 1960), 3.

32. Letter from Robert L. Carter (Legal Counsel) to William P. Rogers (Attorney General), 26 October 1960, Folder 12 "Discrimination Airports 1959–63," Box III: A 107, NAACP Records, LOC; Nichols, *A Matter of Justice.*

33. Letter from Najeeb E. Halaby to Robert F. Kennedy, 24 March 1961, Box 28, Office of the Administrator, Administrator's Subject/Correspondence file, 1959–1982, RG 237, FAA Records, NARACP.

34. Almer Monroney served as the chairman of the Senate Committee on Commerce's Aviation Subcommittee. Oren Harris was chairman of the House Committee on Interstate and Foreign Commerce.

35. *Chicago Daily Tribune*, 27 June 1961, 7; *New York Times*, 27 June 1961, 1.

36. Complaint, 20 May 1960, *Harris v. City of New Orleans*, CCF 10055–10062, Box 893, U.S. District Court for the Eastern District of Louisiana, New Orleans, Records of the District Courts of the United States, RG 21, NARA Fort Worth; Complaint, 23 May 1960, case files, *Adams v. City of New Orleans*.

37. Interstate Hosts Inc. was another airport restaurant operator. It had grown out of the merger of the Van Noy Railway Hotel and News Company (St. Louis) and the Interstate News Company (New York) in 1915. Besides airport restaurants, the company's portfolio included concession stands, railway station and bus terminal restaurants and lunch rooms, and hotels. In 1954, Interstate Hosts was awarded its first airport contract at San Francisco International Airport. In the following years, it operated restaurants at airports in California, Colorado, Hawaii, Illinois, Louisiana, Michigan, Texas, and Washington. After a name change to Host International, the company was acquired by Marriott International in 1982, which in turn was bought by Italian food service provider Autogrill S.p.A. Its U.S. subsidiary branch is now called HMS Host. There is little readily available history of these companies. Information is available on their websites.

38. For A. P. Tureaud's legal work, civic activism (in the black and Creole communities), and political career, see Rachel L. Emanuel and Alexander P. Tureaud Jr., *A More Noble Cause: A. P. Tureaud and the Struggle for Civil Rights in Louisiana: A Personal Biography* (Baton Rouge: Louisiana State University Press, 2011); and Arnold R. Hirsch and Joseph Logsdon, eds. *Creole New Orleans: Race and Americanization* (Baton Rouge: Louisiana State University Press, 1992).

39. For biographical information see chapter 4.

40. Answer to Complaint, 19 July 1961, case files, *Adams v. City of New Orleans*.

41. Herman L. Barnett was a graduate of Tulane University Law School. He was admitted to the bar in 1916. He served as the chairman of the New Orleans Civil Service Commission between 1942 and 1951. He represented Interstate Hosts as one of the senior partners at Guste, Barnett, and Shushan, a law firm in New Orleans. See *The American Bar*, vol. 40 (Minneapolis: J. C. Fifield, 1958), 582.

42. Court hearing for summary judgment, 12 July 1961, transcript of proceedings, case files, *Adams v. City of New Orleans*, 12, 13.

43. Opposition to motion for a summary judgment, 12 July 1961, case files, *Adams v. City of New Orleans*.

44. Amended answer to complaint, 21 July 1961, case files, *Adams v. City of New Orleans*.

45. Ibid.

46. Court hearing for summary judgment, 12 July 1961, transcript of proceedings, case files, *Adams v. City of New Orleans*, 12.

47. Ibid., 14.

48. *Adams v. City of New Orleans*, 208 F. Supp. 427 (1962).

49. *The City of New Orleans v. William R. Adams et al.*, 321 F.2d 493 (5th Cir. 1963).

50. *New York Times*, 27 July 1961, 31; *Washington Post*, 27 July 1961, A2.

51. Norfolk *Journal and Guide*, 29 July 1961, C2.

52. See Catsam, *Freedom's Main Line*; Arsenault, *Freedom Riders*; Bryant, *The Bystander*.

53. *Los Angeles Times*, 26 May 1961, 1.

54. See Catsam, *Freedom's Main Line*; Arsenault, *Freedom Riders*; Bryant, *The Bystander*.

55. Norfolk *Journal and Guide*, 29 July 1961, 2.

56. Montgomery's first airport was Gunter Airport, a facility that served both military and commercial purposes. In 1946 Dannelly Field opened. Dannelly Field became the city's main commercial airport. Its expansion begun in 1955 was an infrastructure project promoted by the city's business community. "The Men of Montgomery," as the business boosters called themselves, intended to increase the city's appeal as a business center by increasing capacity at its aerial gateway. See Billy J. Singleton, *Montgomery Aviation* (Charleston: Arcadia Publishing, 2007); Thornton, *Dividing Lines*, 52.

57. Exhibit Photographs, case files, *United States v. City of Montgomery*.

58. The water fountains had a complicated history, which emerged in the testimony of airport manager James Crouch. Originally, he said, there had only been one fountain across from the ticket counters and it was clearly marked "White." In early 1961 the second fountain was moved from its location in the waiting area reserved for blacks to the more easily accessible spot in the ticketing lobby. Couch explained: "The reason why this second fountain was moved from another portion of the terminal building is because I had heard criticism that there were no places at Dannelly Field for a Negro to get a drink of water." To ensure proper use, the airport management mounted what he called "directional signs." Deposition of James Joshua Couch Jr., 19 October 1961, case files, *United States v. City of Montgomery*, 26.

59. The photographs were probably taken in the spring of 1961. Exhibit Photographs, case files, *United States v. City of Montgomery*.

60. Norfolk *Journal and Guide*, 19 July 1961, C2.

61. Correspondence between E. B. Henderson and Charles C. Diggs Jr. and correspondence between E. B. Henderson and William B. Davis/Hubert H. Howell (CAA), April–September 1958, Series 7, Civil Rights, Box 42, Folder 5, Charles Diggs Collection, Howard University.

62. *Baltimore Afro-American*, 5 March 1960, 4; Letter from James Anton (CAB) to H. J. Palmer, John Lee Tilley, S. S. Seay Sr., and Ralph D. Abernathy, 24 May 1960, Folder 9, "Airports 1959–62", Box IX: 2, NAACP Records, LOC. Also see footnote 61.

63. Letter from L. H. Foster to Robert F. Kennedy, 23 February 1961, Folder "Federal Aid Airport Program 1961," Box 28, Office of the Administrator, Administrator's Subject/Correspondence file, 1959–1982, RG 237, FAA Records, NARACP.

64. Letter from Burke Marshall to L. H. Foster, 13 March 1961, Folder "Federal Aid Airport Program 1961," Box 28, Office of the Administrator, Administrator's Subject/Correspondence file, 1959–1982, RG 237, FAA Records, NARACP.

65. Letter from Burke Marshall to Najeeb E. Halaby, 15 March 1961, Folder "Federal Aid Airport Program 1961," Box 28, Office of the Administrator, Administrator's Subject/Correspondence file, 1959–1982, RG 237, FAA Records, NARACP.

66. 49 U.S.C. §1374 b (1958). A year earlier, CAB's Bureau of Enforcement came to the conclusion that the term "air carrier" could not be so construed citing *Palmer v. Eastern Airlines* 31 CAB 835 (1960). It therefore declined to order the integration of Montgomery's airport for want of jurisdiction (Letter from James Anton [CAB] to H. J. Palmer, John Lee Tilley, S. S. Seay Sr., and Ralph D. Abernathy, 24 May 1960, Folder 9, "Airports 1959–62," Box IX: 2, NAACP Records, LOC; CAB Order No. E-1518 [16 September 1960]). Although

by the summer of 1961 *Boynton v. Virginia* provided a legal basis for CAB action, its chairman Alan S. Boyd (in cooperation with the FAA) referred the matter to the Justice Department asking the attorney general to file the complaint against Montgomery. Letter from Alan S. Boyd to Robert F. Kennedy, 23 June 1961, case files, *United States v. City of Montgomery*.

67. Dixon, "Civil Rights in Air Transportation," 227.

68. Complaint, 26 July 1961, case files, *United States v. City of Montgomery*.

69. Ranch Enterprises Inc. was a local food and beverage business in Montgomery. It was established in 1956. Alabama, Secretary of State, Government Records, Business Entity Records, Ranch Enterprises Inc., Entity ID 786–734.

70. Complaint, 26 July 1961, case files, *United States v. City of Montgomery*.

71. The defendants filed the motion to dismiss putting forward the statutory argument that the provisions of the Federal Airport Act did not apply to them because they were not air carriers. They also claimed from a procedural perspective that the plaintiffs had not exhausted all administrative remedies available to them. Motion to dismiss, 14 August 1961, case files, *United States v. City of Montgomery*.

72. See Abernathy, *And the Walls Came Tumbling Down*; Branch, *Parting the Waters*.

73. Affidavit of Juanita Abernathy, 20 October 1961, case files, *United States v. City of Montgomery*.

74. Affidavit Ralph Abernathy, 20 October 1961, case files, *United States v. City of Montgomery*.

75. Deposition of James Joshua Couch Jr., 19 October 1961, case files, *United States v. City of Montgomery*, 2–3.

76. J. Harold Flannery was a civil rights lawyer. He joined the Civil Rights Division of the Justice Department as a trial lawyer in 1958 where he remained until 1970. He was appointed to the Massachusetts Superior Court in 1984, and in 1995 he became an Associate Justice of the Massachusetts Appeals Court. Obituary, *New York Times*, 23 December 1998.

77. Deposition of James Joshua Couch Jr., 19 October 1961, case files, *United States v. City of Montgomery*, 6–7, 14.

78. Ibid., 10, 20.

79. Calvin M. Whitesell was a partner at Whitesell and DeMent, a Montgomery law firm. He served as Montgomery's city attorney for most of the 1950s and 1960s. See Mills, *Dividing Lines*.

80. Deposition of James Joshua Couch Jr., 19 October 1961, case files, *United States v. City of Montgomery*.

81. Deposition of Franklin W. Parks, 19 October 1961, case files, *United States v. City of Montgomery*, 6–7.

82. Affidavit Kredelle Petway, 20 October 1961, case files, *United States v. City of Montgomery*.

83. Deposition of Franklin W. Parks, 19 October 1961, case files, *United States v. City of Montgomery*, 9–10.

84. Ibid.

85. Earl D. James took office in 1959. For his role in the city's struggle against the civil rights movement, see Thornton, *Dividing Lines*.

86. Deposition of Earl Daniel James, 19 October 1961, case files, *United States v. City of Montgomery*.

87. Decree, 2 January 1962, case files, *United States v. City of Montgomery*.

88. *United States of American v. City of Montgomery*, 201 F. Supp. 590 (1962).

89. Ronald J. Krotoszynski Jr., "Equal Justice under Law: The Jurisprudential Legacy of Judge Frank M. Johnson, Jr.," *Yale Law Journal* 109 (April 2000): 1237–1251, 1239.

90. *Browder v. Gayle*, 142 F. Supp. 707 (1956); David J. Garrow, "Visionaries of the Law: John Minor Wisdom and Frank M. Johnson, Jr.," *Yale Law Journal* 109 (April 2000): 1219–1236, 1220.

91. Thornton, *Dividing Lines*, 127–128.

92. Affidavit St. John Barrett, 24 July 1962, *United States v. City of Shreveport et al.*, CCF, C.A. 8888, U.S. District Court for Western District of Louisiana, Shreveport Division, Records of the District Courts of the United States, RG 21, NARA Fort Worth.

93. *Cleveland Call and Post*, 7 July 1962, 1C.

94. *Cleveland Call and Post*, 30 June 1962, 1C.

95. Complaint, 19 September 1960, case files, *Shuttlesworth v. Dobbs Houses, Inc.* Shuttlesworth's lawsuit also targeted the manager of the Dobbs House restaurant.

96. Letter from Harold W. Grant (Acting Administrator) to Robert F. Kennedy, 14 June 1962, Folder "5100 Jackson, Miss. Airport," Box 82, Office of the Administrator, Administrator's Subject/Correspondence File, 1959–1982 (OA/Correspondence), RG 237, FAA Records, NARACP.

97. Affidavit John T. Peterson, 9 July 1962, *United States v. City of Birmingham*, CCF, Box 527, Case Nos. 10195–10208, U.S. District Courts for the Northern District of Alabama, Southern Division (Birmingham), Records of the District Courts of the United States, RG 21, NARA Atlanta.

98. Affidavit Barbara Ann Robinson, 12 July 1962, case files, *United States v. City of Birmingham*.

99. Section 369 of the General Code provided: "It shall be unlawful to conduct a restaurant or other place for the serving of food in the city, at which white and colored people are served in the same room unless such white and colored persons are effectually separated by a solid partition extending from the floor upward to a distance of seven feet or higher, and unless a separate entrance from the street is provided for each compartment."

100. Complaint, 19 July 1962, case files, *United States v. City of Birmingham*.

101. For biographical information see chapter 4.

102. Order, 19 June 1962, case files, *United States v. City of Birmingham*.

103. *United States of America v. Birmingham*, Civil Action No. 10196 (1962).

104. Complaint, 19 June 1962, case files, *United States v. City of Shreveport*.

105. Stipulation of facts, 21 August 1962, case files, *United States v. City of Shreveport*.

106. Construction plans for Shreveport airport, case files, *United States v. City of Shreveport*.

107. Complaint, 19 June 1962, case files, *United States v. City of Shreveport*.

108. Memorandum in support of motion to dismiss on behalf of all defendants, 21 July 1962, case files, *United States v. City of Shreveport*.

109. Ibid. The motion referred to *United States v. Klans* as a case in point. See *United States v. U.S. Klans, Knights of the Ku Klux Klan, Inc.*, 194 F. Supp. 897 (1961).

110. Memorandum in support of motion to dismiss on behalf of all defendants, 21 July 1962, case files, *United States v. City of Shreveport*.

111. Affidavit St. John Barrett, 24 July 1962, case files, *United States v. City of Shreveport*. Barrett had joined the Justice Department in 1955 and was part of the Civil Rights

Division when it was created in 1957. As a government civil rights lawyer he had a major role in a number of landmark cases including the desegregation of Central High School in Little Rock, Arkansas (1957), the desegregation of public school in New Orleans (1960), and the integration of interstate bus carriers and terminals by the ICC (1961) among them. See St. John Barrett, *The Drive for Equality: A Personal History of Civil Rights Enforcement, 1954–1965* (Frederick, Md.: Publish America, 2009).

112. *United States v. City of Shreveport*, 210 F. Supp. 36 (1962).

113. Notice of Appeal, 16 November 1962, case files, *United States v. City of Shreveport*.

114. *City of Shreveport, Louisiana v. United States*, 316 F.2D 928 (1963).

Notes to Chapter 7

1. Don M. Thomas, Memorandum for Hobart Taylor Jr., 15 March 1965, Folder "5450 Other Airports 1965," Box 160, Office of the Administrator, Administrator's Subject/ Correspondence File, 1959–1982 (OA/Correspondence), RG 237, FAA Records, NARACP.

2. See David H. Golland, *Constructing Affirmative Action: The Struggle for Equal Employment Opportunity* (Lexington: University Press of Kentucky, 2011), 44–48.

3. Don M. Thomas, Memorandum for Hobart Taylor Jr., 15 March 1965, Folder "5450 Other Airports 1965," Box 160, Office of the Administrator, Administrator's Subject/ Correspondence File, 1959–1982 (OA/Correspondence), RG 237, FAA Records, NARACP.

4. Hobart Taylor Jr. was the executive vice chairman of the President's Committee of Equal Employment Opportunity and as such responsible for overseeing Plans for Progress. See Golland, *Constructing Affirmative Action*.

5. *United States of America v. Birmingham*, Civil Action No. 10196 (1962). See chapter 6.

6. Letter of Najeeb E. Halaby to Hobart Taylor Jr., 24 April 1965, Folder "5450 Other Airports 1965," Box 160, Office of the Administrator, Administrator's Subject/Correspondence File, 1959–1982 (OA/Correspondence), RG 237, FAA Records, NARACP.

7. Risen, *The Bill of the Century*.

8. Civil Rights Act of 1964, 78 Stat. 241, Title II (Injunctive Relief against Discrimination in Places of Public Accommodation).

9. E. W. Kenworthy, "Dirksen Shaped Victory for Civil Rights Forces in Fight to Bring Measure to Vote," *New York Times*, 20 June 1964, 11.

10. My thanks go to Bryant Simon for encouraging me to think in this direction. His comments were extremely useful.

11. See Richard Kluger, *Simple Justice: The History of Brown v. Board of Education and Black America's Struggle for Equality* (New York: Vintage, 2004). Mary Alice Nye and Charles S. Bullock III, "Civil Rights Support: A Comparison of Southern and Border State Representatives," *Legislative Studies Quarterly* 17. 1 (1992): 81–94.

12. 14 C.F.R. § 15.1–23, 1963 Supp.

13. The order also established the President's Committee on Equal Employment Opportunity. "to scrutinize and study employment practices of the Government of the United States, and to consider and recommend additional affirmative steps which should be taken by executive departments and agencies to realize more fully the national policy of nondiscrimination within the executive branch of the Government" (Sec. 201). 3 C.F.R., 1961 Supp., 86; 3 C.F.R. 1963 Supp., 185.

14. FAA Order CS 3300.1; FAA Order PT 3300.6.

15. Nathaniel Goodrich, "Civil Rights Policy," 1 January 1965, 11, Folder "5100 Federal Aid Airport Program 1965," Box 159, Office of the Administrator, Administrator's Subject/Correspondence File, 1959–1982 (OA/Correspondence), RG 237, FAA Records, NARACP.

16. Ibid., 1, 3–5. The Commission initially was not very effective because the Johnson administration was slow in appointing members. Moreover, it had a small budget and when it opened its doors in the summer of 1965 it was inundated with cases. See Risen, *Bill of the Century*, 250.

17. For many years, they would continue to be served by all white and female cabin crews, however. As Victoria Vantoch and Phil Tiemeyer show, U.S. airlines were slow to react to the shifting legal grounds on which their hiring practices stood. Few translated the Civil Rights Act Title VII into human resources policy speedily, which led to legal disputes involving black and eventually male job aspirants. See Vantoch, *The Jet Sex*, chap. 3, and Phil Tiemeyer, *Plane Queer: Labor, Sexuality and AIDS in the History of Male Flight Attendants* (Berkeley: University of California Press, 2013).

18. Online history of Birmingham Shuttlesworth International Airport, http://www.flybirmingham.com/about-bhm/history/.

19. See Andrew M. Manis, *A Fire You Can't Put Out: The Civil Rights Life of Birmingham's Reverend Fred Shuttlesworth* (Tuscaloosa: University of Alabama Press, 2001), and Manis and White, *Birmingham's Revolutionaries*.

20. Affidavit Fred Shuttlesworth, 6 June 1962, case files, *Shuttlesworth v. Dobbs House Inc.*

BIBLIOGRAPHY

Manuscript and Archival Collections

Adams v. City of New Orleans, United States District Courts, Civil Case Files, Record Group 21, National Archives Forth Worth.

Brooks v. City of Tallahassee, United States District Courts, Civil Case Files, Record Group 21, National Archives Atlanta.

Charles Diggs Collection, Moorland-Spingarn Research Center, Howard University.

Civil Rights Commission Records, Record Group 453, National Archives College Park.

Coke v. City of Atlanta, United States District Courts, Civil Case Files, Record Group 21, National Archives Atlanta.

Congress of Racial Equality (CORE) Papers, State Historical Society of Wisconsin, Madison (microfilm at Manuscript Division, Library of Congress).

Coxe Collection, Greenville Historical Society.

Department of Justice, Civil Rights Division, Record Group 60, National Archives College Park.

Federal Aviation Administration, Office of the Administrator, Record Group 237, National Archives College Park.

Harris v. City of New Orleans, United States District Courts, Civil Case Files, Record Group 21, National Archives Fort Worth.

Henry v. Greenville Airport Commission, United States District Courts, Civil Case Files, Record Group 21, National Archives Atlanta.

Horydczak Photograph Collection, Library of Congress.

Moise H. Goldstein Papers, Tulane University.

National Association for the Advancement of Colored People (NAACP) Records, Manuscript Division, Library of Congress.

Photograph Collection, Smithsonian National Air and Space Museum.

Shuttlesworth v. Dobbs Houses, Inc., United States District Courts, Civil Case Files, Record Group 21, National Archives Atlanta.

Turner v. City of Memphis, United States District Courts, Civil Case Files, Record Group 21, National Archives Atlanta.

United States v. City of Birmingham, United States District Courts, Civil Case Files, Record Group 21, National Archives Atlanta.

United States v. City of Montgomery, United States District Courts, Civil Case Files, Record Group 21, National Archives Atlanta.

United States v. City of Shreveport, United States District Courts, Civil Case Files, Record Group 21, National Archives Fort Worth.

Court Cases

Adams v. City of New Orleans, 208 F. Supp. 427 (1962).
Air Terminal Services v. Rentzel, 81 F. Supp. 611 (1949).
Bailey v. Patterson, 369 U.S. 31 (1962).
Boynton v. Virginia, 364 U.S. 454 (1960).
Brooks v. City of Tallahassee, 202 F. Supp. 56 (1961).
Browder v. Gayle, 142 F. Supp. 707 (1956).
Brown v. Board of Education of Topeka, 347 U.S. 483 (1954).
City of New Orleans v. Adams, 321 F.2d 493 (1963).
City of Shreveport v. United States, 316 F.2d 928 (1963).
Coke v. City of Atlanta, 184 F. Supp. 579 (1960).
Derrington v. Plummer, 240 F.2d 922 (1956).
Dresner v. City of Tallahassee, 375 U.S. 136 (1963).
Fitzgerald v. Pan American World Airways, 229 F.2d 499 (1956).
Henry v. Greenville Airport Commission, 175 F. Supp. 343 (1959).
Henry v. Greenville Airport Commission, 279 F.2d 751 (1960).
Henry v. Greenville Airport Commission, 284 F.2d 631 (1960).
Morgan v. Virginia, 328 U.S. 373 (1946).
Nash v. Air Terminal Services, Inc., 85 F. Supp. 545 (1949).
Plessy v. Ferguson, 163 U.S. 537 (1896).
Shuttlesworth v. Dobbs Houses, Inc., Civil Action No. 9765 (N.D. Alabama).
Smith v. City of Birmingham, 226 F. Supp. 838 (1964).
Turner v. City of Memphis, 369 U.S. 350 (1962).
Turner v. Randolph, 195 F. Supp. 677 (1961).
United States of America v. City of Birmingham, Civil Action No. 10196 (1962).
United States of America v. City of Montgomery, 201 F. Supp. 590 (1962).
United States of America v. City of New Orleans, Civil Action No. 11254.
United States v. U.S. Klans, Knights of the Ku Klux Klan, Inc., 194 F. Supp. 897 (1961).

Interstate Commerce Commission and Civil Aeronautics Board Decisions

Palmer v. Eastern Airlines, 31 CAB 835 (1960).
Sarah Keys v. Carolina Coach Company, 64 MCC 769 (1955).

Government Documents

Alabama, Secretary of State, Government Records, Business Entity Records, Ranch Enterprises Inc., Entity ID 786–734.

Campell, Gibson, and Kay Jung, "Historical Census Statistics on Population Totals by Race, 1790 to 1990, and by Hispanic Origin, 1970 to 1990, for the United States, Regions, Divisions, and States," Working Paper Series No. 56, United States, Census Bureau, Washington, D.C., September 2013 (http://www.census.gov/population/ www/documentation/twps0056/twps0056.html).

City of New Orleans, *Annual Report of the Mayor*, 1959–1960. New Orleans: City of New Orleans, 1960.

Congressional Record.

United States, Civil Aeronautics Administration, *Airport Design*. Washington, D.C.: GPO, 1949.

United States, Civil Aeronautics Administration, *Airport Terminal Buildings*. Washington, D.C.: GPO, 1953.

United States, Commission on Civil Rights, Mississippi Advisory Committee, *Administration of Justice in Mississippi: A Report to the United States Commission on Civil Rights*. Washington, D.C.: United States Commission on Civil Rights, 1963.

United States, Commission on Civil Rights, *Civil Rights: Report of the United States Commission on Civil Rights '63*. Washington, D.C.: United States Commission on Civil Rights, 1963.

United States, Congress, House of Representatives, 87th Congress, 1st Session, *Hearings before a Subcommittee of the Committee on Interstate and Foreign Commerce*, Federal Airport Aid Extension, H.R. 6580 and 6680. Washington, D.C.: Government Printing Office, 1961.

United States, Congress, House of Representatives, 87th Congress, 1st Session, *Report No. 728, Amendments to the Federal Airport Act*, 18 July 1961.

United States, Congress, House of Representatives, 88th Congress, 1st Session, *Report No. 1002, Amendments to the Federal Airport Act*, 5 December 1963.

United States, Congress, Senate, Committee on Interstate and Foreign Commerce, *Hearing on the Nomination of Charles J. Lowen, Jr. to be Administrator of Civil Aeronautics*, 11 May 1956. Washington, D.C.: Government Printing Office, 1956.

United States, Congress, Senate, 87th Congress, 1st Session, *Hearings before the Aviation Subcommittee of the Committee on Commerce*, Federal Aid to Airport Program, S. 1703. Washington, D.C.: Government Printing Office, 1961.

United States, Congress, Senate, 87th Congress, 1st Session, *Report No. 654, Amendments to the Federal Airport Act*, 1 August 1961.

United States, Congress, Senate, 88th Congress, 1st Session, *Hearings before the Aviation Subcommittee of the Committee on Commerce*, Federal Aid to Airport Program, S. 1153. Washington, D.C.: Government Printing Office, 1963.

United States, Congress, Senate, 88th Congress, 1st Session, *Report No. 422, Amendments to the Federal Airport Act*, 20 August 1963.

United States, Federal Aviation Agency, *Annual Reports of Operations under the Federal Airport Act*. Washington, D.C.: FAA, 1946–1965.

Periodicals

The American Bar
Atlanta Daily World
Atlanta Journal Constitution
Baltimore Afro-American
Boston Globe
Carolina Times
Charleston Evening Post
Chicago (Daily) Defender
Chicago Tribune
Cleveland Call and Post
Ebony
Los Angeles Times
New York Times
Norfolk Journal and Guide

Pittsburgh Courier
Race Relations Law Reporter
Times-Picayune
Washington Post

Online Resources

Airchive: The Webseum of Commercial Aviation: http://www.airchive.com.
American Experience (PBS) program "Freedom Riders": http://www.pbs.org/wgbh
/americanexperience/freedomriders/people/roster/.
Associated Press digital archive: http://www.apimages.com.
Birmingham Shuttlesworth International Airport: http://www.flybirmingham.com
/about-bhm/history/.
The Civil Rights Digital Library: http://crdl.usg.edu/.
Dobbs Houses, Inc.: http://www.dobbsmanagement.com/portfolio.html.
Greenville Airport: http://www.greenvilledowntownairport.com/History.html.
Jackson Municipal Airport Authority: http://jmaa.com/jmaa-history/.
"Just the Beginning Foundation, Biographies of African American Judges": http://www
.jtbf.org/index.php?submenu=Integration&src=gendocs&ref=BiographiesofAfrican
AmericanJudges&category=Integration.
Leigh Fisher & Associates: http://www.leighfisher.com/meet-leighfisher/overview.
Louis Armstrong International Airport: http://www.flymsy.com/PageDisplay.asp?p1=
5715.
Metropolitan Washington Airports Authority, Dulles Airport: http://www.metwash
airports.com/dulles/661.htm.
Mississippi Heritage Trust: http://www.mississippiheritage.com/.
Norfolk Municipal Airport: http://www.norfolkairport.com/mission-history.
North Carolina State Archives: http://www.ncdcr.gov/archives/home.aspx.
Scheuermann Jr., Milton G. "Moise H. Goldstein." In *KnowLA: Encyclopedia of Loui-
siana*, edited by David Johnson. Louisiana Endowment for the Humanities, 2010–.
Article published 12 January 12 2011. http://www.knowla.org/entry/874/.
Tennessee State Library and Archives digital collections: http://www.tennessee.gov/tsla/.
The Times-Picayune digital photo archive: http://www.nola.com/multimedia/photos/.
United States, Congress, Biographical Dictionary of the U.S. Congress: http://bioguide
.congress.gov/biosearch/biosearch.asp.
United States, Federal Judicial Center, History of the Federal Judiciary, Judges of the
United States Courts, Biographical Directory of Federal Judges: http://www.fjc.gov
/history/home.nsf/page/judges.html.

Books and Articles

Abel, Elizabeth. *Signs of the Times: The Visual Politics of Jim Crow*. Berkeley: University
of California Press, 2010.
Abernathy, Ralph D. *And the Walls Came Tumbling Down: An Autobiography*. New
York: Harper & Row, 1989.
Agnew, Jean-Christophe. "Coming Up for Air: Consumer Culture in Historical
Perspective." In *Consumer Society in American History*, ed. Lawrence B. Glickman.
Ithaca: Cornell University Press, 1999, 373–398.

Alexis, Marcus. "Patterns of Black Consumption 1935–1960." *Journal of Black Studies* 1.1 (1970): 55–74.

———. "Some Negro-White Differences in Consumption." *American Journal of Economics and Sociology* 21.1 (1962): 11–28.

Allen, Barbara. "Martin Luther King's Civil Disobedience and the American Covenant Tradition." *Publius* 30 (2000): 71–113.

Ambrose, Andy. *Atlanta: An Illustrated History*. Athens: Hill Street, 2003.

American Airport Designs. 1930; rpt. Washington, D.C.: American Institute of Architects Press, 1990.

Anagnostou, Yiorgos. *Contours of White Ethnicity: Popular Ethnography and the Making of Usable Pasts in Greek America*. Athens: Ohio University Press, 2009.

Anderson, Jean Bradley. *A History of Durham County, North Carolina*. Durham: Duke University Press and Historic Preservation Society of Durham, 1990.

Arsenault, Raymond. *Freedom Riders: 1961 and the Struggle for Racial Justice*. New York: Oxford University Press, 2006.

Ayers, Edward L. *The Promise of the New South: Life after Reconstruction*. New York: Oxford University Press, 2007.

Bailey, Elizabeth F. "Aviation Policy: Past and Present." *Southern Economic Journal* 69.1 (2002): 12–20.

Bake, Liva. *The Second Battle of New Orleans: The Hundred-Year Struggle to Integrate the Schools*. New York: HarperCollins, 1996.

Baldwin, James. *The Fire Next Time*. New York: Dial, 1963.

Barnes, Catherine A. *Journey from Jim Crow: The Desegregation of Southern Transit*. New York: Columbia University Press, 1983.

Barrett, St. John. *The Drive for Equality: A Personal History of Civil Rights Enforcement, 1954–1965*. Frederick, Md.: Publish America, 2009.

Bartley, Abel A. *Keeping the Faith: Race, Politics, and Social Development in Jacksonville, Florida, 1940–1970*. Westport, Conn.: Greenwood Press, 2000.

Bass, Jack. *Taming the Storm: The Life and Times of Judge Frank M. Johnson, Jr. and the South's Fight over Civil Rights*. New York: Doubleday, 1994.

Bass, Jack, and Marilyn W. Thompson. *Strom: The Complicated Personal and Political Life of Strom Thurmond*. New York: Public Affairs, 2005.

Beckett, Katherine, and Steve Herbert. *Banished: The New Social Control in Urban America*. New York: Oxford University Press, 2010.

Bednarek, Janet R. Daly. *America's Airports: Airfield Development, 1918–1947*. College Station: Texas A&M University Press, 2001.

Bednarek, Janet R. Daly, with Michael H. Bednarek. *Dreams of Flight: General Aviation in the United States*. College Station: Texas A&M University Press, 2003.

Bedwell, Don. *Silverbird: The American Airlines Story*. Sandpoint, Idaho: Airways International, 1999.

Belafonte, Harry, with Michael Shnayerson. *My Song: A Memoir of Art, Race, and Defiance*. New York: Vintage, 2011.

Belcher, Ray. *Greenville County, South Carolina: From Cotton Fields to Textile Center of the World*. Charleston: History Press, 2006.

Bellury, Phillip R. *Georgia Flight: The History of Aviation in Georgia, 1907–2007*. Atlanta: Wm. Robb Group, 2007.

Billington, Monroe. "Civil Rights, President Truman and the South." *Journal of Negro History* 58.2 (1973): 127–139.

Bilstein, Roger E. *Flight in America: From the Wrights to the Astronauts*. Baltimore: Johns Hopkins University Press, 2001.

———. "Travel by Air: The American Context." *Archiv für Sozialgeschichte* 33 (1993): 275–288.

Bodroghkozy, Aniko. *Equal Time: Television and the Civil Rights Movement*. Urbana: University of Illinois Press, 2012.

Bonastia, Christopher. *Knocking on the Door: The Federal Government's Attempt to Desegregate the Suburbs*. Princeton: Princeton University Press, 2006.

Borstelmann, Thomas. *The Cold War and the Color Line: American Race Relations in the Global Arena*. Cambridge, Mass.: Harvard University Press, 2001.

Braden, Betsy, and Paul Hagan. *A Dream Takes Flight: Hartsfield Atlanta International Airport and Aviation in Atlanta*. Atlanta: Atlanta Historical Society; Athens: University of Georgia Press, 1989.

Branch, Taylor. *Parting the Waters: America in the King Years, 1954–63*. New York: Simon & Schuster, 1988.

———. *Pillar of Fire: America in the King Years, 1963–65*. New York: Simon & Schuster, 1998.

———. *At Canaan's Edge: America in the King Years, 1965–68*. New York: Simon & Schuster, 2006.

Brown, Leslie. *Upbuilding Black Durham: Gender, Class, and Black Community Development in the Jim Crow South*. Chapel Hill: University of North Carolina Press, 2008.

Brown-Nagin, Tomiko. *Courage to Dissent: Atlanta and the Long History of the Civil Rights Movement*. New York: Oxford University Press, 2011.

Bryant, Nick. *The Bystander: John F. Kennedy and the Struggle for Black Equality*. New York: Basic Books, 2006.

Campbell, Karl E. *Senator Sam Ervin, Last of the Founding Fathers*. Chapel Hill: University of North Carolina Press, 2007.

Capparell, Stephanie. *The Real Pepsi Challenge: The Inspirational Story of Breaking the Color Barrier in American Business*. New York: Free Press, 2007.

Carson, Clayborne. *In Struggle: SNCC and the Black Awakening of the 1960s*. Cambridge, Mass.: Harvard University Press, 1981.

Cash, Floris Barnett. "Constance Baker Motley: Lawyer, Politician, Judge." In *Notable Black American Women*, book 1, ed. Jessie Carney Smith. Detroit: Gale Research Inc., 1991, 779–782.

Catsam, Derek Charles. *Freedom's Main Line: The Journey of Reconciliation and the Freedom Rides*. Lexington: University Press of Kentucky, 2009.

Cecelski, David S. *Along Freedom Road: Hyde County, North Carolina and the Fate of Black Schools in the South*. Chapel Hill: University of North Carolina Press, 1994.

Chesnutt, Charles. *The Marrow of Tradition*. 1921; rpt., Ann Arbor: University of Michigan Press, 1969.

Claire, Vincent P. *Louisiana Aviation: An Extraordinary History in Photographs*. Baton Rouge: Louisiana State University Press, 2012.

Cobb, James C. *The South and America since World War II*. New York: Oxford University Press, 2012.

Cohen, Lizabeth. *A Consumers' Republic: The Politics of Mass Consumption in Postwar America*. New York: Vintage, 2003.

Cohen, William. *At Freedom's Edge: Black Mobility and the Southern White Quest for Racial Control 1861–1915*. Baton Rouge: Louisiana State University Press, 1991.

Cohodas, Nadine. *Strom Thurmond and the Politics of Southern Change*. New York: Simon & Schuster, 1993.

Cole, Stephanie, and Natalie J. Ring, eds. *The Folly of Jim Crow: Rethinking the Segregated South*. College Station: Texas A&M University Press, 2012.

Corn, Joseph J. *The Winged Gospel: America's Romance with Aviation*. Baltimore: Johns Hopkins University Press, 1983.

Courtwright, David T. *Sky as Frontier: Adventure, Aviation, and Empire*. College Station: Texas A&M University Press, 2005.

Crouch, Tom D. *The History of Aviation from Kites to the Space Age*. Washington, D.C.: Smithsonian National Air and Space Museum, 2003.

Crow, Jeffrey J., Paul D. Escott, and Flora J. Hatley. *A History of African Americans in North Carolina*. Raleigh: Office of Archives and History, North Carolina Dept. of Cultural Resources, 2011.

Cunningham, David. *Klansville, U.S.A.: The Rise and Fall of the Civil Rights Era Ku Klux Klan*. New York: Oxford University Press, 2013.

Dailey, Jane, Glenda E. Gilmore, and Bryant Simon. *Jumpin' Jim Crow: Southern Politics from Civil War to Civil Rights*. Princeton: Princeton University Press, 2000.

Daniel, Pete. *Lost Revolutions: The South in the 1950s*. Chapel Hill: University of North Carolina Press; Washington, D.C.: Smithsonian Institution Press, 2000.

Davis, Sidney F. *Delta Air Lines: Debunking the Myth*. Atlanta: Peachtree, 1988.

Dekar, Paul R. *Creating the Beloved Community: A Journey with the Fellowship of Reconciliation*. Telford, Pa.: Cascadia, 2005.

Delaney, David. *Race, Place, and the Law, 1836–1948*. Austin: University of Texas Press, 1998.

D'Emilio, John. *Lost Prophet: The Life and Times of Bayard Rustin*. New York: Free Press, 2003.

Dickerson, Dennis C. *Whitney M. Young, Jr.: Militant Mediator*. Lexington: University Press of Kentucky, 1998.

Dittmer, John. *Local People: The Struggle for Civil Rights in Mississippi*. Urbana: University of Illinois Press, 1994.

Dixon, Robert G. "Civil Rights in Air Transportation and Government Initiative." *Virginia Law Review* 49 (1963): 205–231.

Dodd, Don, and Amy Bartlett Dodd. *Deep South Aviation*. Charleston, S.C.: Arcadia, 1999.

Dowdy, Wayne. *Crusades for Freedom: Memphis and the Political Transformations of the American South*. Jackson: University of Mississippi Press, 2010.

Doyle, William. *An American Insurrection: James Meredith and the Battle at Oxford, Mississippi, 1962*. New York: Anchor Books, 2003.

Du Bois, W. E. B. *Dusk of Dawn: An Essay toward an Autobiography of a Race Concept*. New York: Harcourt, Brace, 1940.

———. *Darkwater: Voices from Behind the Veil*. 1921; rpt., New York: Schocken Books, 1969.

———. *The Souls of Black Folk*. 1903; rpt., New York: Penguin, 1989.

DuBose, Carolyn. *The Untold Story of Charles Diggs: The Public Figure, the Private Man*. Arlington, Va.: Barton Publishing House, 1998.

Dudziak, Mary L. *Cold War Civil Rights: Race and the Image of American Democracy*. Princeton: Princeton University Press, 2000.

Dulles, John F. *The Civil Rights Commission: 1957-1965*. Ann Arbor: Michigan University Press, 1968.

Dunn, Marvin. *Black Miami in the Twentieth Century*. Gainesville: University Press of Florida, 1997.

Eagles, Charles W. *Outside Agitator: Jon Daniels and the Civil Rights Movement in Alabama*. Chapel Hill: University of North Carolina Press, 1993.

Edwards, Paul K. *The Southern Urban Negro as a Consumer*. New York: Negro University Press, 1932.

Emanuel, Rachel L., and Alexander P. Tureaud Jr. *A More Noble Cause: A. P. Tureaud and the Struggle for Civil Rights in Louisiana: A Personal Biography*. Baton Rouge: Louisiana State University Press, 2011.

Eskew, Glenn T. *But for Birmingham: The Local and National Movements in the Civil Rights Struggle*. Chapel Hill: University of North Carolina Press, 1997.

———. "'Bombingham': Black Protest in Postwar Birmingham, Alabama." *Historian* 59.2 (1997): 371–390.

Etheridge, Eric. *Breach of Peace: Portraits of the 1961 Mississippi Freedom Riders*. New York: Atlas & Co., 2008.

Fairclough, Adam. *Race & Democracy: The Civil Rights Struggle in Louisiana, 1915-1972*. Athens: University of Georgia Press, 2008.

———. *Better Day Coming: Blacks and Equality, 1890-2000*. New York: Viking, 2001.

———. *To Redeem the Soul of America: The Southern Christian Leadership Conference and Martin Luther King, Jr.* Athens: University of Georgia Press, [2001], 1987.

Farmer, James. *Lay Bare the Heart: An Autobiography of the Civil Rights Movement*. New York: Arbor House, 1985.

"The Federal Assimilative Crimes Act." *Harvard Law Review* 70.4 (February 1957): 685–698.

Felder, James L. *Civil Rights in South Carolina: From Peaceful Protests to Groundbreaking Rulings*. Charleston, S.C.: History Press, 2012.

Feldman, Glenn, ed. *Before Brown: Civil Rights and White Backlash in the Modern South*. Tuscaloosa: University of Alabama Press, 2004.

Finkle, Lee. "The Conservative Aims of Militant Rhetoric: Black Protest during World War II." *Journal of American History* 60.3 (1973): 692–713.

Fitzgerald, Tracey A. *The National Council of Negro Women and the Feminist Movement, 1935-1975*. Washington, D.C.: Georgetown University Press, 1985.

Foster, Mark S. "In the Face of 'Jim Crow': Prosperous Blacks and Vacations, Travel, and Outdoor Leisure, 1890-1945." *Journal of Negro History* 84.2 (1999): 130–149.

Froesch, Charles, and Walther Prokosch. *Airport Planning*. New York: John Wiley & Sons, 1946.

Gardner, Michael R. *Harry Truman and Civil Rights: Moral Courage and Political Risks*. Carbondale: Southern Illinois University Press, 2002.

Garrow, David J. "Visionaries of the Law: John Minor Wisdom and Frank M. Johnson, Jr." *Yale Law Journal* 109 (April 2000): 1219–1236.

————, ed. *The Montgomery Bus Boycott and the Women Who Started It: The Memoir of Jo Ann Gibson Robinson*. Knoxville: University of Tennessee Press, 1987.

————. *Bearing the Cross: Martin Luther King, Jr., and the Southern Christian Leadership Conference*. New York: W. Morrow, 1986.

Gelder, John W. "Air Law: The Federal Aviation Act of 1958." *Michigan Law Review* 57.8 (June 1959): 1214–1227.

Georgakas, Dan. *My Detroit: Growing Up Greek and American in Motor City*. New York: Pella, 2006.

Gerstle, Gary. *American Crucible: Race and Nation in the Twentieth Century*. Princeton: Princeton University Press, 2001.

Gilbert, Robert E. "John F. Kennedy and Civil Rights for Black Americans." *Presidential Studies Quarterly* 12.3 (1982): 386–399.

Goduti, Philip A., Jr. *Robert F. Kennedy and the Shaping of Civil Rights, 1960–1964*. Jefferson, N.C.: McFarland, 2012.

Goldfield, David R. *Region, Race, and Cities: Interpreting the Urban South*. Baton Rouge: Louisiana State University Press, 1997.

————. *Black, White, and Southern: Race Relations and Southern Culture, 1940 to the Present*. Baton Rouge: Louisiana State University Press, 1990.

————. *Cotton Fields and Skyscrapers: Southern City and Region, 1607–1980*. Baton Rouge: Louisiana State University Press, 1982.

Golland, David H. *Constructing Affirmative Action: The Struggle for Equal Employment Opportunity*. Lexington: University Press of Kentucky, 2011, 44–48.

Gordon, Alastair. *Naked Airport: A Cultural History of the World's Most Revolutionary Structure*. New York: Metropolitan Books, 2004.

Grady-Willis, Winston A. *Challenging U.S. Apartheid: Atlanta and Black Struggles for Human Rights, 1960–1977*. Durham, N.C.: Duke University Press, 2006.

Gray, Fred D. *Busride to Justice: The Life and Works of Fred D. Gray*. Montgomery: New South Books, 1995.

Greenberg, Jack. *Crusaders in the Courts: Legal Battles of the Civil Rights Movement*. New York: Twelve Tables Press, 2004.

Greene, Laurie B. *Battling the Plantation Mentality: Memphis and the Black Freedom Struggle*. Chapel Hill: University of North Carolina Press, 2007.

Greif, Martin. *The Airport Book: From Landing Field to Modern Terminal*. New York: Mayflower Books, 1979.

Grisinger, Joanna L. *The Unwieldy American State: Administrative Politics since the New Deal*. New York: Cambridge University Press, 2012.

Gritter, Elizabeth. *River of Hope: Black Politics and the Memphis Freedom Movement, 1865–1954*. Lexington: University Press of Kentucky, 2014.

Gundaker, Grey, ed. *Keep Your Head to the Sky: Interpreting African American Home Ground*. Charlottesville: University Press of Virginia, 1998.

Hale, Grace. *Making Whiteness: The Culture of Segregation in the South, 1890–1940*. New York: Vintage, 1998.

Hardesty, Von, and Dominick A. Pisano. *Black Wings: The American Black in Aviation*. Washington, D.C.: Smithsonian Institution Press, 1984.

Harris, Dianne. *Little White Houses: How the Postwar Home Constructed Race in America*. Minneapolis: University of Minnesota Press, 2013.

———. *Second Suburb: Levittown, Pennsylvania*. Pittsburgh: University of Pittsburgh Press, 2010.

———. "Race, Space, and the Destabilization of Practice." *Landscape Journal* 26 (2007): 1–9.

Harris, Joel Chandler. *Uncle Remus and His Legends of the Old Plantation*. London: David Bogue, 1881.

Height, Dorothy I. *Open Wide the Freedom Gates: A Memoir*. New York: PublicAffairs, 2003.

Hein, Virginia H. "The Image of 'A City Too Busy to Hate': Atlanta in the 1960's." *Phylon* 33.3 (1972): 205–221.

Hirsch, Arnold R., and Joseph Logsdon, eds. *Creole New Orleans: Race and Americanization*. Baton Rouge: Louisiana State University Press, 1992.

Hoffer, Williamjames Hull. *Plessy v. Ferguson: Race and Inequality in Jim Crow America*. Lawrence: University Press of Kansas, 2012.

Horonjeff, Robert, and Francis X. McKelvey. *Planning and Design of Airports*. New York: McGraw-Hill, 1994.

Horsman, Reginald. *Race and Manifest Destiny: The Origins of American Racial Anglo-Saxonism*. Cambridge, Mass.: Harvard University Press, 1981.

Hudson, Kenneth. *Air Travel: A Social History*. Bath, U.K.: Adams and Dart, 1972.

Ingalls, Robert P. *Urban Vigilantes in the New South: Tampa, 1882–1936*. Gainesville: University Press of Florida, 1993.

Jacobson, Matthew Frye. *Whiteness of a Different Color: European Immigrants and the Alchemy of Race*. Cambridge, Mass.: Harvard University Press, 1998.

James, Rawn, Jr. *Root and Branch: Charles Hamilton Houston, Thurgood Marshall, and the Struggle to End Segregation*. New York: Bloomsbury Press, 2010.

James, Tracey. *Direct Action: Radical Pacifism from the Union Eight to the Chicago Seven*. Chicago: University of Chicago Press, 1996.

Javits, Jacob, and Rafael Steinberg. *The Autobiography of a Public Man*. Boston: Houghton Mifflin, 1981.

Jonas, Gilbert. *Freedom's Sword: The NAACP and the Struggle against Racism in America, 1909–1969*. New York: Routledge, 2005.

Jordan, Casper L. "Freddye Scarborough Henderson." In *Notable Black American Women*, book 2, ed. Jesse C. Smith. Detroit: Gale Research, 1996, 284–287.

Juhnke, William E. "President Truman's Committee on Civil Rights: The Interaction of Politics, Protest, and Presidential Advisory Commission." *Presidential Studies Quarterly* 19.3 (1989): 593–610.

Kahrl, Andrew W. *The Land Was Ours: African American Beaches from Jim Crow to the Sunbelt South*. Cambridge: Cambridge University Press, 2012.

Katzenbach, Nicholas deB. *Some of It Was Fun: Working with RFK and LBJ*. New York: Norton, 2008.

Kelley, Blair L. M. *Right to Ride: Streetcar Boycotts and African American Citizenship in the Era of Plessy v. Ferguson*. Chapel Hill: University of North Carolina Press, 2010.

Kennedy, Stetson. *Jim Crow Guide: The Way It Was*. Boca Raton: Florida Atlantic University Press, 1990.

Kent, Richard J., Jr. *Safe, Separated, and Soaring: A History of Federal Civil Aviation Policy 1961–1972*. Washington, D.C.: U.S. Department of Transportation, FAA, 1980.

Klarman, Michael J. *From Jim Crow to Civil Rights: The Supreme Court and the Struggle for Racial Equality*. New York: Oxford University Press, 2004.

———. *Brown v. Board of Education and the Civil Rights Movement*. New York: Oxford University Press, 2007.

Kluger, Richard. *Simple Justice: The History of Brown v. Board of Education and Black America's Struggle for Equality*. New York: Vintage, 2004.

Krotoszynski, Ronald J., Jr. "Equal Justice under Law: The Jurisprudential Legacy of Judge Frank M. Johnson, Jr." *Yale Law Journal* 109 (2000): 1237–1251.

Kruse, Kevin M. *White Flight: Atlanta and the Making of Modern Conservatism*. Princeton: Princeton University Press, 2005.

Landsberg, Brian K. *Enforcing Civil Rights: Race Discrimination and the Department of Justice*. Lawrence: University Press of Kansas, 1997.

Lau, Peter F. *Democracy Rising: South Carolina and the Fight for Black Equality since 1965*. Lexington: University Press of Kentucky, 2006.

———, ed. *From the Grassroots to the Supreme Court: Brown v. Board of Education and American Democracy*. Durham, N.C.: Duke University Press, 2004.

Leigh, Fisher, & Associates, Memphis, Tennessee. "Air Trade Study, Airport Master Plan, Terminal Requirements, Schematic Plans, Design Comments for Memphis Municipal Airport for the Memphis Airport Commission." South Bend, Ind.: Fisher, 1956.

Leigh, Fisher, & Associates, Moisant International Airport. "Air Trade Study, Airport Master Plan, Terminal Requirements, Schematic Plans, Design Comments for the City of New Orleans Aviation Board." South Bend, Ind.: Fisher, 1954.

Levine, Ellen. *Freedom's Children: Young Civil Rights Activists Tell Their Own Stories*. New York: Putnam, 1993.

Lewis, Andrew B. *The Shadows of Youth: The Remarkable Journey of the Civil Rights Generation*. New York: Hill & Wang, 2009.

Lewis, Earl. *In Their Own Interests: Race, Class, and Power in Twentieth-Century Norfolk, Virginia*. Berkeley: University of California Press, 1991.

Lewis, John. *Walking with the Wind: A Memoir of the Movement*. New York: Simon & Schuster, 1998.

Lovett, Bobby L. *The Civil Rights Movement in Tennessee: A Narrative History*. Knoxville: University of Tennessee Press, 2005.

Loving, Neal V. *Loving's Love: A Black American's Experience in Aviation*. Washington, D.C.: Smithsonian Institution Press, 1994.

Luders, Joseph E. *The Civil Rights Movement and the Logic of Social Change*. New York: Cambridge University Press, 2010.

Mack, Kenneth W. *Representing the Race: The Creation of the Civil Rights Lawyer*. Cambridge, Mass.: Harvard University Press, 2012.

———. "Sadie Tanner Mossell Alexander." *Notable American Women: A Biographical Dictionary Completing the Twentieth Century*, ed. Susan Ware. Cambridge, Mass.: Harvard University Press, 2004, 18–19.

———. "A Social History of Everyday Practice: Sadie T. M. Alexander and the Incorporation of Black Women into the American Legal Profession, 1925–60." *Cornell Law Review* 87 (2002): 1405–1474.

Manis, Andrew M. *A Fire You Can't Put Out: The Civil Rights Life of Birmingham's Reverend Fred Shuttlesworth*. Tuscaloosa: University of Alabama Press, 2001.

Manis, Andrew M., and Marjorie L. White, eds. *Birmingham's Revolutionaries: The Reverend Fred Shuttlesworth and the Alabama Christian Movement for Human Rights.* Macon, Ga.: Mercer University Press, 2000.

Marshall, Burke. *Federalism and Civil Rights.* New York: Columbia University Press, 1964.

Marshall, James P. *Student Activism and Civil Rights in Mississippi: Protest Politics and the Struggle for Racial Justice, 1960–1965.* Baton Rouge: Louisiana State University Press, 2013.

Martin, Michael S., ed. *Louisiana beyond Black and White: New Interpretations of Twentieth-Century Race and Race Relations.* Lafayette: University of Louisiana at Lafayette Press, 2011.

Martin Luther King, Jr., Papers. Ed. Claiborne Carson. Berkeley: University of California Press, 1997–2007.

Mayer, Michael S. "With Much Deliberation and Some Speed: Eisenhower and the *Brown* Decision." *Journal of Southern History* 52.1 (1986): 43–76.

McAdam, Doug. *Freedom Summer.* New York: Oxford University Press, 1988.

McMillen, Neil R. *The Citizens' Council: Organized Resistance to the Second Reconstruction, 1954–64.* Urbana: University of Illinois Press, 1994.

McNealey, Earnestine Green. *The Pearls of Alpha Kappa Alpha: The History of America's First Black Sorority.* Washington, D.C.: Alpha Kappa Alpha, 2010.

Meier, August, and Elliott Rudwick. *CORE: A Study in the Civil Rights Movement 1942–1968.* New York: Oxford University Press, 1973.

Miller, Helen Sullivan. *The History of Chi Eta Phi Sorority, Inc.* Washington, D.C.: Association for the Study of Negro Life and History, 1968.

Mitchell, Dennis J. *A New History of Mississippi.* Jackson: University of Mississippi Press, 2014.

Mohl, Raymond A. *South of the South: Jewish Activists and the Civil Rights Movement in Miami, 1945–1960.* Gainesville: University Press of Florida, 2004.

Moore, Winfred B., Jr., and Orville V. Burton, eds. *Toward the Meeting of the Waters: South Carolina during the Twentieth Century.* Columbia: University of South Carolina Press, 2008.

Motley, Constance Baker. *Equal Justice under Law.* New York: Farrar, Straus & Giroux, 1998.

Mullins, Paul R. *Race and Affluence: An Archaeology of African America and Consumer Culture.* New York: Kluwer Academic, 1999.

Murray, Pauli, ed. *States' Laws on Race and Color.* Athens: University of Georgia Press, 1997.

Myrdal, Gunnar. *An American Dilemma: The Negro Problem and Modern Democracy.* New York: Harper, 1944.

Nichols, David A. *A Matter of Justice: Eisenhower and the Beginning of the Civil Rights Revolution.* New York: Simon & Schuster, 2007.

———. "'The Showpiece of Our Nation': Dwight D. Eisenhower and the Desegregation of the District of Columbia." *Washington History* (Fall/Winter 2004–2005): 44–65.

Nye, Mary Alice, and Charles S. Bullock III. "Civil Rights Support: A Comparison of Southern and Border State Representatives." *Legislative Studies Quarterly* 17.1 (1992): 81–94.

O'Brien, Michael J. *We Shall Not Be Moved: The Jackson Woolworth's Sit-Ins and the Movement It Inspired*. Jackson: University of Mississippi Press, 2013.

Ortlepp, Anke. "Cultures of Air Travel in Postwar America." Habilitation, University of Munich, 2009.

Ownby, Ted, ed. *The Civil Rights Movement in Mississippi*. Jackson: University Press of Mississippi, 2013.

———. *American Dreams in Mississippi: Consumers, Poverty, and Culture 1830–1998*. Chapel Hill: University of North Carolina Press, 1999.

Painter, Nell Irvin. *The History of White People*. New York: W. W. Norton, 2010.

Parks, Rosa, with Jim Haskins. *Rosa Parks: My Story*. New York: Dial Books, 1992.

Parsons, Sara Mitchell. *From Southern Wrongs to Civil Rights: The Memoir of a White Civil Rights Activist*. Tuscaloosa: University of Alabama Press, 2000.

Payne, Charles M. *I've Got the Light of Freedom: The Organizing Tradition and the Mississippi Freedom Struggle*. Berkeley: University of California Press, 2007.

Peake, Thomas R. *Keeping the Dream Alive: A History of the Southern Christian Leadership Conference from King to the Nineteen-Eighties*. New York: Peter Lang, 1987.

Philipps, Kimberley L. *War! What Is It Good For?: Black Freedom Struggles and the U.S. Military from World War II to Iraq*. Chapel Hill: University of North Carolina Press, 2012.

Poitier, Sidney. *The Measure of a Man: A Memoir*. New York: Simon & Schuster, 2000.

Powell, Lawrence N. *The Accidental City: Improvising New Orleans*. Cambridge, Mass.: Harvard University Press, 2013.

Prokosch, Walter. "Airport Design: Its Architectural Aspects." *Architectural Record* (January 1951): 112–116.

Rabby, Glenda A. *The Pain and the Promise: The Struggle for Civil Rights in Tallahassee, Florida*. Athens: University of Georgia Press, 1999.

Rampersad, Arnold. *Jackie Robinson: A Biography*. New York: Knopf, 1997.

Ransby, Barbara. *Ella Baker and the Black Freedom Movement: A Radical Democratic Vision*. Chapel Hill: University of North Carolina Press, 2003.

Reed, Betty Jamerson. *School Segregation in Western North Carolina: A History, 1860s–1970s*. Jefferson, N.C.: McFarland, 2011.

Reporting Civil Rights, Parts I + II. New York: Library of America, 2003.

Risen, Clay. *The Bill of the Century: The Epic Battle for the Civil Rights Act*. New York: Bloomsbury Press, 2014.

Roback, Jennifer. "The Political Economy of Segregation: The Case of Segregated Streetcars." *Journal of Economic History* 46.4 (1986): 893–917.

Roberts, Gene, and Hank Klibanoff. *The Race Beat: The Press, the Civil Rights Struggle, and the Awakening of a Nation*. New York: Knopf, 2006.

Robinson, Jackie. *I Never Had It Made: An Autobiography of Jackie Robinson*. New York: Harper Perennial, 2003.

Rochester, Stuart I. *Takeoff at Mid-Century: Federal Aviation Policy in the Eisenhower Years, 1953–1961*. Washington, D.C.: U.S. Dept. of Transportation, Federal Aviation Administration, 1976.

Roediger, David R. *Working toward Whiteness: How America's Immigrants Became White: The Strange Journey from Ellis Island to the Suburbs*. New York: Basic Books, 2005.

Rogers, Kim L. *Righteous Lives: Narratives from the New Orleans Civil Rights Movement*. New York: New York University Press, 1993.

Rose, Chanelle N. *The Struggle for Black Freedom in Miami: Civil Rights and America's Tourist Paradise, 1896–1968*. Baton Rouge: Louisiana State University Press, 2015.

Rust, Daniel L. *Flying across America: The Airline Passenger Experience*. Norman: University of Oklahoma Press, 2009.

Sarat, Austin. *Civil Rights in American Law, History, and Politics*. New York: Cambridge University Press, 2014.

Schein, Richard H., ed. *Landscape and Race in the United States*. New York: Routledge, 2006.

Schickler, Erich, Kathryn Pearson, and Brian D. Feinstein. "Congressional Parties and Civil Rights Politics from 1933–1972." *Journal of Politics* 72.3 (2010): 672–689.

Scott, Lawrence P., and William M. Womack Sr. *Double V: The Civil Rights Struggle of the Tuskegee Airmen*. East Lansing: Michigan State University Press, 1994.

Shearer, Tobin Miller. *Daily Demonstrators: The Civil Rights Movement in Mennonite Homes and Sanctuaries*. Baltimore: Johns Hopkins University Press, 2010.

Singleton, Billy J. *Montgomery Aviation*. Charleston, S.C.: Arcadia, 2007.

Sitkoff, Harvard. *King: Pilgrimage to the Mountaintop*. New York: Hill & Wang, 2008.

———. *The Struggle for Black Equality, 1954–1980*. New York: Hill & Wang, 1981.

———. "Harry Truman and the Election of 1948: The Coming of Age of Civil Rights in American Politics." *Journal of Southern History* 37.4 (1971): 597–616.

Sokol, Jason. *There Goes My Everything: White Southerners in the Age of Civil Rights, 1945–1975*. New York: Knopf, 2006.

Somers, Dale A. "Black and White in New Orleans: A Study in Urban Race Relations, 1865–1900." *Journal of Southern History* 40.1 (1974): 19–42.

Spear, Jennifer M. *Race, Sex, and Social Order in Early New Orleans*. Baltimore: Johns Hopkins University Press, 2009.

Stern, Mark. "John F. Kennedy and Civil Rights: From Congress to the Presidency." *Presidential Studies Quarterly* 19.4 (1989): 797–823.

Surgue, Thomas J. "Jim Crow's Last Stand: The Struggle to Integrate Levittown." In *Second Suburb: Levittown, Pennsylvania*, ed. Dianne Harris. Pittsburgh: University of Pittsburgh Press, 2010, 175–199.

Szurvoy, Geza. *The American Airport*. St. Paul: MBI Publishing, 2003.

Teter, Betsy W., ed. *Textile Town: Spartanburg County, South Carolina*. Spartanburg, S.C.: Hub City Writers Project, 2002.

Theoharis, Jeanne. *The Rebellious Life of Mrs. Rosa Parks*. Boston: Beacon Press, 2013.

Thomas, Karen K. *Deluxe Jim Crow: Civil Rights and American Health Policy, 1935–1954*. Athens: University of Georgia Press, 2011.

Thornton, J. Mills, III. *Dividing Lines: Municipal Politics and the Struggle for Civil Rights in Montgomery, Birmingham, and Selma*. Tuscaloosa: University of Alabama Press, 2002.

Thuesen, Sarah Caroline. *Greater Than Equal: African American Struggles for Schools and Citizenship in North Carolina, 1919–1965*. Chapel Hill: University of North Carolina Press, 2013.

Tiemeyer, Phil. *Plane Queer: Labor, Sexuality and AIDS in the History of Male Flight Attendants*. Berkeley: University of California Press, 2013.

Tracy, James. *Direct Action: Radical Pacifism from the Union Eight to the Chicago Seven.* Chicago: University of Chicago Press, 1996.

Tuck, Stephen G. N. *Beyond Atlanta: The Struggle for Racial Equality in Georgia, 1940–1980.* Athens: University of Georgia Press, 2001.

Tygiel, Jules. *Baseball's Great Experiment: Jackie Robinson and His Legacy.* New York: Oxford University Press, 2008.

Upton, Dell. *Architecture in the United States.* New York: Oxford University Press, 1998.

Vance, Sandra Stringer. "The Congressional Career of John Bell Williams, 1947–1967." Ph.D. dissertation, Mississippi State University, 1976.

Vantoch, Jennifer. *The Jet Sex: Airline Stewardesses and the Making of an American Icon.* Philadelphia: University of Pennsylvania Press, 2013.

Vaughan, Alden T. *Roots of American Racism: Essays on the Colonial Experience.* New York: Oxford University Press, 1995.

Von Eschen, Penny M. *Race against Empire: Black Americans and Anticolonialism, 1937–1957.* Ithaca, N.Y.: Cornell University Press, 1997.

Ward, Jason M. *Defending White Democracy: The Making of a Segregationist Movement and the Remaking of Racial Politics, 1936–1965.* Chapel Hill: University of North Carolina Press, 2011.

Webb, Clive, ed. *Massive Resistance: Southern Opposition to the Second Reconstruction.* New York: Oxford University Press, 2005.

Weyeneth, Robert R. "The Architecture of Racial Segregation: The Challenges of Preserving the Problematical Past." *Public Historian* 27 (Fall 2005): 11–44.

Whaley, Deborah E. *Disciplining Women: Alpha Kappa Alpha, Black Counterpublics, and the Cultural Politics of Black Sororities.* Albany: SUNY Press, 2010.

White, Forrest R. *Pride and Prejudice: School Desegregation and Urban Renewal in Norfolk, 1950–1959.* Westport, Conn.: Praeger, 1992.

Whitnah, Donald R. *Safer Skyways: Federal Control of Aviation, 1926–1966.* Ames: Iowa State University Press, 1966.

Wilkins, Roy. *Standing Fast: The Autobiography of Roy Wilkins.* New York: Viking Press, 1982.

Williams, Clay. "The Guide for Colored Travelers: A Reflection of the Urban League." *Journal of American & Comparative Cultures* 24, nos. 3/4 (2001): 71–79.

Williams, Juan. *Thurgood Marshall: American Revolutionary.* New York: Times Books, 1998.

Winsboro, Irvin D. S., ed. *Old South, New South, or Down South?: Florida and the Modern Civil Rights Movement.* Morgantown: West Virginia University Press, 2009.

Wolcott, Victoria W. *Race, Riots, and Roller Coasters: The Struggle over Segregated Recreation in America.* Philadelphia: University of Pennsylvania Press, 2012.

Woodward, C. Vann. *The Strange Career of Jim Crow.* 1955; rpt., New York: Oxford University Press, 2002.

———. *Origins of the New South.* Baton Rouge: Louisiana State University Press, 1951.

Young, Andrew. *An Easy Burden: The Civil Rights Movement and the Transformation of America.* New York: HarperCollins, 1996.

INDEX

Abernathy, Juanita, 1, 124–125

Abernathy, Ralph David: in altercation at Montgomery airport, 1; appeals to the Civil Aeronautics Board (CAB), 123; at Atlanta airport, 27, 70; as frequent flyer, 30; on segregation in Florida, 53; as witness in *United States v. City of Montgomery*, 124, 125

Adams, William R., 86, 118

Adams v. City of New Orleans, 62, 69, 81, 86–88, 118–129

advertising, 6, 29, 49

African Americans: in advertising, 6, 29, 49; and air mobility, 28; as air travelers, 1–3, 19, 28, 30, 137, 139–140; as business travelers, 19, 28, 29, 38, 71, 72, 79, 82, 132; as civil rights lawyers, 12, 31, 70–71, 84–85, 118, 167n109; as consumers, 2, 6–7, 46, 60, 132; restricted mobility of, 19; as travelers on trains and buses, 4, 5, 13–14, 15, 63; travel statistics of, 73

"air carrier," definitions of, 91, 123, 129

airport surveys: by Charles Diggs, 23, 26–28, 53, 92–93; by the Civil Aeronautics Administration (CAA), 32; by the FBI, 130; by the NAACP, 20–22, 32–33, 53, 152n93

Air Terminal Services, Inc., 16, 62, 65–66, 67. See also *Nash v. Air Terminal Services*

Air Transport Association of America, 24

air travel: in advertising, 29–30; and black middle class mobility, 79, 137; and the Civil Rights Act (1964), 138–140; and civil rights activists, mobility of, 29–30, 31; and class, as signifier of, 137; and consumer culture, 6, 46, 60; development of, 3, 92; and gender, 3, 49–50, 67; integrated, 2, 15, 18; King, Martin Luther Jr., and, 30–32, 39; as lifestyle, 6, 60; and local culture, 3, 19; in *Negro Travelers' Green Book*, 35; and race, 7

Alexander, Sadie T. M., 66, 67

American Airlines, 16, 24, 29, 62

Andrews, O. L., 44, 76

Anniston, Ala., 37, 47

Armstrong, Thomas A., 24

Assimilative Crimes Act, 63, 64, 65

Atlanta, Ga., 9, 25, 168n11

Atlanta Daily World, 75

Atlanta Municipal Airport: architecture and design of, 37–38; direct action at, 27; FAAP funding of, 92; integration of, 74; segregation of, 37–42. See also *Coke v. Atlanta*

Azalea Room, 17–18

Bailey v. Patterson, 81, 89, 105

Baker, George T., 25

Barnett, Herman L., 119

Barnett, Ross, 48, 108

Baton Rouge Municipal Airport, 32, 33, 130

Belafonte, Harry, 28

Birmingham, Ala., 7, 37, 47, 138, 168n11

Birmingham Municipal Airport: airport motel at, 168n126; Don Thomas incident at, 135–136; FAAP funding for, 95, 98; integration of, 133; renaming of, 140; segregated facilities at, 132; and Shuttlesworth, Fred, 88. See also *Shuttlesworth v. Dobbs Houses, Inc.*; *United States v. City of Birmingham*

blackness, notions of, 2, 5, 7, 21, 106, 136

Boston Globe, 48

Boyd, Marion Speed, 84–85
Boynton v. Virginia, 47, 101, 113, 118
Braden, Henry E., III, 86, 118
Brooks v. Tallahassee, 55–56, 81, 108
Broward County International Airport, 28
Browder v. Gayle, 69, 129
Brown, Edgar G., 65, 66
Brown v. Board of Education, 48, 61, 69, 70
Bryan, Albert V., 65, 68
Burton v. Wilmington Parking Authority, 120
buses: integration of, 47, 63, 69, 101; segregation of, 2, 5, 14–15, 36–37
Byrd Field (Richmond), 28

Call and Post (Cleveland), 19–20, 46, 130
Charleston Municipal Airport, 32, 33
Chattanooga Airport (Lovell Field), 23–24
Chestnutt, Charles W., 14
Chicago Defender, 19–20
Christenberry, Herbert W., 87–88, 118, 119–120
Cincinnati Airport, 26
Civil Aeronautics Act (1938), 15, 91, 146n10
Civil Aeronautics Administration (CAA): and airport funding practices, 92–94; and airport investigations, 32; authority of, 90–91; and civil rights, 94; in Jackson, Miss., 48; and National Airport, integration of, 64–66; and Raleigh-Durham airport, investigation of, 58. *See also* Federal Aviation Administration
Civil Aeronautics Board (CAB), 99
Civil Rights Act (1947), 67
Civil Rights Act (1957), 103
Civil Rights Act (1964), 110, 111, 136–137, 138–140
Civil Rights Division (Dept. of Justice): and airport desegregation, role in, 130; responsibilities of, 54, 104, 112
civil rights lawyers, 12, 31, 70–71, 84–85, 118, 167n109
civil rights movement: in Atlanta, Ga., 40–41; in South Carolina, 42; in Tallahassee, Fla., 53

class, as status signifier, 3, 28, 95–96, 139–140. *See also* middle class
Code of Virginia, 16, 17, 63
Coke, H. D., 40, 69–75, 137
Coke v. Atlanta, 62, 69–75, 81, 86, 88, 119
Cold War, 22–23, 59, 96
Columbus (Lowndes County) Airport, 130
Columbus (Metropolitan) Airport, 130
Commission on Civil Rights, U.S., 103–104, 108
Congress, U.S.: as agent of change, 10, 90, 111; and debates about airports in, 94–96, 97–99, 109–110; legislation of, and race, 12; NAACP criticism of, 95–96; and National Airport, 64; and segregation, 94, 96, 112. *See also* Federal Airport Act; House of Representatives, U.S.; Javits, Jacob; Senate, U.S.
Congress of Racial Equality (CORE): and Atlanta airport protest, 41–42; and direct action, focus on, 9–10, 36; and Freedom Fly-Ins, 47–51; and Freedom Rides, 47–48, 49; and Greenville airport protest, 42–46; Greenville chapter of, 154n26; and Tallahassee airport protest, 51–55
consumer culture, development of, 3, 4, 6–7
consumer rights, 60, 75, 89, 140
consumption, and race and class, 3, 6–7, 8, 60, 89
CORE-lator, 44
Cotton, Norris, 98, 99
Couch, James, 125–126
Court of Appeals, U.S.: for the Fifth Circuit, 88, 120, 134; for the Fourth Circuit, 79, 80–81; for the Second Circuit, 55; for the Sixth Circuit, 85
Cumberland Municipal Airport, 26
Cunningham, Lilly, 66, 67
Current, Gloster, 19, 32, 44, 115

Dallas, Tex., 24
Dannelly Field Airport (Montgomery): Abernathy incident at, 1; architecture and design of, 33–35, 121–122; FAAP

68; and private and public actors, application to, 81; in *Turner v. Memphis*, 81, 83, 85; and waiting rooms, applied to, 80

Stoutamire, Frank, 54–55

streetcars, 3, 4, 13

Student Nonviolent Coordinating Committee (SNCC), 36

Sugarmon, Russell, 84

Sullivan, L. B., 123

Supreme Court, U.S.: and desegregation of airports, 81, 85, 88, 89, 96; and desegregation of bus terminals, 47, 101, 113; and desegregation of interstate buses, 15, 63; and desegregation of schools, 61, 77; and desegregation of terminal facilities, 120; "separate but equal" ruling of, 4, 61, 78. *See also specific cases*

surveys. *See* airport surveys

Tallahassee, Fla., 9, 46, 51, 53

Tallahassee Municipal Airport: architecture and design of, 53–54; and FAAP funding, 92, 95, 98; and Freedom Rides protest, 51–54; integration of, 56; James Baldwin on, 158n74. See also *Brooks v. Tallahassee*

Tallahassee Ten. *See* Interfaith Freedom Riders

taxi service, 21, 26, 27, 82

Tennessee, 13

Terrace Dining Room (National Airport), 9, 15, 65, 67

Texarkana Airport (Webb Field), 130

Texas, 13

Thomas, Don, 135–136, 140

Thompson, Allen, 107, 108

Timmerman, George Bell, 76–77, 78, 80–81, 84

trains. *See* railways

transportation. *See* air travel; buses; railways; streetcars

Truman, Harry S, administration of, 10

Tupelo Airport, 130

Tureaud, Alexander P., 87, 115, 118

Turner, Jesse, 81, 82–83, 138

Turner v. Memphis, 62, 81–86, 89, 96, 120

TWA (Trans World Airlines), 29, 49

Uncle Remus, 38, 75

Union News Company, 52, 157n67

United States v. City of Birmingham, 131–133

United States v. City of Montgomery, 120, 123–130

United States v. City of New Orleans, 118

vagrancy laws, 19

Washington, D.C., 62

Washington, Ralph, 49, 96, 105

Washington Post, 65

White, Walter, 20, 57, 64

whiteness, notions of: and consumption, 7; and FAA policy, 106; Greek Americans and, 17–18; local definitions of, 2; "separate but equal" doctrine and, 5; and white supremacy, 21, 136

white supremacy: affirmation of, 2, 23, 134; in the courtroom, 76–79, 84–85, 125–128; heterogeneity of, 8–9, 136; impermeability of, 136; in Mississippi, 48, 103–104; nonnegotiability of, 46; and organization of space, 13, 18, 57, 111, 140; passenger terminal as symbol of, 46

Whitesell, Calvin, 126–128, 130

Wilkins, Roy, 32

Williams, John Bell, 99, 109

Willis, A. W., 84

Wofford, Thomas A., 76–77, 80, 94

Woolman, Collett, E., 25

POLITICS AND CULTURE IN THE TWENTIETH-CENTURY SOUTH

A Common Thread: Labor, Politics, and Capital Mobility in the Textile Industry
BY BETH ENGLISH

"Everybody Was Black Down There": Race and Industrial Change in the Alabama Coalfields
BY ROBERT H. WOODRUM

Race, Reason, and Massive Resistance: The Diary of David J. Mays, 1954–1959
EDITED BY JAMES R. SWEENEY

The Unemployed People's Movement: Leftists, Liberals, and Labor in Georgia, 1929–1941
BY JAMES J. LORENCE

Liberalism, Black Power, and the Making of American Politics, 1965–1980
BY DEVIN FERGUS

Guten Tag, Y'all: Globalization and the South Carolina Piedmont, 1950–2000
BY MARKO MAUNULA

The Culture of Property: Race, Class, and Housing Landscapes in Atlanta, 1880–1950
BY LEEANN LANDS

Marching in Step: Masculinity, Citizenship, and The Citadel in Post–World War II America
BY ALEXANDER MACAULAY

Rabble Rousers: The American Far Right in the Civil Rights Era
BY CLIVE WEBB

Who Gets a Childhood: Race and Juvenile Justice in Twentieth-Century Texas
BY WILLIAM S. BUSH

Alabama Getaway: The Political Imaginary and the Heart of Dixie
BY ALLEN TULLOS

The Problem South: Region, Empire, and the New Liberal State, 1880–1930
BY NATALIE J. RING

The Nashville Way: Racial Etiquette and the Struggle for Social Justice in a Southern City
BY BENJAMIN HOUSTON

Cold War Dixie: Militarization and Modernization in the American South
BY KARI FREDERICKSON

Faith in Bikinis: Politics and Leisure in the Coastal South since the Civil War
BY ANTHONY J. STANONIS

*"We Who Believe in Freedom": Womanpower Unlimited
and the Black Freedom Struggle in Mississippi*
BY TIYI M. MORRIS

New Negro Politics in the Jim Crow South
BY CLAUDRENA N. HAROLD

Jim Crow Terminals: The Desegregation of American Airports
BY ANKE ORTLEPP

*Remaking the Rural South: Interracialism, Christian Socialism,
and Cooperative Farming in Jim Crow Mississippi*
BY ROBERT HUNT FERGUSON